彭

明

敏

Ming-min Peng
Nov 28. 2014

A TASTE
OF
FREEDOM

by Peng Ming-min

Recent picture at his home in Oregon, U.S.A.

Dr. Peng's mother Chen King-Ying

Dr. Peng's father
Peng Ching-Kou:
a family Doctor

Dr. Peng (right 1) with his parents, brothers and sister.

Taken in 1970 before dramatically escaping from Taiwan.

Taken in 1970 after arriving in Sweden.

Dr. Peng is thinking of his homeland in Oregon.

A TASTE OF FREEDOM

Memoirs of a Formosan Independence Leader

Peng Ming-min

TAIWAN PUBLISHING CO.

P.O. Box1418, Upland, CA. 91785 U.S.A.

TASTE OF FREEDOM

Memoirs of a Formosan Independence Leader

First edition published in the United States of America
1972 by Holt, Rinehart and Winston, Inc.
383 Madison Ave. New York, New York 10017
Copyright© 1972 by Peng Ming-Min.
Second edition published in 1994
by Taiwan Publishing Co. Inc.
Copyright© 1994 by Peng Ming-Min.
Third edition published in 2005
by Taiwan Publishing Co.
P.O. Box1418, Upland, CA. 91785 U.S.A.
Tel : 909-985-9458 Fax : 909-985-5600
Copyright© 2005 by Peng Ming-Min.

台灣總經銷

望春風文化事業股份有限公司
100台北市林森南路12號2樓之1
Tel：(02)3393-2100・Fax：(02)2321-0136
郵政劃播：19318334・客服信箱：spwind@ms35.hinet.net
精裝本特價：NT$450 US$20

Professor Edwin O. Reischauer's words

It is a fascinating human story which, through one man's life, gives a clearer idea of the essence of the Taiwan problem than any learned treaties could. It clearly shows that the Taiwan problem has grown out of the past experiences, present feelings, and hopes for the future of the twelve million native Taiwanese-the forgotten people ground between the political rivalries of the Peoples' Republic of China and Chiang's Nationalist government on Taiwan.

One cannot read Professor Peng's moving account of his own experiences from childhood under Japanese colonial rule, through prominent participation in the intellectual life of Taiwan under Chiang, to eventual exile from his native land without hoping, and also believing, that the meek and also the not-so-meek Taiwanese will indeed some day inherit their own piece of earth.

Congratulations on a fine and important book.

HARVARD UNIVERSITY

Contents

AUTHOR'S NOTE

I am greatly indebted to Mr. George Kerr for taking down what I have dictated and typing the first draft of the manuscript, as well as for his valuable suggestions and checking of certain facts. However, I am solely responsible for the final version and the viewpoints expressed in this book.

Since I destroyed all my diaries and notes kept from childhood just before I left Formosa, certain dates are not too specific. For the protection of certain people their names cannot be given in my narrative.

I would like to express my deep appreciation to all who extended concern, assistance, and support to me during the most difficult period.

I wish to pay homage to those brave Formosans who never cease the struggle for the future of their compatriots, in the course of which many have endured great personal sacrifice and others have lost their lives.

My thoughts are always with members of my family and personal friends who still bear the burdens and punishment imposed on them because of their relationship to me.

I appreciate the initial suggestion of Professor and Mrs. Carl Gustaf Bernhard that I write my memoirs. I want to thank Mr.

Julian Bach and Miss Mary Clemmey for their encouragement, and also the staff of Holt, Rinehart and Winston, Inc. for their arrangement to publish this manuscript.

I am grateful to Mrs. Linda G. Erickson for her careful editing and assistance in preparing the final version of the manuscript.

PENG MING-MIN

Ann Arbor, Michigan
January 1972

A TASTE OF FREEDOM

1

My Formosan Heritage

The last dim light of the island gradually faded behind me. I was almost to the high sea and beyond the reach of the Nationalist Chinese agents. In my whole life I had never felt such a sense of *real* freedom. After fourteen months in prison and over four years under surveillance I still could not believe that I had finally managed to escape from captivity.

This feeling of freedom was so overwhelming that it was physically almost unbearable. Even more exhilarating was my thought that I could now repudiate publicly all the "confessions" and "repentance" forced from me and used by the Nationalist government and party to humiliate me. The fact that I risked my life to flee Formosa is itself a complete repudiation of the regime and all their propaganda aimed at discrediting me.

As I looked to the future I suddenly realized that fate would thrust upon me the role of a spokesman for the rights and aspirations of my compatriots. In the past I had considered myself purely an academician, but now a new destiny was to radically change my whole life. A deep sense of fatalism and unreality permeated my being.

The three worlds in which I had lived in the past decades came distinctively and simultaneously into my thoughts: the Chi-

1

nese world of my ethnic heritage; the Japanese world in which I spent most of my youth, received my early education, and which was once politically dominant over Formosa; and the Western world to which I had been closely linked ideologically and intellectually and to which I was now returning.

I was now heading toward a blank and uncertain future, but I was certain of one thing: the life ahead would never be the same as the life I had lived.

I became sharply aware that my experience symbolized the destiny of a whole generation of Formosans—their life and tragedy.

I KNOW VERY LITTLE about my ancestors, but since on my father's side, I am of the fifth generation born in Formosa, I must assume that his forefathers were among the extremely poor farmers and fishermen who left Fukien more than a hundred years ago to settle on the rugged island frontier.

My humorous old grandfather used to say with a laugh that his grandfather was a fisherman who had reached southern Formosa with nothing more than a thin pair of pants—too poor to possess even a shirt. In his later days he entertained himself by drawing up a family tree, but it begins only with this shirtless ancestor. He seemed unable to remember or was uninterested in tracing the family lineage back across the Straits to China. We do know that in Fukien province, near Amoy, there is a village in which the family name *Peng* is quite common, but on Formosa this name is used almost exclusively by Hakka people whose forefathers came principally from the hinterlands of Kwangtung province, and whose traditional social life, costume, and dialect set them apart from the people of Fukienese descent. However, my family is not Hakka.

Technically speaking, the great majority of Chinese who crossed to the Formosan frontier before 1875 were "outlaws" and "renegades" in the eyes of imperial Peking, and this must be understood as the background for much of contemporary Formosa's unhappy relationship with the continent. The island was a wild jungle-covered place, inhabited only by headhunting savages of Indonesian or Malayan origin when Europeans first explored it. The Dutch and Spanish opened it to settlement and agricultural development in the seventeenth century, established missions and schools, opened roads in the southwestern region, and began to import cheap Chinese labor from nearby Fukien. In 1663 they were driven out by an adventurous sea-baron named Cheng Cheng-K'ien, known to the Western world as Koxinga. This man, half-Japanese and half-Chinese, dreamed of conquering the continental provinces, but was driven off to Quemoy and Formosa. Cheng died before he could realize this ambition, but for twenty years his son ruled in Formosa, developing a maritime principality quite cut off from China, but thriving on commerce with Japan, the Philippines, and Southeast Asia. He had the same dream as his father, until at last, in 1683, Peking sent a great expeditionary force to Formosa. This expedition destroyed the independent principality, and after a garrison administration was established at Tainan, imperial edicts forbade further Chinese emigration.

Although these edicts, renewed again and again, remained on the books until 1875, they were ignored by impoverished farmers and fishermen who found conditions in Fukien and Kwangtung intolerable. Some of these people went to Southeast Asia and the Indies, others went to the Philippines, and tens of thousands slipped over to Formosa which was an open frontier, poorly and lightly governed. Here, there was new land available for anyone bold enough to drive back the aborigines and clear the land of trees and scrub.

By the beginning of the nineteenth century, the southwestern lowlands were fairly well settled, and adventuresome farmers were pushing into the northern regions as well.

My great-great-grandfather, the shirtless fisherman, was one of the tens of thousands of emigrés who broke with the past in China and ventured to make a new life in southern Formosa. He settled at the seaside village of Tung-kang, about thirty miles south of present-day Kaohsiung. In this rough region he found a wife and established a family. Tung-kang lay at the mouth of the largest river in the region and not far from a massive mountain wall that runs from north to south throughout the island. At that time Hakka immigrants from south China were pushing eastward across the narrow coastal plain to the foothills nearby, quarreling incessantly with the "tamed" aborigines, the Pepohuan, who were still clinging to their ancestral tribal lands in that region. Southward along the coast were lawless villages of "wreckers" and pirates who farmed a little, fished a little, and plundered any luckless ship stranded nearby.

Around 1850 my great-grandfather and his fellow villagers began to hear more and more often of Western "barbarians," for British and American ships were beginning to touch here and there along Formosa's western shores, seeking to exchange silver dollars and opium for camphor brought out of the hills by the Hakka bordermen. By 1855 adventuresome American traders had established a base within a stockade at Kaohsiung (then known as Ta-kow), and had run up the American flag at the entrance to the lagoon anchorage. Four years later Spanish Catholic missionaries landed at this harbor and pushed inland several miles to establish a Christian mission at the Hakka village of Pithau, a little north of Tung-kang. The appearance of these bold strangers created a great sensation, and I am sure my great-grandfather was curious about them.

In 1865, about the time of my grandfather's birth, English Presbyterian missionaries also established themselves at Kaohsiung, an event that was to have profound influence upon the future of the Peng family. The mission leader was Dr. J. L. Maxwell, a physician who had graduated from the University of Edinburgh and from French and German schools. He first founded a small hospital at the port town, and after some years moved his mission and clinic to the larger city of Tainan, some thirty-five miles north of Kaohsiung. My great-grandfather is reputed to have been one of the early converts to Christianity.

Within the next twenty years, the Presbyterians founded schools and set up a printing-press which issued texts and a newspaper printed in the romanized Amoy dialect. They developed the pioneer medical service program in Formosa and ultimately established about forty outlying chapels and congregations in the southern region. As a youth my grandfather was employed as a cook for the missionary doctor, Dr. Thomas Barkley. He became a convert, and until his death in 1945 remained a devoted and active leader in Formosan Christian life. Mission histories speak of him as "Pastor Peng," but I do not know if he was ever formally ordained. I know nothing of his first wife except that she was reputed to have had a fearful temper. He had five sons and two daughters by her and a daughter by a second marriage to a widow.

Clearly my grandfather was happy in his association with the foreign teachers and doctors and was interested in Western culture and in the changes that were so swiftly taking place around him. He moved steadily away from traditional Chinese life through two revolutionary periods. From about 1850 until 1895 the island of Formosa was the center of frequent international controversies. The Western maritime world and Japan demanded that the Chinese government light and chart its coast and maintain law and order within the area it claimed to govern. They demanded that Peking put an end to piracy in Formosan waters and establish some control over the headhunting aborigines living in the mountains and along the eastern coast. When the Chinese government made all sorts of promises but did nothing, the foreign powers—England, France, the United States, and Japan—proposed various corrective measures. In 1874, when my grandfather was a young boy, Japan sent an expeditionary force to occupy the southern tip of Formosa until Peking grudgingly paid a large indemnity and took some steps toward reform.

Beginning in 1875, two comparatively progressive governors arranged to cancel the edicts forbidding Chinese migration to the island and removed many of the restrictions upon expansion of settlement and general economic development. The imperial Peking government soon lost interest, and the Formosans found themselves once again at the mercy of a set of rapacious Chinese officials. In 1884, when my grandfather was a youth of nineteen, France blockaded the island and elements of the French Foreign Legion occupied Keelung. Again Peking sent a comparatively progressive governor to Formosa and the French withdrew. Within the next five years Governor Liu had made Formosa the most modern territory within the Chinese empire. He built a railway line from Keelung to Hsinchu, introduced a post and telegraph system, bought ships to serve Formosan trade with Southeast Asia, laid a cable from Tamsui to Amoy, tried to introduce electric lights, built a "School for Western Studies" at Taipei, attempted to found a government-supported hospital, and tried to overhaul and reorganize the land-tax system. In 1887, when my grandfather was in his early twenties, Formosa was declared a "Province of China."

Many of these innovations were possible because the Formosans were much less traditional than their distant cousins on the continent. Thanks to the stimulus of maritime trade promoted by the foreign merchants and consuls now settled at the ports, the economy made spectacular gains. But when the progressive Governor Liu was recalled in 1891, the traditional, inefficient and unimaginably corrupt scholar-bureaucracy from China let most of the reforms lapse.

Throughout these years the attention of men like my grandfather had been drawn away from traditional China and turned to the Western world. Peking's neglect and the abusive administration of Chinese agents sent to the island on temporary assignments angered many Formosans.

Then in 1895 Peking handed Formosa over to the Japanese. Formosa was used to buy off the Japanese armies prepared then to march to Peking after defeating the Chinese forces in Manchuria. The Treaty of Shimonoseki was signed in April 1895. For a few days in May before the Japanese arrived to take control, there was a confused and ill-organized attempt to establish a "Republic of Formosa." This attempt failed, and after the Japanese flag was raised at Taipei in June, imperial Japanese troops marched southward. Thousands of Formosans took to the hills to join outlawed bands in guerrilla warfare, a hopeless attempt to prevent Japanese occupation of the island. Chinese authorities and soldiers had fled back to China from the northern region. In the south, around Tainan, a Chinese general known as "Black Flag" Liu held out until October, when all organized resistance collapsed and General Liu escaped to Amoy disguised as an old woman.

Even though Peking had not consulted any Formosans in reaching the decision to cede Formosa to Japan, Tokyo offered all Formosans and Chinese on Formosa a two-year grace period in which to declare a choice of nationality. Those who wished could leave the island and take their property with them; those who preferred to remain Chinese subjects could register as "resident aliens," but if they did not do this within the two-year period, they automatically became subjects of the Japanese emperor. A few thousand Formosans left for the continent, and a few thousand registered as aliens, but the great majority—some 3,000,000—remained on their native island, and my grandparents were among them.

At that time cholera, plague, malaria, tuberculosis, black river fever, trachoma, and many other diseases were endemic in Formosa, giving the island an evil reputation. Except for Governor Liu's short-lived effort to found a hospital at Taipei, no Chinese official had ever done anything to clean up the island. The concept of public health and sanitation was not a continental Chinese idea. The incoming Japanese forces had lost nearly 12,000 men who either died or were totally disabled from the effects of disease during the four-month campaign of subjugation. Mortality rates among the common people were spectacularly high. The nominal commander-in-chief of the Japanese forces was an imperial prince and despite the elaborate precautions taken to protect this exalted personage, he, too, died at Tainan of malaria and dysentery contracted on the march southward. This made an enormous impression at Tokyo.

The imperial government saw at once that if Japan were to establish itself successfully in this new island possession, Formosa would have to be cleaned up. But until 1898 the military governors were preoccupied with subjugation of the guerrilla bands in the agricultural lowlands and in the foothills, and public health problems were left in the hands of military officers who knew little about them. Japan had no hope of establishing a permanent administration if the mortality rates among her soldiers and civilians remained so high. A healthy Formosan labor force also would be required to make the colony a success. However, the only medical services then available to the common people were the Presbyterian mission hospitals and clinics at Taipei and Tainan. Something had to be done, and done quickly, to supply medical services on a large scale.

Therefore, in 1898, when Tokyo sent down the fourth governor general, General Baron Kodama Gentaro, a military man of unusual distinction, he brought with him a medical doctor, Dr. Goto Shimpei, to serve as his civil administrator and deputy in all but purely military matters. For six years these two men relentlessly carried through a program designed to reorganize the Formosan administration, economy, and social life. No Formosan family remained untouched. One of Goto's first moves was to establish a medical school at Taipei, which offered a short course to train men urgently needed for the proposed islandwide public health clean-up campaign. He advertised for students, offering each a small monthly subsidy.

By this time my grandfather had become a lay minister serving the English Presbyterian church mission. He was a poor man with five sons and three daughters to support. The boys gathered firewood in the hills and did the most menial work in the town in order to help support the family. My grandfather was much too poor to send all his sons to school, but when the new government offered this subsidy for medical studies, he urged his third son— my father—to enter the course at Taipei.

The Japanese were having difficulty winning Formosan cooperation, for Tokyo's military authorities and the civil police were very severe. The island people had often in the past tried to throw off Chinese rule and had resisted the Japanese troops in 1895; now for a decade they offered passive resistance in the towns and resorted to sabotage and guerrilla action in the more distant countryside. Generally speaking, there was a mutual dislike and mistrust on both sides that was to continue for many years. My grandfather, however, was an optimist, a man of good will, and intensely interested in new ideas. His long association with the missionary doctors and teachers at Tainan influenced him to look away from China and the past, and try to make the best of the dramatic change the Japanese were determined to bring about. Though lacking in formal education, he was a truly enlightened man.

At a young age my father entered the medical school at Taipei. At Tamsui and Taipei the young stranger was introduced to members of the Presbyterian community. There he met my mother who was a school girl at the Canadian mission in Tamsui. Her family had settled long ago in Patou village, on the road between Keelung and present-day Taipei. Her parents were acquainted with the first foreigners who passed that way and with the missionaries in the northern region. They too had become Christians sometime after 1872 when the Canadian Dr. George MacKay founded his Tamsui mission. My maternal grandparents were brewers of rice wine, and therefore were well off in comparison with Pastor Peng's family. They had accumulated enough capital to buy up rice fields in the fertile northern region. My maternal grandfather was a rather quiet, gentle, easy-going man who left much of the management of the brewery to his hard-working wife. When the Japanese came, brewing was made a government monopoly, and all private breweries were bought by the government. My mother had two brothers and a sister. Her elder brother was sent to Japan to study at the Doshisha University, an American missionary foundation in Kyoto. He returned to become a Presbyterian pastor, chairman of the MacKay Mission Hospital Board, and moderator of the northern Presbyterian synod in Formosa. Meanwhile my mother's second brother attended the Tamsui Mission School and then became a businessman.

When my father had finished his medical training at the government school he spent two years as an intern at MacKay Hospital, Taipei, and during this time my parents married. Moving down to the small coastal town of Ta-chia (Tai-ko) in central Formosa, my father opened his first practice. This old coastal community of less than twenty thousand inhabitants was then quite famous; it was a very prosperous community of household craftsmen producing finely woven hats and mats for export to a world market. In its best years Ta-chia sent nearly ten million hats to the United States alone, and the number exported to Japan was very large.

Once established in Ta-chia, my father prospered too. A doctor's income was rather high and in every community the doctor enjoyed prestige and influence. Since my father was the first in our family to earn money, he sent his brothers to the medical school as soon as he was able to do so. One after the other they too began to prosper, and the brothers together took great pleasure in making my grandfather's life more comfortable.

My proud grandfather discovered that he had in effect founded a "medical dynasty," for his sons' children either took medical degrees or married doctors, and their children in turn are entering the medical profession. At least fifteen members, including five women, of the Peng family have completed their medical degrees, and a third generation, including my son and some nephews and nieces, are now in medical school.

My father enjoyed a close relationship with his brothers throughout his life, and all the brothers were keenly interested in education, determined to secure the best possible opportunities for every child in the Peng family.

Father remained in practice at Ta-chia for eighteen years, and as he prospered he invested in rice land until he had acquired forty *chia*, which is a substantial estate by Formosan standards. He planned to leave ten *chia* to each of his children, which would enable us to support our children when the time came to send them to school. I remember well that often as we rode northward on the train, he used to point out the golden paddy, saying with pride, "Those rice fields are all ours."

I was born at Ta-chia on August 15, 1923, the youngest of three brothers and a sister. As we grew older we discovered what a truly remarkable man our father was, and why he commanded such wide respect and affection in the Ta-chia community. He loved horses and sometimes kept four of them at one time. He always had at least one horse and a groom to attend it. He would ride out in the early morning to make distant house calls, which was not the usual thing in Formosa. I vividly remember a day when he came back riding at a furious gallop with an angry water-buffalo chasing along behind him. On another occasion his horse was actually gored by one of these surly beasts. Throughout his life he rode for pleasure and was at one time an enthusiastic member of the local Japanese riding club of Kaohsiung.

His interests were varied and in some respects quite extraordinary. He learned to box in the Chinese style, he was an enthusiastic gardener who cultivated chrysanthemums and rare orchids, he took up ink-painting, and he learned to play the violin. His relations with his tenant-farmers were good. I recall how often they came to discuss the shares to be paid out of crops in the forthcoming season or to ask his understanding for not paying an agreed amount. His large clinic was also the scene of many charitable acts, for this kind-hearted man often overlooked failures to pay for treatment and gave free attention to patients too poor to meet the usual fees. Both he and my mother were devout Christians who served as elders in the local Presbyterian congregations and supported charities and the educational work of the Formosan church.

I can recall only one issue that seriously disturbed the harmony of our family. It was common practice in Formosa for well-to-do families to "adopt" girls who were really servants. The girls were taken into the households when only five or six years old, and money was paid to their families in return for which the girls served as maids until they were marriageable. In some households these servants were well treated, but in some they were abused. We always had one or two in our household, and when my sister was married, an aunt gave her a servant who remained with her for many years. When my brothers entered higher school they attacked this practice as being a form of slavery. They criticized it harshly, sometimes saying, "You call yourselves Christians and these are slaves!" My embarrassed and troubled parents tried to justify the practice by pointing out that the handmaidens in our house were very well treated. Nevertheless, my brothers were often distressed by this situation and never felt completely comfortable with it.

When I was about five years old I was taken to China. I remember how cold it was in Shanghai, and I recall the long flights of steps to the newly constructed tomb of Sun Yat-sen near Nanking. Mr. Huang Chao-chin, one of my father's acquaintances who was then in the foreign ministry at Nanking, guided us about the capital. He had just returned from study in the United States. I was too young to comprehend all that we saw, but this trip gave my father and mother an opportunity to compare the living conditions of the Chinese in China with conditions in Formosa after thirty-three years of Japanese rule. They were of course impressed by the immensity of China and felt some nostalgia toward the land of their ancestors. However, in terms of social development, industrialization, education, and public health they felt that, compared to Formosa, there was still much to be done in China.

When my sister and brothers were old enough to attend school, Father rented a Japanese-style house in Taipei near the old American consulate. Mother stayed there with us and Father came up for weekends whenever he could. Occasionally we would all return to Ta-chia to be with him, and the sixty-mile train trip was always a great adventure.

On entering school we children began to move away from the protection and warmth of a large family in a rural town and into the more complicated life of a colonial capital. At Ta-chia we were the children of a prominent family pampered and petted by household servants and surrounded by our Formosan friends. At Taipei after being rigidly examined, we were allowed to enter the best Japanese schools, attended principally by sons and daughters of Japanese officials.

The situation for all young Formosans was quite peculiar at that time. From 1895 until 1922 the Japanese had maintained separate primary schools for children of Japanese colonials in Formosa. There had been a legitimate excuse for this in the opening years of the Japanese era when Formosan children could not understand or speak proper Japanese, but after twenty-five years had passed that was no longer true. Nevertheless, the separate school arrangement was perpetuated through prejudice. World War I had brought about the first organized Formosan demands for home rule and an end to economic, social, and political discrimination. Japan's participation in the European war on the Allied side had stimulated an extraordinary expansion of industry in Japan and a corresponding growth of urban population and industrial slums. The new urban proletariat demanded wider suffrage in the same period in which revolutionary movements began to sweep Europe. The Russian imperial system was destroyed, and England, Holland, and France were challenged in their colonies. President Wilson of the United States was proclaiming the equality of man and stressing minority rights to self-determination.

Against this background Japan had demanded at Versailles formal international recognition of racial equality. Formosan university students at Tokyo promptly petitioned the Japanese government to end racial discrimination in the colonial schools. In 1918 a commoner became the prime minister of Japan for the first time in history, and Tokyo began to make slight concessions in Formosa. For example a civilian was appointed governor general after twenty-five years of rule by admirals and generals, and in 1922, the year before my birth, discrimination was theoretically done away with in the schools. The first generation of Formosans had now matured under the Japanese flag and many became bilingual. Their children in turn were bilingual, as was I, from earliest childhood.

At the time I entered school the law said that any child speaking adequate Japanese could study in the primary schools previously reserved for Japanese children. Nevertheless discrimination continued in fact. An examination system screened all applicants. The schools in which Japanese students were in the majority were better equipped and generally had better teachers than the schools in which Formosan pupils were in the majority.

Mother had taken a house in the Japanese section of town. My father's early training in the Japanese medical program, his professional status, and his wealth gave us a privileged position. Nevertheless we underwent severe examinations before my brothers and my sister were admitted to the Kensei Primary School and I was allowed to enter the Taisho Kindergarten nearby. Only one other Formosan child was in that kindergarten. Our teachers were kind and good, but nothing could conceal the fact that we were expected to consider ourselves fortunate.

After one year in kindergarten I passed the Kensei Primary School examinations and joined my brothers and sister there. In the second year my mother decided to return to Ta-chia. She took me with her and left my maternal grandmother to care for the others. I entered the local primary school for Japanese children which had an enrollment of about 200 pupils. I believe I was the only Formosan boy enrolled at that time. Here the Japanese principal developed an unusual affection for me, always turning to me with the questions other boys had failed to answer. On the small public occasions of a primary school, I was again and again put forward to represent the student body.

In this pleasant way I spent two years, but before such treatment could altogether spoil me or spoil my relations with my fellow-pupils, my father decided to suspend his practice in Ta-chia for a period of advanced study in Japan. It was now 1933. My sister was graduating from the best girls' school in Formosa and was about to go to Tokyo to take entrance examinations for a women's medical college. At Taipei one of my brothers was attending the First Middle School and the other had entered the *Koto Gakko* ("higher school"). Both schools were considered to be the best in Formosa.

During these years we heard much talk of the Japanese invasion of China and of the "Shanghai Incident." It aroused a complex feeling in us. The Japanese newspapers carried stories of the noble deeds of Japanese soldiers and of Japan's righteous purpose in subduing the backward Chinese. Teachers and students at school echoed these patriotic sentiments, but at home we heard our parents talking about the brave Chinese who had resisted the Japanese invasion.

On the day of our departure from Ta-chia, the principal of my school brought the entire student body to the station to see us off. This was an unprecedented gesture. We talked about it then, and as I grew older I discovered that many thoughtful Japanese civilians did not approve of the government's discriminatory policy. There were unprejudiced teachers and other intellectuals who sincerely attempted to treat Formosans as equals and were eager to bridge the gap between the Japanese and the island people.

This first trip to Japan in 1933 took me into a world quite different from anything I had known before. At that time in Formosa, the Japanese were a self-conscious minority of about 300,000 ruling a population of about 4,000,000, and no one could conceal the differences between the two groups. In Tokyo our family found itself lost in a sea of Japanese in one of the world's largest cities. Nobody noticed us because we were Formosans; we enjoyed no special privileges nor were we treated as curiosities. My sister passed her examinations and entered the medical school, I was enrolled in a primary school near our temporary home in *Kamatu-Ku* ("Kamata ward"), and my father entered a large private hospital in Ogimachi to take a special course in gynecology. We spent over one year in Japan.

By this time I was an ardent baseball fan. When Babe Ruth visited Japan I boldly wrote a letter to him and in return received his autograph, which became my treasure.

When we returned to Formosa my father decided to open a new hospital in the thriving southern port city of Takao (Kaohsiung). The government had undertaken a great industrial expansion program there. New hydroelectric generators at Sun-Moon Lake were ready to supply power, the old Takao Lagoon had been dredged to accommodate ocean-going freighters, and docks, warehouses, and industrial sites were being constructed to anticipate the great thrust southward into Southeast Asia and the Indies. The public was aware of this ultimate purpose and under this intensive development program Takao had become a booming city.

Here, a short distance from the industrial area, my father purchased a rather large Japanese hotel, converted it into a clinic, and turned one wing into a pediatrics hospital to be run by one of my uncles. My energetic mother assisted in the day-to-day management details. The hospital prospered at once, it was a financial success, and my father's reputation grew as a specialist in treating ovarian tumors.

When I was twelve years old I was enrolled in the local primary school for my fifth year. By now I was beginning to have sharp preferences and dislikes; I took a great dislike to brush-painting, and reserved my greatest enthusiasm for baseball. Our school masters took baseball very seriously, treating it almost as if it were a military training program. Although I was a poor batter, I was an excellent fielder, and played on our team when it won a citywide championship. Needless to say, my Babe Ruth autograph gave me great prestige among my classmates.

From my earliest childhood the problem of being a Formosan had become psychologically more and more complex. I spoke Japanese perfectly and usually stood high in my class; nevertheless I was always self-conscious, constantly aware that I was different from my Japanese classmates. My name embarrassed me; the Chinese character for *Peng* is in Japanese pronounced "Ho," and when it was called out in the classroom it often provoked laughter. Mother wore the conventional dress of an upper-class Formosan woman, but when she came to the Japanese school on public occasions I was embarrassed because she looked so different from the other mothers present.

On entering Takao Middle School I found that about one-fourth of my schoolmates were Formosans, the majority of whom were excellent students for they had been obliged to pass stiff examinations designed to restrict Formosan access to higher education and the professions. The colonial administration saw to it that the cut-off point in educational opportunity came at this middle school level. The theory seemed to be that it was useful to train Formosan laborers to read and write at the most elementary level, but dangerous to encourage development of an intellectual or professional leadership within the island.

A change of principals took place soon after I entered this school; a small, gentle man was replaced by a tall, austere one who had the reputation of being a hard disciplinarian. His severe alcoholism caused his head to shake constantly even when he addressed the students in public. We were immediately subjected to a Spartan regimentation. In addition to meeting a heavy classroom schedule, each of us was obliged to prepare and tend a small garden plot on the school grounds for which we had to carry in buckets of human excrement to apply as fertilizer, and to work in teams cutting grass and doing other manual labor on the grounds. We resented it all, but it was required discipline and was intended to toughen us for ultimate military service. As in middle schools throughout the empire, we were required to wear drab gray uniforms, visored caps, and puttees, all of which were extremely unsuitable for Takao's tropical climate. We were punished if anyone reported seeing us off-campus without the uniform. We could not wear the cool, comfortable, and cheap wooden footgear (*geta*) that most students preferred, we were not supposed to ride bicycles to school but had to walk, and we were absolutely forbidden to go to the movies; any student discovered at the cinema might be expelled from the school.

We ranged in age from about twelve to eighteen, and these restrictions irked us. Like all boys, we took risks. None of us will forget the day our principal, in his official capacity, attended an athletic meet held at a girls' school across town. On such occasions the girls all wore short, tight athletic bloomers, and a number of our middle school students sneaked to the edge of the crowd in an effort to spy on the girls in this brief attire. Our principal happened to catch sight of them, and the next morning the entire student body was subjected to a furious tirade, a screaming and almost hysterical denunciation. In the view of this martinet we were not fit to be soldiers for the emperor. We thought this very unjust, and gossiped about the male swimming instructor at the girls' school who was allowed to enter the pool with his young charges.

The principal was typical of many military men and superpatriots in Japan at that time. The invasion of China had been resumed, and the so-called "China Incident" that began with the Marco Polo Bridge affair near Peking in July 1937 did not end until August 1945. Reservists were being called up throughout the empire, and one by one our teachers were leaving for the front. We students were obliged to march in great lantern parades celebrating countless victories won by the emperor's soldiers in China, and we heard our Japanese friends sending off husbands, sons, fathers, and brothers with the chilling farewell, *"Rippa ni shinde kudasai!"* ("Please die beautifully!")

We had one peculiar middle-aged military instructor named Tokunaga who was rather popular. He was straightforward, unprejudiced, and sometimes entertaining. If he thought a student was not acting briskly enough or seemed effeminate, he would rush forward and grab for the student's crotch "to see if he is really a man!" We missed him when he went off to the war, and were horrified later to hear that he had died on Guadalcanal where, it was said, he had starved to death and had been eaten by his companions.

Our fanatic principal and our military instructors inculcated in us a drill-master enthusiasm for war, lecturing us constantly on the backwardness and cowardice of the Chinese people, the heroic bravery of the Japanese, and Japan's self-sacrifice on China's behalf. We Formosan students found ourselves in an awkward and painful position. My father was well read and kept himself informed of developments in China as best he could. Following his example, I may have kept myself better informed than some of my classmates, for I was a newspaper addict throughout my primary and middle school days, always reading every page of the papers very carefully. It is a habit I have never lost.

The China War and foreign affairs were frequent topics of conversation in our home. Both my parents had foreign friends, members of the English and Canadian Presbyterian missions, who visited our home from time to time, and we visited them in return. I suppose that none of my middle school classmates had such foreign associations and wide foreign interests.

I had begun the study of English in my first year in middle school, and I enjoyed it. It is possible that foreign-language studies have always appealed to me as a subconscious avenue of escape, an avenue leading toward the great world beyond both China and Japan, and from the dilemma in which we were placed by the war in China. My grandparents had known the disorder and lawlessness of the last years of Chinese rule in Formosa, and had obviously prospered under the Japanese administration. I was born a subject of the Japanese emperor, and every day was exposed to the propaganda of Japanese patriotism, but I was also a Chinese by blood, language, and family tradition. At this impressionable age the English language offered an intellectual passport to the Western world, which to our family meant Canada, England, and the United States, thanks to their association with the Christian church.

English was therefore my favorite course, and I achieved some distinction in it. My Japanese teacher, Mr. Amatsuchi, took great pride in my accomplishment, but unfortunately these were the years of growing anti-British and anti-American fanaticism among the Japanese militarists, and our school principal was a fanatic.

A student was expected to spend five full years in middle school, but the regulations also provided that a youth was entitled to sit for entrance examinations to a higher school at the end of his fourth year. The endorsement of the middle school principal was customary but not technically required. I stood high in my classes scholastically, and my father wanted me to go to Japan to sit for examinations. My older sister had previously done this successfully. The competition would be keen, but we were confident that I would succeed. I therefore applied to my principal for his approval and for a transfer of records and recommendation. This he flatly refused. The reason was simple—he would not allow any of his students to do so. My father then called on him at his office to remind him with some emphasis, that "this is the *right* of every qualified student. I want my son to do so. You have no right to refuse." The principal bluntly retorted, "Withdraw your son from this school." Just as bluntly, my father said, "I shall."

With an unpleasant memory of this colonial martinet lingering in my mind, I set out for Tokyo by myself. I was to stay with my sister while I took the examinations for the Second Higher School at Sendai. She had finished her medical work, and had married a rather successful Formosan businessman, a graduate of Keio University. To my chagrin, but possibly to my benefit, I failed. I had been an outstanding student in a small colonial middle school at Takao, far from metropolitan Tokyo, but it was not quite enough. Undoubtedly I was overconfident. Youth and homesickness, too, probably had something to do with it. I was then sixteen years of age.

Now I had a problem. I had to find a middle school in Japan to finish my study at this level. In principle, middle school administrators were always reluctant to accept a student transferring in his last year. After a painful search I was accepted for registration in a mission school, the Kansei Gakuin, located midway between the great international commercial port of Kobe and the industrial city of Osaka. It was not much more than an hour's ride to Japan's ancient capital of Kyoto. This was a school much favored by aristocratic and wealthy families. The college was not first rate, and the lower school had a poor scholastic reputation. It was considered a refuge for the spoiled sons of indulgent wealthy parents.

I did not live on campus, but found instead rather simple accommodations with a farmer's family living not far away in the suburbs. It was a rather primitive lodging by standards I had known at home. I had no servants to do things for me which meant I had to wash my own linen and take care of my room. We depended upon a well in the dooryard for our water supply, and I thought the food poor compared to our varied Formosan table.

By this time my second brother was at Keio Medical School in Tokyo, and my sister continued to live there. I was miserably homesick for several months, and when I found myself alone in the evenings, I sometimes cried. But this passed, and when it did I began thoroughly to enjoy myself. It would be impossible to imagine a greater contrast with life at that barbarous Takao Middle School. The Kansei Gakuin seemed to have assembled a faculty of entertaining eccentrics, nonconformists who loved teaching but did not fit into the drab para-military regimentation of the state schools. Class requirements were very easy, nevertheless I worked hard, eager to absorb everything offered on the campus. At the chapel services I enjoyed singing familiar Christian hymns in Japanese, and for a time I admired the extremely handsome and well-dressed young music teacher. His exceedingly smart Western clothes and manner fascinated me. When we occasionally sang in English I felt a great sense of accomplishment.

The one strict rule in this school forbade us to go to the famed Takarazuka Theatre, an all-girl revue patterned after New York's Radio City Music Hall Rockettes. The brief attire of Takao's school girls and the costumes of the girls at the Takarazuka Theatre seemed to lack something in the eyes of school administrators.

The school itself was situated in the most westernized district in all Japan, a strip of suburban residential communities where many foreign businessmen and consular people maintained substantial homes. Some of my classmates came from wealthy westernized families in this area. We were free to travel on weekends, so I often went to Osaka or Kobe to wander about by myself. Sometimes I went to classical Kyoto. I was learning to enjoy Japanese food, and best of all, I now had no feeling of self-conscious strangeness. Everywhere I was treated as an equal; I was no longer a subordinate colonial.

On the contrary I found myself something of a favorite on campus, a Formosan who unexpectedly spoke Japanese surprisingly well. Also I was at the top of my classes. Even the military instructor liked me. I had been so thoroughly disciplined by the Takao martinets that I performed with a precision noteworthy among my easy-going classmates. In consequence I was usually assigned to carry the flag during parade drill, the highest honor the military instructor could think to confer upon a student.

Throughout these pleasant months I was working at my studies late into the night, and managed to emerge as the outstanding student of the school. The school year ended in February. I applied to take examinations for admission to two prestigious higher schools, the economics department at Keio University and the literary and arts course in the Third Higher School at Kyoto, known to everyone as *San-ko*. I passed both exams with some distinction. This created a great sensation at the Kansei Gakuin, for no graduate of that school had ever successfully passed into the Kyoto school. It was considered one of the two finest higher schools in Japan, sharing this distinction with the First High School in Tokyo, and I, a Formosan, had done this after only one year at Kansei Gakuin.

I cabled the news to my parents. They were extremely pleased although not altogether happy that I had decided not to study medicine. I was the maverick in the family. A long exchange of correspondence followed. Both my parents were disturbed, for as matters stood in Formosa, there was little hope for a distinguished career outside the medical profession, and even in the medical academic profession, only one Formosan had reached the rank of a full professor.

Suppressing their disappointment, they gave me full support, observing only that the youngest sons and daughters always have their own way. My brother at the Keio Medical School understood me rather well, and at every turn gave me good advice when I faced a choice between Keio University and the Dai San Koto Gakko (*San-ko*).

Scholastically the Keio was not to be compared with *San-ko*, but once admitted to it, I could expect to move right up the ladder through the university to a bachelor's degree without further difficult examinations. The rate of admission to Keio was about one in every sixteen applicants, hence the numerical competition was stiff, but the quality of *San-ko* applicants was the highest in the nation. Nevertheless, when a student finished at *San-ko*, he had once again to face a stiff competitive examination when he

applied for admission to one of the imperial universities at the
summit of the Japanese school system.

Without hesitation I enrolled at *San-ko*. Moving from Kobe to
Kyoto, I entered upon the happiest period of my life. The school
was well known for its liberal tradition. The *San-ko* motto was
Ji-yu ("Liberty" or "Freedom") and when I entered, it was
fighting hard to maintain that liberal tradition. In 1940 it was
under great pressure from the militarists. The China War was
drawing Japan deeper into the continent. While Japanese re-
cruits were being called upon to "die beautifully," the national
economy was being strained to prepare for further escalation of
war. Our school administration and faculty were struggling to
preserve a degree of intellectual and personal freedom for themselves and their students, a freedom then rare in Japan, and
about to vanish.

In Kyoto I found a rooming house near the famous fifteenth-
century temple, the Ginkaku-ji. In a peculiar Kyoto tradition,
meals were not served in student lodgings. Instead each man had
to go out to one of the many tiny shops nearby catering to students. It was the same with bathing. I soon established a routine,
studying until very late, sometimes reading through the night,
and I spent many hours browsing through Kyoto's many old
bookshops. The master of my lodging house treated me with
great kindness, and we became good friends.

My father now indulged me by providing an allowance of sixty
yen per month, far more than I needed for food and lodging, and
perhaps twice as much as the average student had to spend. I
began to buy books. Soon I had a collection that was unusual for
a student in the higher school. One day while walking through
the grounds of the ancient Yoshida Shrine, I suddenly was swept
with an overwhelming sense of exhilaration, perhaps the happiest
moment of my life, for I felt that I had no cares, and could buy
all the books I wanted. I was seventeen, an age when all things
seem possible.

I had entered the literary and arts course rather than the

science course. This was an intensive program of directed reading in history, literature, and philosophy. We were stimulated by a sense of pride and friendly competition among ourselves. Each of us was eager to be the first to call attention to new discoveries. Everything and anything in print beckoned to us and we had insatiable intellectual curiosity. Each man thought he was a philosopher. We were visionaries at that age, and the friendships formed were deep and emotional, perhaps unconsciously assuring ourselves a little desperately that we knew much more of the world than our elders and the common man beyond the campus gates. A strong sense of membership in an elite led us to look at the world with a degree of supercilious youthful contempt.

We were living in the shadow of war. It was inevitable that every graduate who did not go on to college somewhere would be drafted and leave for China. Some of my fellow students were true individualists. In this age group, from sixteen to nineteen years, there was a sudden blossoming of personality. Talents appeared. Each man was free to follow his own interests and these were frequently outside the formal courses of instruction. At the core of the system was intensive reading and passionate discussions among ourselves and with our instructors.

Great emphasis was placed upon intensive language training, and I excelled in this. We had all completed four or five years of English training in the middle schools, and however imperfectly we spoke the language, our ability to read was well developed. Now another foreign language was required, and I chose French. This meant four hours per week of training in grammar, five hours of reading, and three hours of conversation, much of it with first-rate teachers. I did well in spoken French, but in all language courses the emphasis was on reading. As one of our teachers said, we were not being trained as tour guides, we were being trained to absorb foreign culture and thought.

I soon found myself intoxicated with everything French, especially French history, language, and literature. I read these sub-

jects in translation and in the original, and I joined a small informal group of students brought together by one of our Japanese
professors. It was our custom to meet very early in the morning
before regular classes assembled in order to read and discuss
French literature and philosophy.

In our first year we read Western philosophy in Japanese
translation, but in our second year we were expected to read in
French. Anatole France and Jules LeMaître took first place in my
personal estimation. I bought many volumes of their original
works and of critical Japanese essays concerning them. The
rather cynical views of Anatole France influenced my philosophi-
cal development.

The writings of Ernest Renan have had a strong influence on
my political philosophy. His essay entitled *Qu'est qu'une nation?*
("What is a Nation?") touched me as a Formosan, rather than as
the loyal Japanese I was supposed to be. He raised the fundamental idea that neither race, language, nor culture form a nation, but rather a deeply felt sense of community and shared destiny. In the context of the savage war in China, what could this
idea mean to a Formosan?

One remarkable faculty member was a professor of philosophy
named Doi, an individualist who wordlessly taunted the military
establishment and defied regimentation of mind and body by
affecting certain disheveled mannerisms in dress and conduct.
This advertised his dissent to all of us, and he had our admiration. On the whole, our faculty and student body shared a
strongly antimilitarist sentiment. We wanted to preserve our
independence and our ivory tower, and the militarists wanted to
break it down. This created a sense of tension between the school
body and the army martinets assigned as our instructors in military training.

One day we witnessed an astonishing confrontation. The senior military officer who had recently arrived on campus was a
colonel in the regular army. He called an assembly. Some small
rules had been broken, and a junior military instructor had

complained to the colonel. Singling out the guilty students, he heaped contempt upon them, scorning them as not true Japanese. After ranting on and on, he ended his tirade by ordering them to begin running around the parade ground bearing heavy arms until told to cease or collapsing in exhaustion. It was a harsh discipline. Suddenly one of the students broke out of line, dashed screaming at the colonel and struck him several times with his gun butt. He then threw the gun to the ground and ran across the field toward the campus gates. For a moment everyone stood frozen by this unprecedented and shocking action, and then the other military instructors raced after him. He was, of course, expelled and then called up at once for military service. We never knew what finally became of him. The school was shaken by the incident which no doubt hardened attitudes of anti-intellectual militarists toward liberal institutions such as ours.

My psychology professor was a quiet, stiff person who had served in the regular army. His courses were rather dull and systematic, but the subject itself was of great interest. One day, rather surprisingly, he asked us to write an essay in which we were to open our hearts to him and express ourselves freely on subjects that concerned us most deeply. He promised to treat the papers confidentially. My response was an essay condemning the invasion of China, and once into it I wrote on and on, at least ten pages of bitter comment on discrimination and the contempt shown by Japanese toward all Chinese in China and in colonial Formosa. Knowing that I might be arrested by the "thought police" if my sentiments were known, I nevertheless turned in the finished paper. A few days later the professor called me to his office, quietly assured me that no one else would know of my outpouring, and expressed deep regret that the situation was as it was. He warned me however that it would be best to keep my thoughts to myself in the future, and not to speak of such things to other persons.

My aversion to military service was intense. I had hated military drill since middle school days. School units were taken on long maneuvers from time to time, obliged to march with heavy equipment, camp in the rough for two or three days at a time, and perform drills and exercises along the way. Some students could not take it, breaking down physically while on the march or showing signs of emotional disturbance. I was in my last year at San-ko now, I was nineteen, and I considered myself an intellectual entirely superior to the needs and demands of the military establishment. I simply did not report for the field maneuvers, knowing very well that I would get a poor grade for the military course, but confident that it would be the only bad grade on my entire San-ko record, except mathematics.

At the close of the school year, near graduation time, I chanced one day to meet one of my professors who said, in a tone of obvious relief, "Congratulations! You *did* manage to pass!" I was astonished, for it had never occurred to me that I might not. There had been a great debate in the faculty meeting called each year to consider questionable cases and final records. The military instructor had given me a failing mark and had vehemently demanded that I should not graduate. My professors had won the argument with great difficulty. They argued on my behalf at some personal risk, for this was early 1942, and the military were in full control.

A Kyoto University student of economics who was the son of a wealthy Tokyo family and an outspoken critic of militarism lived in my rooming house. We were quite good friends despite the difference in our ages and academic status. One December day he rushed into my room shouting out, "Tojo is a fool! Now he has done the most stupid thing! This will be the end of us!" My friend had just heard the radio report that Pearl Harbor had been attacked, and that Japan had won a great victory.

From that day the school was plunged into a mood of fatalistic despair, underscored by noisy crowds demonstrating in the streets outside. After the long years of fruitless campaigning in continental China a great victory in the Pacific was doubly welcome. Everyone boasted of how many American ships had been sunk and how many planes destroyed. There was pride and surging enthusiasm. China had been defeated in 1895, Russia had been defeated in 1905, and now the United States! There were lantern parades and public celebrations. But inside our campus gates faculty and students alike were not so sure. We had read too widely and knew too much of America. Pearl Harbor would be only a surprise success at the beginning of the conflict, not the final victory.

II

Nagasaki, 1945

Japan celebrated victory after victory. Hong Kong surrendered on Christmas Day, 1941, Manila was occupied a week later, and Singapore fell into Japanese hands in February 1942. The spectacular success in this great thrust to the tropics was marred by the Doolittle hit-run raid on Tokyo on April 19. This was a reminder that Americans had the capacity to reach the imperial capital itself. In the far south the inhabitants of Dutch, British, and American territories were showing reluctance to cooperate with the Japanese forces and in many places were offering determined resistance. The war in China dragged on. Tokyo saw that a total mobilization of manpower was required throughout the empire.

It was announced suddenly that although preparatory school science courses would continue as usual, courses in the humanities and social science would be shortened by six months. At *San-ko* therefore we would have to be prepared to enter a university in the summer of 1942 or face the military call-up. This meant that I had to decide as soon as possible upon a university and a professional field.

As long as the sea-lanes leading southward past Formosa were open we could keep in communication with our worried parents at Takao. Their letters urged me to choose a career in medicine, the only career that promised a future in Formosa. They wanted me to abandon thoughts of the imperial universities and to enroll in a medical school such as my brother's school at Nagasaki.

It was unthinkable that I should make such an important decision concerning my future without full consultation with my parents, nevertheless I refused to yield on this issue. My letters argued against a medical career. I wanted only to enter the Department of French Literature at Tokyo Imperial University and to turn my face away from Formosa and Japan and toward the Western world of arts and ideas. I was truly bemused by the French language, and at the age of nineteen I was repelled by the situation in which my close Japanese friends and schoolmates were expected to die beautifully following military orders. My parents now probably had reason to regret my years at the liberal Kansei Gakuin and at *San-ko*, where the motto was "Freedom." They patiently observed, again and again, that French literature offered no livelihood and no future for me either in Formosa or Japan.

At last I offered a compromise. I would give up French as a major, and would enter the Department of Law or Political Science at the Tokyo Imperial University. I would become either a lawyer or a bureaucrat. After many letters had passed back and forth, they accepted this, but with regret.

I now had to work extremely hard to prepare for the imperial university entrance examinations, to be given this year in the early summer. They were the stiffest exams required in the Japanese system. When the time came I went to Tokyo, took a small room near the main campus, and sat for the two-day ordeal. It was well known that a Formosan applicant had to do far better than Japanese students if he was to penetrate this screen. Colonial subjects, Koreans and Formosans, were not welcomed into the imperial civil service. More than ten Formosans were sitting for examination at this time, but we knew that only one at most would be accepted, no matter how high the others' marks might be.

When the results were posted I was the lucky one, standing rather high on the list of nearly five hundred applicants accepted for the coming session. I purchased the proper uniforms, found lodgings, and settled down to work.

One day it was announced that military service deferments were canceled for all students in the university humanities and social science courses. A majority of the young men about me vanished from the campus, including my friends from happier *San-ko* days. As a colonial subject I was not legally subject to conscription, but I had the privilege of volunteering. In Formosa, itself, thousands were being obliged to volunteer. A few were accepted into the regular military service, but the majority were drafted to form a labor corps sent overseas for duty behind front lines. At first Formosan students were merely harangued on the moral obligation and glory of service to the emperor, but soon the Formosan students at all the Japanese universities were summoned to the offices of the military instructors on each campus, where they were invited to sign individual applications for volunteer duty. On our campus the names of those who had been "invited" were soon posted in a prominent public place. My name appeared as the only one who had not yet presented himself.

I promptly left Tokyo to consult with my brother, then a student in the Nagasaki Medical School. We met with other students from Formosa and spent long hours discussing my situation. I could not imagine myself submitting to the mindless regimentation of military service for Japan. I was a second-class subject in peacetime, and I could not serve as a first-class soldier in war.

After a week I returned to the campus in Tokyo, attending lectures and continuing to read for my courses. My name remained posted as the only one who had not yet volunteered, and I began to fear arrest. I moved my lodging from time to time and went to the campus less and less often. Fortunately the Japanese univer-

sity system permitted this, for we only had to pass our final examinations, and class attendance was not mandatory. Life in
Tokyo was bleak. Consumer goods were scarce, rationing had become severe, and the black markets were flourishing. The
government's optimistic news reports were received with growing skepticism, for the public sensed that the military situation
had taken a turn for the worse. The years 1943 and 1944 produced no victories to lift the public gloom and depression.

Fortunately for us, my father had made good financial arrangements. My brother was finishing his work in Nagasaki and
about to take charge of a public clinic in the small village of Tameishi twenty miles to the south. My second brother had to give
up his medical studies at Keio University because of ill health,
and made his way back to Formosa to rest and recover before all
communication with our island had been cut off. Allied subma-
rines and planes were taking a heavy toll on shipping near Japan.
Many died when the ships went down, and I lost several of my
friends.

I left Tokyo at last, going westward to the beautiful old castle
town of Matsumoto in the heart of the mountain country. It was
far from any military targets. No one in Tokyo knew of my
whereabouts, but I notified my brother in Nagasaki, and at Matsumoto found a cousin who was then enrolled at the local higher
school. He had written me that the food situation was comparatively good, but my first lodging proved to be very poor. Although I had managed to ship my books to Matsumoto, most of
them had to be left in their unwieldy boxes. I had little taste for
reading now, for on leaving the university I plunged into a period of extreme anxiety and despair.

A few other students and one laborer shared my lodging
house. As winter came it became very cold. There was little char-
coal and no hot water in which to wash our clothes in freezing
weather. This was snow country. The high mountains all around
were brilliantly white and beautiful, but cruel and repellent to

anyone born in the tropics. Then came word of the great Tokyo raids. We read the newspaper accounts with horror. Thousands had died in a single night, and the city was carpeted with fire.

The few young men remaining in Matsumoto were embarrassingly conspicuous and were stared at in the streets. When the weather permitted, I took long, lonely walks in the castle park or in the countryside. My first lodging house had become intolerable. The rooms were dirty and full of fleas seeking warmth. I found a better place and moved my ten boxes of books and my few other possessions into two upstairs rooms which I had to myself in the home of an old man and his daughter. These kind people took care of me, glad to have a little additional income in these hard times.

This tedious and lonely life continued for about six months. Now and then a letter came through from my parents, but my letters rarely reached them. Then came news that Takao city had been heavily bombed and my father's hospital destroyed. The family had survived, however, and had moved out into the countryside. This was the last I heard of my parents until after the war.

I was at a loss as to what to do with myself. It was a useless life and my funds were dwindling. My brother had married a doctor, the daughter of one of my father's classmates at medical school, and with their tiny daughter had moved to the fishing village, Tameishi, to take charge of the public clinic. We now agreed that the most economical course would be for me to join them there. Together we could conserve our dwindling resources while we waited to see what was going to happen to us all.

Japan was in full retreat at sea. Great raids were leveling the industrial cities and the ports, and the future looked hopeless. On April 1, 1945, the battle for Okinawa had begun. In desperation the Army organized suicidal *kamikaze* units which were sent out to strike the Allied fleet that now stood between Japan and Formosa.

In preparing to leave the old castle town, my first thought was for my beloved books which I shipped off to my closest friend of *San-ko* days, Jiro Nishida. He had gone on to study in the Department of Linguistics at Kyoto Imperial University. Because of ill-health he had escaped the draft and had returned to his country home in Kyushu. I wrote and asked him to take care of them. If I were alive at the end of the war I would come to claim them; if not, they were to be his. Meanwhile they would be stored not too far from my brother's place on the same island. I still don't know whether he ever received them. I reserved a few books, my dictionaries and the works of Anatole France and LeMaître, which I mailed directly to my brother's clinic.

Train tickets were not easy to get. A reluctant stationmaster issued me a ticket from Matsumoto to Nagasaki when I pleaded that my brother was in a hospital, and my young cousin saw me off. It was an emotional parting, for he would be left entirely alone in cold Matsumoto, and I was setting out on a long and dangerous journey, a thirty-hour trip. The route passed through Nagoya, Osaka, Kobe, Hiroshima, and Yawata in northern Kyushu, cities and towns then being subjected to devastating raids. I had to change trains at the rail centers which were also major targets.

I reached Nagasaki station about five o'clock in the afternoon of a late April day. Since my brother's village was twenty miles away, it was necessary to stay in the city overnight. On the next day I could choose to ride on a truck leaving rather early in the morning to cross the hills nearby, or I could board a small ferry at ten o'clock for an easier ride to my brother's village. Although I invariably become seasick on any craft large or small, I decided on the latter. I could sleep late, and I was exceedingly tired after sitting up throughout the long journey in third-class coaches.

Although picturesque Nagasaki was an important shipbuilding center, it had not been bombed. The government had eased rationing there, and rice was plentiful and good. An extraordinarily beautiful girl brought me a delicious dinner, and sat and chatted with me in my room as I ate. After a quiet night and an excellent breakfast, I set out, baggage in hand, for the ferry pier not far away. A small ship of thirty or forty tons was waiting, just ready to cast off. About thirty other men, women, and children were already aboard, lining the rails or settling down on deck mats for the short voyage. It was a beautiful day, and I was happy to see that the sea was calm.

As I went aboard and looked about for a sheltered spot, I heard overhead the peculiar whistling sound of a plane gliding down. It banked and began a steep climb with a sudden roar of motors. An instant later I was knocked unconscious to the deck by a tremendous explosion.

When I regained my senses and opened my eyes, I was in the midst of screaming confusion and a scene of horror. I was covered with blood, and the deck was awash with it, and strewn with bodies, the shattered parts of bodies, and people writhing, moaning, and struggling to drag themselves away. I tried to rise, and found to my disbelief and horror that my left arm had been torn off at the shoulder and was hanging there by a few tendons and a shred of skin. The shattered bones were exposed, and blood was pouring out. "This is the end," I thought, "I am dying here, and my parents and brother don't even know I am here."

The instinct for survival is powerful. With my right hand I seized my dangling left forearm, found it very heavy and strangely cold and without feeling. It was an extraordinary moment. I was in a state of shock and felt no pain, although I was conscious that I also had a wound of some sort on my left temple, for warm blood was trickling down into my eye and across my cheek. Struggling to my feet, feeling so strangely off-balance, I managed to cross the slippery deck, get down to the dock, and stagger into the street, feeling immensely alone in a screaming crowd. Over and over I said to myself, "I must get to a hospital! I must find a doctor!"

Knowing nothing of the town, I tried to speak to people running frantically to and fro. Two or three looked at me and turned away in shocked revulsion, for by now I was drenched in blood from head to feet, and they showed a natural human reaction to such a sight. Suddenly one middle-aged man shouted at me as if in anger, literally cursing me. I was astonished and even in that condition angry and disbelieving. "Why? Why such a response to a man in such an extreme condition?" It was only long after the war that I understood. He was using a Japanese military technique, a shout, a blow, or a violent shake to create shock and tension to revive a person about to faint, but at that moment I was in no condition to understand. After what seemed an eternity, though perhaps it was only a matter of moments, someone directed me to a small clinic in the street near the wharf. As I staggered through the door I lost consciousness.

When I came to, I was lying on the concrete floor of a dark reception area, only one of a large number of victims being brought in. One doctor and one nurse were trying desperately to offer first aid to all while waiting for an emergency medical team from the Nagasaki Medical School nearby.

I was lying motionless, drifting in and out of consciousness, when doctors and nurses came in. To my astonishment I saw that one of them was an eye specialist, Dr. Yo, my brother's classmate, and best friend, one of the Formosans who had counseled me on my previous visit to Nagasaki. This was a miracle! I tried to attract his attention each time he passed, kicking at his ankles and calling his name. I thought I was shouting, but I was probably speaking in a whisper. "Dr. Yo! Dr. Yo! This is Peng!"

He had passed me three or four times before he looked down and finally recognized me despite the blood and tatters. "What? You are here?" he exclaimed in shocked disbelief. In a moment, summoning a nurse, he gave me a hasty examination and first aid as best he could, an emergency stimulant twice, directly to the heart. The blood-loss was obviously great and my life in peril when he gathered me up and sent me off at once to the nearby hospital.

I have no clear memory of this interlude. When I regained my senses, I was on an operating table and the surgeon was completing the removal of my left arm, shattered at the shoulder-joint. I was alive but little more.

Somehow Dr. Yo had managed to get word to my brother. He had come to Nagasaki as quickly as he could, riding the truck over the mountain road. I was dimly aware of his presence and it was comforting. A fearful night followed. My brother had left me to consult with the surgeon, to attend to urgent business, and to get some badly needed rest. Although I still felt no pain, I developed a burning thirst. There were no nurses available, and once or twice I attempted to get up for water. My weakness from blood-loss and the strange imbalance of my body caused by the loss of my left arm, caused me to fall to the floor. Lying there in the darkened room I began to realize that this accident marked an irrevocable and fundamental change in my life.

My sister-in-law joined us in Nagasaki the next day, but they lived too far away and were too busy to come often thereafter. It was decided that I should remain as long as necessary in the Nagasaki hospital where I had a room to myself on the third floor. Since there were no trained nurses available to care for me, my sister-in-law engaged an old woman who began soon to complain of the flights of stairs and of my requests that she go out early each morning to buy the local papers, issued now in limited number. She had to be dismissed. To replace her we hired a girl of obscure background who did the best she could quite willingly but sometimes was given to odd behavior. We were plagued with mosquitoes, and to my embarrassment, when she had hung the bed-net each evening, she would slip in, bared to the waist, to sleep on the floor within its protective folds. In contrast, there was a very kind young nurse who used to come in sometimes on her off-duty hours to feed me and help me move. Whenever she came I was visibly in better spirits and cheerful, and this seemed to delight her.

All hospitals in Japan were undergoing a severe shortage of medical personnel and supplies of every kind. The dressings on my wound could be changed only every few days and the medications and equipment were not sufficiently sterile. When maggots were found in the wound, I suffered a psychological shock. Moreover, I began to suffer terrible itching sensations where my lost arm and hand should be, and there was nothing there to scratch. At times this drove me to the point of desperation. At last blood poisoning set in, because of unsterile dressings, and I developed an extremely high fever. The doctors almost gave up on my case. I needed a massive blood transfusion.

At that time the Japanese people were generally undernourished. There were no blood banks and no selling of blood. However I was extremely fortunate because several Formosan students at the Nagasaki Medical College heard of my need and volunteered. My blood-type is O, and four students saved my life by gifts of blood. One of these was a Pepohuan, an assimilated lowland aborigine.

It was now mid-June. Nagasaki was not being bombed very often, but when the alerts sounded, usually in the night, it was necessary for the hospital staff to carry all patients down into the basement shelter. After being in bed without exercise for six weeks or more, I was extremely weak. These midnight trips, down four flights of stairs, were very painful. Psychologically too there was great strain, for whenever we heard planes overhead while sheltering in the dark basement, we expected a bomb to drop. It was a nightmare to be endured every night. Bombs were falling on towns and cities throughout Japan, and the Americans had begun to shower leaflets over Nagasaki warning people to leave the city.

One day the hospital administrators were ordered suddenly to empty the hospital of all who could possibly be sent elsewhere to shelter. Only a skeleton staff would remain to care for air raid victims. My sister-in-law had been coming in once or twice a week to bring me food. We now agreed that I must go to my brother's home. They could dress my wound, and since the food situation in the village was comparatively good, and seaweed and vegetables were plentiful, I might gain strength. The journey was an ordeal, however, for by now even the truck service was erratic. I would have to ride out of Nagasaki as far as I could, then walk for more than an hour over a steep and stony path to a point where another truck might be available for the onward journey to Tameishi.

On the day of that painful journey my brother was unable to come into Nagasaki, so his pregnant wife took his place. Without her valiant help I could never have completed the trip. More than two months had passed since my injury; nevertheless I was extremely weak and had no proper sense of balance. When at last we reached my brother's home, exhausted, I cried as much from emotional relief as from pain, but I was overwhelmed by a black despair. Would my life be always like this?

Somehow my parents in distant Formosa had heard that I had been the victim of a bombing raid. They attempted to cable my brother, but no message came through. They were convinced that I was dead, and for weeks spent sleepless nights in tears and agonizing remorse. They blamed themselves for not having sent more funds to me so that it would have been unnecessary for me to make the fatal trip to Nagasaki. Such was their love for me. This had been a double blow since my beloved grandfather had died about this time. He had spoken of me so often by my nick-name "Bin," for I had been one of his favorite grandsons, and when he was dying he was heard to say, "My only consolation is that I'm going to meet Bin in Heaven!"

Little by little I regained my strength and began to recover my spirits. New great silver planes, the huge B-29s, flew over nearly every day on their deadly missions. The Japanese had lost Okinawa on June 18. Official announcements and stories in the Nagasaki press played up the story of heroic last-ditch resistance and patriotism, but the military significance of the island's loss could scarcely be concealed from even the more uninformed Japanese.

It was a great psychological blow, for it was realized that an invasion of Kyushu must soon take place. The newspapers candidly told of massive attacks on the larger cities and the appalling conditions in Tokyo, Nagoya, and Osaka. Our little village was not bombed, although occasionally American planes bombed and strafed the fishing fleet not far offshore. We expected the enemy to land any day. Many women sharpened bamboo spears and practiced using them, and some women and children retreated to the hills.

July came. Sometimes the heat and tension seemed unbearable. As the weeks passed my wound began to heal satisfactorily at last, and my brother very skillfully began to fashion a light artificial arm for me, using bamboo, wire and cloth. He felt that it would help me adjust psychologically to my new condition. I was suffering from severe digestive troubles, possibly induced by the unrelieved tension in which we lived. There was no news from home. Fortunately my precious selection of books, my dictionaries, and the volumes of LeMaître and Anatole France, had come through safely by mail, but I had no further news of the larger shipments sent down to my friend Nishida. I was in no mood to read seriously, however, since I spent my days and evenings in long walks along the shore.

On August 8 the Nagasaki newspapers carried a brief official announcement, "Yesterday Hiroshima was bombed. The Americans have used a new weapon. There was considerable damage," but no particular attention was paid to such a routine bombing announcement. As we were to learn much later, 150 thousand men, women, and children had perished in an instant when that first atomic bomb exploded.

Three days later I was indoors, glancing through the newspaper when I heard the drone of a plane overhead. Suddenly there was a blinding light, as if a huge photo-flashbulb had been triggered in the room. This was followed instantly by a tremendous metallic clanging sound as if the whole earth had been hit by a gigantic hammer. Our house shook violently. Something prompted me to cry out in Formosan "What is it?" as I looked out to see an enormous black cloud over Nagasaki. Then the great white mushroom rose above it. Later there was a sudden light shower in our garden, falling out of a clear sky.

Within an hour, my brother rushed into the house. He had received an urgent call. All doctors had been summoned to meet at a certain place for transportation into Nagasaki. Taking a quick lunch and gathering up his medical kit, he rushed away.

That afternoon we heard that Nagasaki had been destroyed, *zenmatsu* ("obliterated"). The Americans had used their new weapon again. It was rumored that everyone in Nagasaki was dead. When my brother returned, late that night, he was in a state of shock and nausea. He could barely speak and had to struggle for words with which to tell us what he had seen. The city as we knew it was gone. The whole area was dead.

He left again at dawn the next day to help search for and treat survivors who were dragging themselves out of the ruins. There were appalling injuries and incredible stories were told by the people who began to come into the village from the ruined city. Although my sister-in-law was in the last days of a second pregnancy, she did what she could at the clinic during my brother's absence. He was overjoyed to find our friend Dr. Yo alive.

The effects of the blast had produced an irrational pattern of damage. Some concrete structures still stood, but all wooden fixtures and other combustible materials had been instantly consumed. It was said that in some classrooms only neat piles of white ashes marked the spots where students had been seated at their desks at the fatal moment. The heat had been that intense. A majority of medical school students had perished, and among them were the four young Formosans who had so generously given blood to me. It was a tragic irony that their useful lives should be snuffed out and that I should live.

One of my brother's best friends, Dr. Lin, and his wife lived in the center of the city at the time of the atomic explosion. However, miraculously, they survived unharmed. Although they had not had children before the war, they had several normal children afterward.

It was midsummer. Soon the dead city gave off an intolerable stench. Relief work meant an extraordinary test of human will. There had been about 70,000 victims, and many injured survivors could be moved only a short distance. Within a few days a new horror appeared. Scores of survivors suddenly began to bleed from the nose and mouth, the hair dropped out, and soon many died. My brother and his fellow-doctors were at a loss with this new phenomena.

The government had made a brief announcement that Nagasaki had been destroyed but vowed that the nation would fight on. On August 14, it was announced that the emperor himself would address the nation. My sister-in-law and I were in the village street when we heard this unprecedented broadcast begin. Reception was extremely poor. We understood little more than that Japan had agreed to unconditional surrender. The nation was asked to "bear the unbearable," but this meant that peace had come at last.

As Formosans we were not so awed by the high-pitched imperial voice as our Japanese friends about us; nevertheless, we were deeply moved. Our astonishment was followed by a sense of immeasurable relief. An era had ended. What would come next? What would become of Formosans in Japan? What would become of Formosa?

III

Return
to Formosa and
to University Life

We decided to return to Formosa as soon as possible.
No other thought occurred to us. We had been born under the
Japanese flag, we had many Japanese friends, and we had been
law-abiding subjects. If we had wished, my brother could continue to carry on here in the medical profession, and I could
complete my education in the best university in Japan. A number
of our Formosan friends elected to stay, but we were determined
to leave as soon as possible. We felt we must go home.

It was as if Japan had suddenly lost all memory of Formosa.
We searched the papers daily for any scrap of news, but during
the late summer saw only one brief note. General Chen Yi had
been appointed governor general on Chiang Kai-shek's behalf,
and my father's acquaintance Huang Chao-chin was to become
the first postwar mayor of Taipei.

There were now six in our household, for about ten days after
the surrender, my sister-in-law gave birth to a second daughter.
She was being cared for very well by the Formosan maidservant
who had accompanied her to Japan and was considered to be a
member of her family. We were the only Formosans in Tameishi
village.

Immediately after the emperor's surrender broadcast many

American planes began to fly over us at very low altitude. We heard that Allied prisoners of war had been released and that these planes were parachuting food to them. It was believed that an American landing was imminent. Many village girls and women retreated to the hills, taking their sharpened spears with them. They had been told often that all American soldiers were devils, beasts, and rapists, and they believed it.

Americans did begin to appear in the area about twenty days after the surrender. My brother and I encountered a jeep on a nearby mountain road and were surprised and interested in this new vehicle. Soldiers, black and white, began coming into the village, and at once the American image changed radically. There was a curious emotional swing to another extreme. The anticipated devils proved to be wonderfully kind and helpful human beings. There was candy for the children, cigarettes for older people, and extraordinary stories of first encounters. There were occasional reports of a rape or a robbery, but as a whole the Japanese were astounded that conquerors were often so considerate. For example, when the overburdened village truck broke down on the mountain road one evening, an American jeep came along, the driver carefully maneuvered to light the scene with his headlights, and helped the harassed driver make repairs. The passengers and the driver were overwhelmed.

There was no interference with village life. American patrols drove through the streets from time to time, but the villagers were left unmolested. One day I fell into conversation with two Americans in a jeep beside the road, and in passing, explained to them that I was not a Japanese, but a Chinese from Formosa. It was something of a shock to find myself for the first time openly and proudly making this distinction.

My brother remained in charge of the Tameishi Clinic throughout the autumn months. We were safe, he was being paid properly, and we were comparatively comfortable. Still we longed to go home. No letters came from Takao. My young cousin at Matsumoto had decided to remain in Japan to complete

his medical education, not realizing that fifteen years would pass
before he would visit Formosa. We had no word from my sister
who had gone to Shanghai and Peking with her husband during
the war. Now that my wound had healed and I was regaining my
strength, I was restless. Occasionally I went into Nagasaki where
there were many Americans and many of the new jeeps and bull-
dozers, a powerful wartime American invention being used to
clear away shattered buildings and open the streets once more.
Enormous heaps of rubble everywhere created the effect of a gigantic city dump.

One afternoon in late December I returned from Nagasaki on
the village truck to find our house in an uproar. We had been
notified that we would leave at once for home. We would be allowed to take with us only hand baggage and had to be at the
Nagasaki railway station before midnight ready to board a train
for Sasebo naval port. There we would take a ship for Keelung.

I wanted to carry my precious books and at last prevailed
upon my brother to allow me to scatter a few volumes here and
there through the bags and bundles the three fit adults must
carry. I could carry very little. My brother had to cope with all
the gear necessary to supply two babies and four adults. All that
we could not carry we gave away to our Japanese friends and
neighbors.

At Nagasaki station we found twenty or thirty other Formosans, the medical students who had survived, our friend Dr. Yo
and his family, and a few others, all eager to reach Formosa. Japanese officials were in charge of the arrangements under the
general direction of American military authorities. In a special
compartment set aside for evacuees and their luggage, I found
myself talking with a very young Korean girl on her way home to
Seoul. We had all come to a dramatic point of change in our
lives. It was a new era, and we were no longer second-class subjects of the Japanese emperor, but we were not sure of what lay
ahead. The Koreans had been promised independence, and we
Formosans had been promised freedom in a new, reformed, post-

war China, and had been handed over to Generalissimo Chiang Kai-shek.

At Sasebo we were hustled aboard an overcrowded converted cargo ship and left to find ourselves some space for the long homeward voyage. A majority of the passengers were young Formosans who had been conscripted for labor corps service with the Japanese Army. They were a tough, restless lot and many quarrels erupted among them. Nevertheless they were all glad to be going home.

Having been rushed to Sasebo and aboard ship, we sat rocking in the harbor for one week in utter misery. When we left the sheltered anchorage at last and moved out upon the rough high seas, we were thoroughly seasick. In this unhappy condition we were then told that the waters through which we would pass were full of mines and some repatriation ships had been sunk with a heavy loss of life. Watches were organized among the passengers to take turns at the rail throughout the voyage.

We reached Keelung at nightfall on January 2, 1946, still without word from our parents and with no friends or relatives to greet us. The devastation in Keelung was astonishing, for this port city had suffered an estimated eighty percent total destruction during the battle for Okinawa. It had been bombed thoroughly in order to keep it from Japanese use during that fearful encounter nearby.

We came off the ship, hired rickshas at the dock, and made our way to the home of a noted doctor, my father's old friend and classmate. When along the way we noticed a crowd of dirty men in ragged uniforms and remarked that they were not Formosans, our ricksha men said in contempt and disgust that they were Chinese Nationalist soldiers, recently delivered to Keelung by American ships coming over from continental ports.

We were welcomed with great cordiality into the doctor's home, and our first great pleasure was to learn that our parents were well and had moved back into Takao, now called Kaohsiung. Even though we were very tired, we talked excitedly until long after midnight. Much that we heard was terribly depressing. Between August 15, the day of the imperial surrender announcement at Tokyo, and October 26, when General Chen Yi at Taipei officially took over the administration of Formosa on behalf of Chiang Kai-shek, the Japanese had continued to administer the city. The main streets had been repaired and considerable progress had been made in clearing building sites and restoring public services. But then a paralysis had set in. The utility services were faltering, public officials newly arriving from China proved incompetent and incredibly corrupt, and the rag-tag conscript Nationalist troops were petty thieves, becoming a rabble of scavengers as soon as they came off the ships. It was a gloomy picture, but even so we were glad to be back in Formosa.

In a gray dawn the next morning we had our first experience of the change that had overtaken Formosa now that Nationalist Chinese were in charge. Before the war the Japanese government had maintained a precise schedule for twelve or fourteen trains running each day between Keelung and Takao. Some were expresses, some semi-expresses, and some were locals. There had been little wartime damage to the main lines. The railway installations near Taipei were larger and better equipped than any in China, and these too had escaped serious damage.

At the time of surrender in October the rolling stock was extremely shabby, but it was intact. Now we discovered that under Chinese management only one through train per day linked Keelung with Kaohsiung. The Keelung station was filthy and crowded with dirty soldiers who had been hanging about all night for want of a better shelter. When our train pulled in, there was a wild scramble to get aboard. As the pushing crowd surged forward, baggage and children were thrust in through the windows, and adults scrambled in after them in a fierce struggle to obtain space. Somehow we managed to find seats and began the long slow ride. The chill January air poured in through broken windows, the seats had been stripped of green plush that had once covered them, and it was obvious that the cars had not been cleaned for many weeks. This was "Chinese Formosa" and not the Japanese Formosa we had known. We had never seen anything like this dirt and disorder on a public train in our lives.

For us, however, nothing could detract from the joy of riding southward again through the beautiful countryside of our island. As we drew near Ta-chia we looked out on our father's fields and watched eagerly for familiar sites associated with our childhood. We fell into conversation with fellow passengers who came and went at the stations along the way, some entering through the windows and some through the doors. The story was always the same, a tale of dissatisfaction and disappointment with the new government. Security of property was a thing of the past. There were frequent long, unexplained delays along the way, and these brought up stories of well-organized gangs of looters who had stripped the right-of-way of copper wires and carried off signal equipment for shipment to Shanghai or Amoy to be sold as scrap. "Nobody knows when this train may be derailed," a passenger remarked. Since the Chinese had taken over management of the railways, shippers had to send private guards along with cargo sent in the baggage cars and freight trains. The newly arrived government officials themselves were sharing in the loot.

After fourteen hours on the train we reached our destination after nightfall. I had been absent from my home for nearly six years. Only the sight of the beautiful countryside and the anticipation of reunion with our parents kept us from deep depression. We left the station not knowing the address of our parents' new home, but one of the local ricksha men knew of the clinic and we set off at once. It was about nine o'clock at night when our little fleet of rickshas pulled up before a small, two-storied concrete house. A sign before it advertised the clinic on the ground floor and the residence was above.

The gate was securely barred. Since we could find no bell, we knocked loudly and even the ricksha men joined us in calling loudly "Open up! Open up!," for they seemed to share in giving

us a welcome. My parents had no cause for alarm, for they had
heard that repatriation ships were beginning to arrive from
Japan and my sister-in-law's voice, the voice of a woman,
surely meant that this was no marauding band of Nationalist soldiers. They assumed correctly that my brother and his family
had arrived.

When they threw open the door they were astonished to see
me, too. They had believed me dead. It was an emotional
reunion. My parents at once asked us all to pray with them,
thanking God for our safe return. My father then with tears
sought to console me for the loss of my arm and the consequent
great changes in my life. There were two new grandchildren to
be admired. Through the hours of excited conversation that followed my father could not conceal his feeling that the whole
prospect for Formosa was grim. Repeatedly he said, "We are in a
terrible situation."

In the next few days and weeks relatives and friends came to
see us and we went about visiting them in turn. Gradually I
heard my father unfold the story of the Japanese surrender, the
arrival of Chinese troops in south Formosa, and the rapid corruption of public life thereafter. The Nationalists were undoubtedly
pulling us down to the general level of chaotic life in continental
Chinese provinces. He had always remained aloof from politics
and public office before the war, but immediately after the surrender the Japanese officials in Kaohsiung sought him out with
an invitation to become chairman of a local committee formed to
maintain local law and order until the Chinese should arrive to
assume control. He was a respected senior citizen, acceptable to
Japanese and Formosans alike. Like a majority of his Formosan
associates, he was glad that Japanese rule had come to an end.
The great economic and social benefits of Japanese administration had never been enough for self-respecting Formosans who
bitterly resented social and political discrimination. Formosan
leaders and students had been demanding home rule for the
island since World War I. In 1945 the victorious Allies, princi-

pally the Americans, used radio broadcasts and leaflet drops to promise Formosans a bright future in a postwar freedom under China. Accepting these promises at face value my father agreed to be a committee chairman, believing that he could help bring about this new era of great promise.

In late October word came at last that Chinese military units were expected to land at Takao. My father was made chairman of a welcoming committee. The job soon became a nightmare. He was notified that the troops would arrive on a certain date. Preparations included the purchase of firecrackers and of banners bearing appropriate sentiments, construction of temporary booths at the exits from the landing stage, and preparation of huge amounts of roast pork and other delicacies, soft drinks, and tea. Then came notification that the arrival was delayed. The perishable foods had to be sold or given away. This happened twice again, tripling the expenses, before a fourth notification proved to be correct.

An American naval vessel came slowly into Takao harbor, making its way among the sunken hulks. Local Japanese military authorities, awaiting repatriation with their men, turned out a smartly disciplined honor guard to line the wharf, ready to salute the victorious Chinese army. A great crowd of curious and excited citizens had come to support my father's welcoming committee and to see the show.

The ship docked, the gangways were lowered, and off came the troops of China, the victors. The first man to appear was a bedraggled fellow who looked and behaved more like a coolie than a soldier, walking off with a carrying pole across his shoulder, from which was suspended his umbrella, sleeping mat, cooking pot, and cup. Others like him followed, some with shoes, some without. Few had guns. With no attempt to maintain order or discipline, they pushed off the ship, glad to be on firm land, but hesitant to face the Japanese lined up and saluting smartly on both sides. My father wondered what the Japanese could possibly think. He had never felt so ashamed in his life. Using a Jap-

anese expression, he said, "If there had been a hole nearby, I
would have crawled in!" This victorious Chinese army was made
up of country conscripts who showed not the least sign of understanding the welcome arranged for them. They moved into the
town, grabbing up what food they wanted and tossing aside
things they did not like. There was no acknowledgment by the
few Chinese officers accompanying them and no thanks for anyone. Within an hour these troops, spreading through the town,
had begun to pick up anything that struck their fancy. As far as
they were concerned, the Formosans were a conquered people.

Now that some Chinese troops were ashore and a garrison
present in Kaohsiung, Chinese civil officials began to venture
down from Taipei in larger numbers. They asked my father for
advice and directed him to represent the Formosan side during
the takeover. He was quickly disillusioned, he said, for invariably
the first question seemed to be, "How much money is there in the
city bank?" That is the kind of question any new administration
would eventually ask, but it was always their very first question,
and because of the way it was asked, it left an extremely bad impression on my father and other Formosans. It was apparent that
these petty officials coming down from the capital were little better than the common soldiers. Soon they began to dress well and
to commandeer good houses. The reason for the new affluence
was apparent to all Formosans who had to deal with them. They
were carpetbaggers. From one end of Formosa to the other looting was in progress at all levels. The common conscript roaming
in Kaohsiung was simply taking what he wanted from shops and
homes and the public streets. The newcomers from Taipei had
been sent down by the highest officials to loot the sugar mills and
warehouses, the factory stockpiles and industrial equipment.
Junks were leaving the harbor every day loaded with foodstocks,
scrap metal, machine tools, and consumer goods of every variety,
destined for private sales along the China coast.

Father's sense of humor prompted him to suggest that someone
should collect stories of the incoming Chinese, especially of the

ignorant conscripts who had been shipped over to Formosa from inland provinces on the continent. Many were totally unacquainted with modern technology. Some had never seen or had never understood a modern water system. There were instances in which they picked up water faucets in plumber's shops and then, pushing them into holes in walls and embankments, had expected water to flow. They then complained bitterly to the plumbers from whose shops the faucets came. There was a story of one soldier who took a seat in a barber's shop, had his hair cut, and then when the barber picked up an electric hair-dryer, instantly put up his hands pale with fright thinking it was a pistol.

My father had his own special problems. A large sign at our entrance advertised a gynecological clinic, but soldiers insisted upon coming in for VD treatments, or brought remarkable and unidentifiable salves and liquids which they insisted he should inject into them. Injections were believed to be the cure-all for every ill.

Every week produced some new story of such behavior or some new instance of theft on a grand scale. For a time my father was very active in public affairs. The mayor consulted him often, and he became speaker in the local city council. His integrity was unchallenged, his clinic was busy, and he was beginning to recover financially from the losses suffered during the war. Since our house was overcrowded, he decided to rebuild on the site of his burned-out older hospital. One day he happened to remark to the mayor that he proposed to clear the site. "That's no problem," said the mayor, and within a day or two about thirty Japanese soldiers came to the clinic. The officer in charge said that they were awaiting repatriation, and they would like to help.

We went to the old hospital site. They worked hard and efficiently. My mother provided tea and food. For my part I was astonished to find myself "commanding" so many Japanese soldiers, and recalled with a smile my unfortunate military record at *San-ko*. To our embarrassment, the Japanese would accept no pay.

Our relations with the Japanese in this period were peculiar. They were awaiting repatriation, waiting for General MacArthur to give them permission to return to Japan. Those who had been in authority throughout our lives were now taking orders from us. The Japanese policeman, once a petty overlord, had now put aside his official sword and uniform, and was glad to find work of any sort. Teachers who had enjoyed high prestige were forced to sell their possessions one by one. I saw a number of my Takao Middle School teachers peddling small objects in the streets. In some cases former students rallied to help them in this difficult period, but in a few instances old scores were settled, and teachers who had been intolerant disciplinarians were badly beaten.

Throughout this period my father was in an uneasy position. Loyalty to his friends and to his profession prompted him to help the Japanese doctors awaiting repatriation, but he also knew that incoming Chinese were seizing private clinics and stripping Japanese doctors of valuable medical equipment and supplies. When a Chinese with some influence wanted a particular property, he had only to accuse a Formosan of being a collaborationist during the past fifty years of Japanese sovereignty.

THE TIME HAD COME for me to make some decision about my future. My indulgent parents urged me to remain at home to rest for a longer period, but I was physically well recovered. I was twenty-three years old and restless. Periods of natural youthful optimism alternated with periods of hopeless depression. And I was beginning to be bored. Kaohsiung offered little intellectual stimulation, and I longed to get back among books.

Since I lacked one year's credit for my Tokyo Imperial University degree, I looked into the possibility of completing work for a diploma at the former Taihoku Imperial University, founded by the Japanese in 1927 and now, twenty years later, occupied by the incoming Chinese. It had recently been renamed the National Taiwan University or *Taita* for short. The Japanese had developed it as a center of research and teaching principally in agriculture and medicine. The humanities and the social sciences were weak. However, a splendid library was there along with the buildings and grounds and laboratories. Now it was being managed by scientists recently arrived from the continent. The new emphasis was to be on physics and agriculture.

In the summer of 1946 it was announced that all Formosans who had come home from the imperial universities in Japan were entitled to enter the new *Taita* without examination. They would merely enroll at Taipei and be accepted as transfers as soon as the university resumed operations. At once I went to Taipei. About thirty of us who qualified under these terms met to discuss the offer. We had come from faculties of law, economics, and political science, and we were an elite group, for we had survived the fierce competition to enter the best institutions in Japan.

After discussing our problems, we called upon the dean and the president of the reconstituted university. They were scientists. Neither had any idea what to do with anyone not prepared to enter the science courses. We asked if our work in the Japanese universities would be given credit toward degrees at *Taita*. They did not know. Despite the published invitation that had drawn us to Taipei on this occasion, they were not prepared for our enrollment. They would have to refer the question to the Ministry of Education at Nanking. We then asked if they expected to bring in professors of social science and the humanities. They didn't know. This too would have to be referred to the authorities at Nanking.

By this time most Formosans had come to realize that under General Chen Yi's administration few policy promises made locally could be relied upon, and that communications between officials in the government on Formosa and the central government offices at Nanking were in confusion. We decided to take as few risks as possible. The Chinese university system was based upon the four-year, hour-and-credit formula derived from the American university system, whereas our Japanese university program had derived from European patterns. We obtained copies of all pertinent Chinese Ministry of Education publications, studied them carefully and found that the hours of course work were explicitly stated. After several meetings we decided that to be on the safe side we must meet all the requirements as specified by Nanking and take all the specified courses leading to degrees. Thus in the long run we would avoid embarrassing either ourselves or members of the new *Taita* administration.

We discussed our problem repeatedly with the new university administrators and discovered quickly that they were not only unfamiliar with the Ministry of Education requirements in fields other than their own, they simply did not care. This reflected the disarray and incompetence throughout General Chen Yi's administration. His commissioner of education was a nonentity in China's academic world, who in his first public address in Formosa told the Formosans bluntly that he thought them a backward people. The other commissioners cared little or nothing about the university as there was little money to be squeezed from it. What the new university administration chose to do was of minor interest.

Soon a curious situation arose. We students organized courses, recruited staff, and ran part of the Taiwan National University. We notified the administration that we were prepared to earn all the course-credits prescribed by Nanking and were ready to begin. When the dean protested that *Taita* had no professors in our fields, we assured him that we could find some for him.

To begin, we found some Formosan lawyers and an economist who were all graduates of the Tokyo Imperial University and each well qualified to teach. The young economist, for example, had been a protégé of Japan's distinguished economist Dr. Tadao Yanaihara, one-time president of the Tokyo school, the most prestigious institution in Japan. One of the lawyers had served on the bench in Japan, reaching the highest judicial office ever occupied by a Formosan in prewar years.

Our recommendations were accepted. This show of interest

and determination on our part stimulated the president and dean of *Taita* to begin recruiting faculty in China for service at Taipei. For a time the situation continued to be unusual, to say the least, for we students found ourselves informally charged with the responsibility of carrying through the innovations, setting up courses when we could find capable instructors, prescribing hours and schedules according to basic Ministry of Education requirements. If the new teachers could provide notes, we undertook to cut stencils and distribute mimeographed copies. As the first lecture series were completed we organized our own notes, mimeographed these, and supplied them as supplementary materials for the students who followed us. We continued to search for qualified and capable instructors and recruited several specialists who were glad to teach at the university. Some of the lectures were delivered in Formosan and some in Mandarin. At that time all of us could read formal Chinese texts, and very quickly learned to speak it.

Under these circumstances our student-life was very busy but easy, and not to be compared with the preexamination periods of intensive study we had all experienced in Japan. We disregarded only one important Nanking Ministry regulation, the precisely even, four annual divisions of degree courses, and by stepping up the pace, we completed the Ministry of Education credit-hour requirements in two years. It was an unorthodox performance, to be sure, but we were an unusual group. Each of us had proved himself in competition near the summit of the Japanese empire's educational system, but at the war's end we had been at different levels and stages of development in the three-year Japanese university curriculum. Now we were working more or less as a body, adapting ourselves to the four-year Chinese system, calling ourselves at my suggestion the *San-San Kai* ("Three-Three Club"), representing three fields, law, economics and political science, and three years in the Japanese system. We got along well enough with our faculty and fellow-students at the university, but as students of law, economics, and political science, we looked about us with growing disillusionment and anger, for as we completed our degree requirements, the island passed through a bloody crisis.

IV

The March
Uprising, 1947

Formosa's legal status was peculiar. China had ceded
Formosa and the Pescadores to Japan in 1895. Tokyo then gave
the inhabitants two years in which to choose nationality, and a
few thousand Formosans chose to leave or to register as Chinese
subjects. The great majority did not, however, and for fifty years
thereafter they and their children and grandchildren were Japanese subjects by law. Had they wished to migrate to China at
any time, they could arrange to do so. Some did, but the vast majority remained. Under the Japanese they enjoyed the benefits of
a rule of law. The police were strict, often harsh, and the Japanese colonial administration treated Formosans as second-class
citizens. However, under Japanese reorganization and direction
our island economy had made spectacular gains, and our living
standard rose steadily until among Asian countries we were
second only to Japan in agricultural and industrial technology, in
communications, in public health, and in provisions for the general public welfare. Our grandparents had witnessed this trans-
formation from a backward, ill-governed, disorganized island
nominally dependent on the Chinese. They did not like the
Japanese, but they appreciated the economic and social benefits
of fifty years of peace which they enjoyed while the Chinese on

the mainland proper endured fifty years of revolution, warlord-
ism, and civil war.

In our father's generation, and in our own, hundreds of well-
educated young Formosans had supported a home rule movement. This was first organized during World War I when
they were encouraged by the American president's call for
the universal recognition of the rights of minority people.
Throughout the 1920s Formosan leaders pressed the Japanese
government for a share in island government, and, at last, in 1935,
Tokyo began to yield. Local elections were held for local
assemblies, the voting rights were gradually enlarged, and in
early 1945 it was announced that Formosans at last would be
granted equal political rights with the Japanese.

But it was too late. By then Japan faced defeat and young Formosan home rule leaders were reading and listening to promises
broadcast to them by the American government, promises of a
new postwar life in a democratic China. To us this meant freedom to participate in island government at all levels and to elect
Formosans to represent the island in the national government of
China.

Japan surrendered Formosa to the Allied Powers at Yokohama
on September 3, 1945. Transfer of sovereignty to China would
not take place, however, until a peace conference produced a formal treaty. In view of promises made by President Roosevelt to
Generalissimo Chiang at Cairo in 1943, promises then reaffirmed
by President Truman at Potsdam, Washington decreed that the
island of Formosa and the Pescadores should be handed over to
the Nationalist Chinese for administration pending legal transfer.
There was no reservation of Allied rights during this interim period and no reservation of Formosan interests. There was no pro-
vision offering Formosans a choice of citizenship as there had
been in 1895. The Formosans, whether they liked it or not, were
to be restored to China.

Formosa was a rich prize for the ruling Nationalists. Keelung
and Kaohsiung had been heavily damaged and Taipei city had

suffered, but the basic industrial and agricultural structure was there. Warehouses were full of sugar, rice, chemicals, rubber, and other raw materials that had not been shipped to Japan. The power plants and sugar mills were not badly damaged. The Japanese prepared an elaborate and carefully detailed report of all public and private properties handed over to General Chen Yi on October 25. It was estimated that these confiscated Japanese properties had a value of some two billion American dollars at that time. At Chungking and Nanking the factions around Generalissimo Chiang, the armed forces, the civil bureaucracy, the party, and the powerful organizations of Madame Chiang's family had competed fiercely to gain immediate control of this island prize. A temporary provincial administration was set up, and the Generalissimo made Lieutenant General Chen Yi the new governor general, carefully surrounding him with representatives of other leading factions, principally of the army, the air force, and Madame Chiang's interests. T. V. Soong had hired representatives of an American firm to survey Formosan industrial resources on his behalf, and the surveying team reached the island even before Chen Yi arrived to accept the formal local surrender and transfer.

American planes and ships ferried the Nationalists from China to the new island possession. Formosans welcomed them enthusiastically in October 1945, thinking that a splendid new era was at hand. Within weeks we found that Governor Chen Yi and his commissioners were contemptuous of the Formosan people and were unbelievably corrupt and greedy. For eighteen months they looted our island. The newcomers had lived all their lives in the turmoil of civil war and of the Japanese invasion. They were carpetbaggers, occupying enemy territory, and we were being treated as a conquered people.

In the nineteenth century, Formosa had been controlled by a disorderly garrison government, notorious even in China for its corruption and inefficiency, but after a half-century of strict Japanese administration we had learned the value of the rule of law. People made contracts and kept them. It was generally assumed that one's neighbor was an honest man. In the shops a fixed price system had made it possible for every merchant to know where he stood. We had learned that modern communications, scientific agriculture, and efficient industries must operate within a system of honest measurement, honored contracts, and dependable timing.

All these standards were ignored by our new masters. We were often treated with contempt. Incoming government officials and the more intelligent and educated carpetbaggers made it evident that they looked upon honesty as a laughable evidence of stupidity. In the dog-eat-dog confusion of Chinese life during the war years, these men had survived and reached their present positions largely through trickery, cheating, and double-talk, often the only means of survival in the Chinese cities from which they came. To them we were country bumpkins and fair game.

The continental Chinese have traditionally looked upon the island of Formosa as a barbarous dependency. Addressing a large gathering of students soon after he arrived, the new commissioner of education said so, with blunt discourtesy, and this provoked an angry protest. On the other hand, Formosans laughed openly and jeered at newcomers who showed so often that they were unfamiliar with modern equipment and modern organization. I witnessed many examples of Chinese incompetence myself and heard of other extraordinary instances. There were well-advertised incidents when officials insisted upon attempting to drive automobiles without taking driving lessons, on the assumption that if a stupid Formosan could drive any intelligent man from the continent could do so. The conscript soldiers from inland Chinese provinces were the least acquainted with modern mechanisms. Many could not ride bicycles, and having stolen them or taken them forcibly from young Formosans, they had to walk off carrying the machines on their backs.

The year 1946 was one of increasing disillusionment. At all levels of the administration and economic enterprise Formosans were being dismissed to make way for the relatives and friends of men in Chen Yi's organization. The secretary general, Chen Yi's civil administrator, had promptly placed seven members of his family in lucrative positions. One of them was given charge of Formosa's multimillion dollar tea export industry. The new manager of the Taichung Pineapple Company, one of the world's largest producers before World War II, was a Y.M.C.A. secretary from Shanghai who had never seen a pineapple plant. The new police chief in Kaohsiung was believed to have more than forty members of his family and close associates on the payroll. The commissioner of agriculture and forestry attempted to sequester a large number of privately owned junks on the East Coast on the pretext that they would be "better kept" under government management at Keelung, when in fact it was common knowledge that his subordinates were operating a smuggling fleet.

At the beginning of 1947 tension had reached a breaking point. The governor general had a direct family interest in the management of the Trading Bureau to which many producers were obliged to sell their products at fixed prices, after which they were sold in turn at great profit within Formosa or on the continent. The commissioners of finance, communications, and industry developed between them an elaborate network of rules and regulations which gave them a stranglehold on the total island economy. Nothing could move out of the island or be imported without some payment of fees, percentages, or taxes.

For a time we students of law, economics, and political science, the *San-San Kai* group, continued to devote ourselves to books, theories, and abstract discussions. We were not yet politicized, but it was impossible to close our eyes and ears to evidence of a mounting crisis. The Generalissimo's representatives on Formosa were extending to our island the abuses that weakened his position throughout China and brought about his ultimate downfall. By the end of 1946, Chen Yi's commissioners were acting with unlimited and desperate greed. They wanted to become as rich as possible before the Nationalist government collapsed. They called it "necessary state socialism."

All this directly affected our own interests or the interests of our families. My father, Speaker of the Kaohsiung City Council, was not molested but he was well acquainted with countless incidents of extortion and illegitimate confiscation of Formosan property, and of properties and businesses in which Formosans and Japanese had developed shared interests during the preceding fifty years. The "collaborationist" charge was used by any unscrupulous Chinese who thought he saw a chance to dispossess a Formosan of attractive property.

During the first weeks of 1947 while we were concentrating on our work for degrees, a series of acts by the Chen Yi administration provoked a violent protest. The commissioners of finance, communications, and industry, working with the Trading Bureau, issued a series of new regulations that drastically tightened the monopolies, the "necessary state socialism," that was draining Formosa's wealth into the pockets of these commissioners, the governor general, and their patrons on the continent. These regulations provoked heated discussion among the students in our group. Concurrently the central government announced adoption of a new constitution for "democratic China," but Governor Chen Yi, on Chiang Kai-shek's orders, informed the people of Formosa that since they were unfamiliar with democratic processes, the provisions would not apply in Formosa until after a period of political tutelage. In other words, we would not be able to have an effective voice in the island administration until the Nationalist party leaders were ready to take the risk. According to us, students of law and political science, the true reason was that Formosa was not yet legally Chinese territory, and the local administration could not take the risk of exposing itself to a public vote of confidence. Then followed a third provocation, and the consequences of this action nearly blasted Chen Yi and the Nationalists from the island.

On the night of February 28, 1947, several of Chen Yi's Monopoly Bureau police savagely beat an old woman who was peddling a few packs of cigarettes without a license in the street-market of Round Park. A riot followed. The Monopoly agents were chased to a nearby police station, and their cars were burned. On the next day the whole of Taipei was seething, and by nightfall a great confrontation between the Formosan people and the occupying Chinese had begun. The first wave of angry protests were directed against the Tobacco Monopoly Bureau. Its branch offices were ransacked and burned and its employees beaten in the streets. Demonstrators marched on the Monopoly Bureau headquarters to demand moderation of Monopoly policies. Getting no satisfaction there, they marched toward the governor's office to protest and present their petition. As they approached the gates, the unarmed marchers were mowed down by machine-gun fire before they could enter the compound.

Pent-up public anger immediately burst forth. By nightfall next day Chen Yi's administration was virtually paralyzed. The principal officials and more influential carpetbaggers had established an armed camp in the northern suburbs to which they sent wives, children, and truckloads of private possessions, under heavy guard. A majority of newcomers from the continent hid in their homes, fearing a general massacre.

There was actually no threat of this. The Formosans were unarmed and police functions were taken over temporarily by students who were observing strict discipline. In the first two days there had been some violence on both sides, for Governor Chen's roving patrols were shooting at random in an attempt to terrorize the people, and the Formosans sometimes resorted to clubs and stones. Several Monopoly Bureau employees were beaten so severely that they died of injuries. Greater public anger was provoked by the disappearance of a number of middle school students who had entered the Railway Bureau offices to ask when service would be resumed on the main line so that they could leave the city for their homes south of Taipei.

On the third day Governor General Chen Yi announced that he was ready to hear the people. He appointed a committee of prominent Formosans to meet with his own representatives to settle the "incident" by drawing up a program of reforms which he promised to submit to the central government for consideration. He promised to withdraw roving patrols from the city streets and pledged that no troops would be brought into Taipei. This widely representative committee included members of the emergency and temporary police force that had assumed the duties of Chen Yi's men, now in hiding. Among his own representatives on the committee, I am ashamed to say, were several men who were Formosans by birth but had gone to China in the 1920s and had worked there for the Nationalist government. They had come back to serve under Chen Yi, and can only be described as "professional Formosans," men who were well paid by the government and who were always brought forward as "native Formosans" to talk convincingly with foreign visitors on behalf of Chen's administration.

In setting up the committee, the governor announced he wished to receive the recommendations for a program of reform on March 14. Seventeen branch committees were set up in cities and towns throughout the island. At each of these, local Formosan grievances were discussed, recommendations drawn up, and forwarded to the central committee at the capital. The Settlement Committee met on the stage of the city auditorium, and the seats in the large hall were crowded at every session.

Within five days after the initial uprising, Taipei was quiet, although tense. Shops reopened and supplies began to come in from the countryside to city markets. Despite the governor's pledges, he tried to bring troops up from the south, hoping to forestall the necessity of receiving the reform proposals. Fortunately word of the events of February 28 and March 1 had spread rapidly throughout the island. Alert citizens in the Hsinchu area prevented troop movements by tearing up the rails at certain places and stalling the troop trains. Governor Chen's attempt at deception heightened the anger and mistrust of the Taipei people. Riots occurred in some of the principal towns where the governor's men attempted to maintain control. A handful of communists, men and women released from local Japanese prisons in late 1945 on General MacArthur's orders, attempted to take advantage of the confusion. They failed to attract a following. Formosans had become accustomed to fear communism ever since Japan adopted its determined anticommunist policies at the close of World War I.

During the height of the excitement at Taipei, we students at the university gathered at the medical school auditorium to discuss the situation. There was no organization, and the meetings were inconclusive. Our situation on the campus was a favorable one, and we still thought we lived in a detached world. We would have liked a better and larger faculty, but we had no real academic grievance. Our only grievances were both personal and general, the troubles, injuries, and losses suffered by our families and by Formosans in general. When our meetings broke up, we each went our own way with the tacit understanding that each would do what he wanted in the crisis.

Chen Yi and his principal officers addressed the people from time to time on the radio, urging them to be calm, saying that their demands for reform were justified, and that their proposals would be given careful consideration. But we began to hear rumors that a large military force was being assembled in Fukien, a hundred miles away across the straits. The committee therefore hastened to finish the Draft Reform Program, knowing that if Nationalist troops arrived in force, Governor Chen would never bother to consider it.

All through the week our local papers issued regular and special editions to keep us informed of the committee's work, and from time to time the proceedings in the city auditorium were broadcast. Occasionally some of our university group attended these sessions, and we talked of nothing else throughout the first week of March. On March 7, after consulting with all the seventeen local committees, such as the one which my father was a member of, the spokesmen for the committee transmitted to the governor the reform proposals he had requested them to make.

One politically active group of students drew up a written petition for reforms and addressed it to General Chen. It was phrased with restraint, and when taken to the governor's offices it was politely received. The governor's officers called it very useful advice, and politely asked the petitioners to write down their names and addresses. This they did, in all innocence.

Meanwhile my father experienced a cruel ordeal at Kaohsiung. Kaohsiung was one of the seventeen cities and towns to form a Settlement Committee and he was asked to be its local chairman. In this strange interim period it was charged with maintaining local law and order and formulating proposals for consideration by the Central Committee at Taipei. The committee therefore decided to call on the local garrison commander, General Peng Meng-chi, to ask that he restrain the soldiers who were attempting to terrorize the city and intimidate the committee. His roving patrols were shooting at random whenever they spotted small groups of Formosans gathered in the streets discussing the crisis. My father's deputation was to ask General Peng to withdraw these patrols and to keep his soldiers in barracks while local leaders debated reform in response to the governor's invitation for recommendations.

The Kaohsiung garrison headquarters is located on a hill overlooking city and harbor. As soon as my father and his companions reached the compound there, they were seized and bound with ropes. Unfortunately one committee member, a man named Tu, was an impulsive man recently returned from China, who had at one time served under Wang Ching-wei, Chiang Kai-shek's bitter rival in the Nationalist party. This man now burst out in a violent tirade against the Generalissimo as well as against his appointee, General Chen.

After this he was taken from the others and bound with bare wires instead of ropes. The wires were twisted with wire-pliers until Tu screamed in agony. After a night of torment, he was shot.

My father and the other committee members were then bound with ropes looped around their necks and were threatened by soldiers with bayonets. They too expected to be shot at any moment, but on the second day my father was released and sent home. General Peng had intervened and shown clemency saying that he knew my father well. He said, "We know this man Peng is a good man. There is no reason to hurt him."

Totally exhausted, Father went home. He had nothing to eat for two days and he was emotionally shattered. His disillusionment was complete. Henceforth he would have nothing more to do with politics and public affairs under the Chinese. His was the bitterness of a betrayed idealist. He went so far as to cry out that he was ashamed of his Chinese blood and wished that his children after him would always marry foreigners until his descendants could no longer claim to be Chinese.

At Taipei I knew nothing of this at this time. We students were listening to radio reports of fighting here and there, of the action along the railway lines near Miao-li that had kept Chen Yi's troops out of the city, and rumors that the aborigines were coming down from the hills to help us confront the Chinese.

My grandmother from Patou village was keeping house for me in Taipei, as she had done for my brothers and sisters so many years ago. She had many relatives and friends in Keelung, and on the afternoon of March 10 a terrified visitor from Patou relayed the news that troop ships were coming in from China, and that soldiers on deck had begun strafing the shoreline and docking area even before the ships had reached the pier.

This began a reign of terror in the port town and in Taipei. As the Nationalist troops came ashore they moved out quickly through Keelung streets, shooting and bayoneting men and boys, raping women, and looting homes and shops. Some Formosans were seized and stuffed alive into burlap bags found piled up at the sugar warehouse doors, and were then simply tossed into the harbor. Others were merely tied up or chained before being thrown from the piers.

By late evening military units had entered Taipei city and from there began to move on through the island. At the same time other troop ships from China arried at Kaohsiung where Nationalist army units joined General Peng's garrison and repeated there the ferocious behavior of the troops at Keelung and Taipei. General Chen Yi was determined to intimidate the Formosan people and to destroy all Formosans who had dared criticize his administration.

Until March 8 the Formosans who were members of the Settlement Committee and many others who were not, continued to call for reform and tried again and again to appeal to Generalissimo Chiang to recall Chen Yi and replace his commissioners with honest men. By March 10 most of these leading Formosans were dead or imprisoned or in hiding, seeking a way to escape from the island. On March 12 Nationalist planes flew low over the principal towns, scattering leaflets bearing a message from the Generalissimo, "President of the Republic, Commander-in-Chief of the Armed Forces, and Leader of the Party." These carried the text of his comments on the "incident" delivered to a body of high officials at Nanking. He fully endorsed Chen Yi's actions. The leaders of the riots, he said, were "Communists" and "people spoiled by the Japanese." He said the Formosan people owed a great debt to the continental Chinese who had "struggled for fifty years to recover Taiwan."

Nobody knows how many Formosans died in the following weeks, but the estimates ranged from ten to twenty thousand. Members of the Settlement Committee were the first to disappear. Editors and teachers, lawyers and doctors who had dared criticize the government were killed or imprisoned. The university students who had carried a petition to the governor's office and had so naïvely given their true names and addresses were sought out and killed. Many of the middle school students who had taken the place of the cowardly Chinese policemen during the previous week were killed. After that it seemed that anyone who had dared laugh at any Chinese at any time since 1945 was in danger of his life.

During these terrifying weeks I remained quietly within my grandmother's house, frightened and worried. I had not been a member of any politically active group on the campus, and my name was on no petition or manifesto. No soldiers came to search our house, and I was not called out in the middle of the night as were some friends who disappeared. For all my hard work toward a degree in political science at the university, I was still far removed from practical politics and very naïve. I had not yet fully realized how much more threatened our personal freedom was now than it had been under the Japanese. In several letters to my father at this time I expressed an angry reaction to the terrible things taking place at Taipei. I did not then know that my father's mail was being censored until one day the chief of police at Kaohsiung quietly warned my father to tell his son not to write such letters, and that my name too was now on a blacklist.

Kaohsiung had suffered terribly during the incident and the weeks following the arrival of Chiang's troops. In these days the garrison commander, General Peng, earned his reputation as "the Butcher of Kaohsiung." For example, when a large number of leading Kaohsiung citizens had gathered in the city auditorium to debate the crisis, the doors were closed and the chamber swept with machine-gun fire. Families were compelled to watch the public execution of fathers and sons in the square before the railway station. There were many stories of torture inflicted on prisoners before their execution. My father, who had been an idealist all his life, became more bitter and more depressed.

Throughout Formosa prominent men or men with property were being intimidated and blackmailed by petty Nationalist officials who threatened to charge them with "antigovernment sentiment." The deputy speaker of the Kaohsiung City Council, for example, was subjected to extortion by several young Nationalist army officers, and barely managed to evade a demand that he hand over a young daughter to one of them. He had been a wealthy man, but was soon bankrupt. It was rumored at one time that my father would soon be arrested and tried for having been chairman of the local Kaohsiung Committee for Settling the Incident. He was closely watched for a long period and only narrowly escaped the hard fate of many friends.

Gradually Taipei became quiet. General Chen Yi was recalled to Nanking, made a senior advisor to the government, and soon President Chiang made him governor of the large and important province of Chekiang. His successor at Taipei was a lawyer, Dr. Wei Tao-ming, who had once been Chinese ambassador to Washington and had many American friends.

We students gradually returned to the campus one by one. We did not dare meet in groups anywhere at any time but confined our angry discussions to moments when we could walk together in twos and threes across the broad university grounds. We quickly realized that there were informers planted among us in the classrooms, and that it was never safe to speak out frankly before a mere acquaintance or before any university group. Occasionally the dreaded secret police, the military police, or the city police raided university dormitories apparently following up leads given to them by members of the student body. Among those arrested in these campus raids were liberal and outstanding Chinese students who were as severely critical of the government as we were. By now we were fully aware that one of the most common Chinese practices was the use of paid informants and the offering of rewards ranging from a few Formosan dollars in cash to promises of lucrative jobs and offices.

In the summer of 1948, sixteen months after the incident, I graduated from *Taita* with a bachelor's degree in political science. My classmates and I who were members of the *San-San Kai* had completed the four-year point requirements in two years' time. We had really done little more than polish up our Mandarin Chinese. But at last we had B.A. degrees from a Chinese university recognized by Nanking.

I now had to choose between the academic world and a career in business. I was invited to remain at *Taita* as an assistant in the College of Law. This meant that I would not teach but do research on my own and assist the department chairman in the administrative chores. At the same time I was offered a position in the First Commercial Bank. This was an important institution. As a reward for his cooperation during the 1947 crisis, former mayor of Taipei, Huang Chao-chin, had been made board chairman. He was one of the few men of Formosan birth who survived service on the Settlement Committee unscathed and emerged well rewarded. The government owned more than one-half the shares in this bank, and therefore it was a semi-official institution, but the former mayor was allowed to run it with an iron hand and more or less as if it were his private business. Undoubtedly the offer of a job there came to me because Huang himself was my father's old friend. His younger sister was my mother's closest friend, and Huang had put his wealthy brother-in-law on the bank board. I was well known to him, and he knew that my academic reputation was quite high.

It was a difficult choice to make. The bank salaries were at least three times as large as academic salaries at *Taita*, and if I performed with even reasonable competence, I could expect rapid promotion. But my heart was really not in commerce.

Nonetheless I decided to enter the bank, and reported for the beginner's training program. At once the favoritism shown me became apparent, for having only one hand, I could not count bank notes properly, one of the first things required of a new recruit. We were expected to begin as clerks and then to move on for training in every lower department in the bank organization.

For one month I reported faithfully to work each day, but it was clear to me that I could not be a good bank clerk. The financial attraction vanished. Neither banking nor any other commercial activity was to my taste. I quit after thirty days and returned to the *Taita* campus where my future seemed to be. My course was set.

V

Montreal and Paris

Confusions and uncertainties in the National Taiwan University administration reflected the general disarray of all Nationalist Chinese organizations at this time. The Communists were growing stronger, the Chinese civil war intensified throughout the Chinese provinces, and the Generalissimo's government was split by factions as he struck down potential non-Communist rivals ruthlessly. These included any liberal who seriously proposed a third party as an alternative to Nationalist or Communist leadership. It was difficult for men of integrity to survive in government service. Between 1945 and 1949 Formosa experienced its full share of confusion and exploitation, none of which could be blamed on the Communists. Although there were undoubtedly Communist agents on the island, there was no significant Communist party apparatus. Governor Chen's successor, Wei Tao-ming, was considered little more than a figurehead, useful principally because of his wide acquaintance in Washington. Mrs. Wei was generally believed to run the government and the economy.

Despite corruption in the Taipei administration, Formosa's academic world began to show signs of improvement. As the Communists advanced on the continent, many institutions were

74

disrupted and many able scholars, uprooted and displaced, sought shelter on the island. The years 1948 and 1949 brought something like two million refugees into Formosa, together with public and private libraries, research collections, and art treasures. A number of well-known institutions that had managed to survive the Japanese invasion by moving from place to place, now made the final move over the straits and were reestablished in Formosa. Some new faculties were organized. The Academia Sinica, China's most eminent intellectual center, having nowhere else to go, was resettled at Taipei. Our own university, founded by the Japanese in 1927 and reorganized by the Nationalists in 1946, now began to grow. Hundreds of young refugees from every province of China were enrolling with us.

I joined the faculty in the lowest rank as an assistant in the Department of Political Science in the College of Law. The college had taken over the buildings and grounds of the Japanese Higher Commercial School in 1947. The chairman of the department, Professor Wan, an able and interesting man, was soon obliged to leave Formosa. On the continent he had been aligned politically with the Generalissimo's great rivals, General Pai Chung-hsi and Vice-president Li Tsung-jen, and was therefore unacceptable to Chiang. There were others, too, who were found to be politically unacceptable and were ousted after Chiang Ching-kuo entered Formosa with his secret police organizations in 1948 to make the island secure for his father's flight from the continent.

In February, 1949, a few months after I returned to *Taita*, I married the eldest daughter of a landholding family living just north of Taipei. The wedding took place in my family's church in Kaohsiung, after which we remained briefly in the south to make a round of ceremonial visits to all my relatives in that area. On returning to the capital we settled into a small suburban house on the northern side of the city, near the Keelung River. I crossed town to the university each day by bus.

Soon after I resumed my duties the College of Law acquired a new dean, Professor Sah Meng-wu, a Chinese who had graduated from my old higher school, *San-ko,* and from the Kyoto Imperial University. He personally paid great attention to me and to my friend Liu Chin-sui who was also a graduate of *San-ko.* Liu had gone on to Tokyo Imperial University as I had, where he was my junior by one year. On returning to Formosa at the war's end, without finishing his degree, he had married my cousin. He was a member of our *San-San Kai* group and after that we were the closest of friends.

The dean urged us both to write academic articles for publication, and when we did, he took great pains to correct our Chinese, page by page and word by word. This was a great and unusual concession on the part of a dean, and we were grateful. We thus wrote many articles, long and short, and it required much time and energy on his part to correct the texts. Under his guidance our command of the Chinese written language improved rapidly. Within a year or two Chinese faculty members in our school began to say with apparent astonishment that our Chinese was almost as good as that of a "true Chinese" brought up on the continent. We owed these compliments to Dean Sah's patient care, and he said repeatedly in public that only the Japanese educational system could produce such promising young scholars.

We began to hear some of the older Chinese scholars and administrators say that we should become the backbone of this college. My friend Liu specialized in constitutional law and I concentrated upon public international law. When the university annexed the former Japanese commercial college, it had acquired an excellent library of about 50,000 books. This was enlarged to hold all the books inherited by the School of Law from the old Taihoku Imperial University collections. The prewar university library had contained more than 400,000 volumes, of which at least two-thirds were in European languages. Now the new *Taita* School of Law Library was augmented by Chinese publications. The growing collection was not catalogued or well organized, however, and I took delight in browsing in the stacks to discover new and interesting items. It was here that I came upon volumes devoted to the subject of air law. I found a long treatise in French, Le Goff's *Le Droit Aérien,* which I read with absorbing interest. In the light of later developments in my career I suspect that I was stirred by some subjective fascination with planes, especially planes at war, after my own traumatic experiences at Nagasaki.

Once again I was fascinated by French literature, this time the literature of law. I decided that it should be my specialty. I began reading extensively on the subject principally in French and English and started to write in earnest. My articles were not highly original, but in Chinese they were new contributions to an unstudied subject. One by one the essays were published, some in the university journals and some in off-campus publications. As I read, an American name began to appear more and more often, the name of John Cobb Cooper, considered the leading expert in the field, who was at that time associated with the Institute for Advanced Studies at Princeton. I therefore wrote directly to Professor Cooper, who responded with great kindness and consideration. After that we exchanged occasional letters for a year.

A new president came to *Taita.* Professor Fu Su-nien was an enlightened and liberal refugee scholar, although at times somewhat authoritarian in manner. He showed at once that he was quite aware of the peculiar situation of Formosa and the Formosan people. He publicly stated his belief that *Taita* must be run eventually by Taiwanese, and this became an accepted university policy. Professor Fu not only tried to recruit Formosan faculty members but set out to cultivate and train younger Formosans already on campus.

Fu was a Peking University man and a good friend of China's most eminent modern scholar, Dr. Hu Shih. Dr. Hu's father had held a minor official position in the imperial Chinese administration on Formosa at the close of the Chinese era (1891-1894). Dr. Hu was at this time acting director of the Sino-American Cultural and Educational Foundation, an organization set up to administer the Boxer Indemnity Fund established by the American government in 1908 to generate income to be used to educate Chinese youths. The fund headquarters were in New York.

Through this personal connection, President Fu had secured two fellowships for *Taita*. One was reserved for a faculty member, and the other was available to a graduating student. Each year the faculty had been invited to apply for one of these. President Fu made it a rule that at least one of the annual recipients must be a Formosan. This rule had just been made when the president died of a heart attack. I felt that I had lost a friend and local sponsor. Nevertheless, in the second year of the program I applied for the faculty Boxer Fund grant, stating that I wished to study air law. To my great pleasure, I received the award.

At once older faculty members challenged the selection, wanting to know why this young Formosan should receive the honor. When *Taita*'s new president, Professor Chien Shih-liang had to answer such questions before the university administrators, he stated publicly that the selection was correct, and that he believed the results would be good.

When the award had been confirmed, I wrote at once to Mr. Cooper, seeking advice. Where should I go for advanced work in the field of air law? To my delight he answered promptly that McGill University in Montreal was just then establishing an Institute of International Air Law, the first graduate program in the world devoted to the subject. He would be the first director, and he urged me to come to McGill. Montreal had become the most important center for international aviation. The U.N.'s International Civil Aviation Organization was located there, and it was also the site of the International Air Transport Association, whose members include almost all airlines in the world engaged in scheduled international flight.

In great personal excitement I prepared to leave. At that time few students were leaving the island for study abroad. I had no friends in Canada or the United States to whom I could appeal for advice and information of a private sort. Although I had spent my life reading books about the Western world, I was ignorant of practical matters. Suddenly I found myself about to leave my home and family for a long stay in a distant land. My little son had been born in March, 1950, and was about eighteen months old, the most attractive, lively, and innocent age. It would be very hard to leave him. He had been named Peng Wen. Traditionally in a Chinese family the grandfather chooses names for the grandchildren, and the great majority of Chinese personal names contain two characters. It was quite characteristic of my father, however, to insist that all of his grandchildren have only one in his name. The use of two characters, he said, was nonsense and a waste of time. One character would always be simpler and easier to write and would always take less time. In consequence of his views on this, only two of his many grandchildren, two granddaughters born in Japan, have two characters in their personal names.

In accepting the fellowship and going abroad, the most difficult and painful prospect was that of saying good-bye to my father, the man who was too quick and impatient to waste time writing two characters when one might suffice, and too imaginative to be bound by ancient tradition if a better way of doing something might be found. He was quick-tempered, but we all loved him very deeply and all now realized that he might not have long to live.

He had led an extremely active life between 1945 and 1947, suffering through the dangers and losses of war and the disenchantment and the dangerous months of General Chen Yi's administration that ended in such disaster. In total disillusionment he had withdrawn altogether from public life and confined himself exclusively to the administration of his clinic. He was more than sixty years of age, and his health had begun to fail. Medical examination revealed a greatly enlarged heart and a serious diabetic condition. The doctors gave him only six months to live. Although he was not told this directly, he saw the x-ray photos of his heart and as a professional man drew his own conclusions.

If I was to meet the McGill University requirements for the master's course, I had to plan to be abroad for at least two years, and we all knew that I could not expect to see my father again. This was a cruel dilemma. It is considered a most unfilial thing for a son to be far away when a father dies, especially if one has left home knowing that this would probably be the case. On the other hand, we knew that it would be technically and financially impossible for me to return to Formosa on sudden call. The Chinese government made no provisions for temporary returns. If I would reenter Formosa for any purpose, my passport would be cancelled and months would be required to obtain a new one.

My father knew all this, and took the position that I had now been given an opportunity I must not miss. He saw that it was professionally unthinkable for one to abandon such an opportunity, and he was aware of my lifelong interest in the Western world which he shared. His deep bitterness toward China and the Chinese carpetbaggers who were our masters now may also have strengthened his desire to have me seize an opportunity to go abroad. Perhaps I could do for my generation on a larger scale what he had been able to do for his when he had seized the opportunity to study medicine at Taipei. It was not simple. Some of our relatives advised me strongly not to go, but Father always countered by urging me not to hesitate. I made the decision as he wished, and began to make my way through red tape and regulations restricting travel abroad at that time. This required many months. I had been reading and writing English for fifteen years or more; now for several months I was tutored privately in conversation by a Catholic sister at Taipei.

When all was ready, the passport secured, the dates set, and the time had come to say good-bye, I went south to Kaohsiung to be with my father for the last time. The doctors had forbidden him to move around at home too much and had absolutely forbidden him to travel, so I spent a quiet week with him there. The day came when I had to leave. I took a night train, and despite our protests, my father insisted upon going to the railway station to say good-bye. Undoubtedly I was doing what he would have liked to do and would have done if such a great opportunity had risen in his youth. For me, however, it seemed an unbearable thought that this might be our last parting.

My mother, my brothers, many colleagues and students came to the airport to see me off. I said good-bye to my little son and to my wife, knowing that they would go now to Kaohsiung to live with my parents. That would give my father great pleasure. After that my son and his grandfather each became the favorite of the other, and since my elder brother had assumed charge of the clinic, my father spent all of his days and evenings with the child in his small home and garden.

I flew to Vancouver by a round-about way, first to Manila, then a few hours in Honolulu, and a night in San Francisco. At Vancouver I decided to save money by taking a train across Canada to Montreal. This would enable me to spend a night enroute with a cousin, a theological student, who had a summer job in a small Canadian church in a town along the way.

By now I had discovered that my English was a problem and this embarrassed me. Two young girls aboard the train proved very helpful and very kind, giving me apples to share with them and making me feel more at ease in speaking English. After an overnight stay with my cousin I went on eastward across the vast plains of central Canada. The elaborate dining car menu proved too much of a problem, there were too many choices and too many unfamiliar items, so after one meal I gave up, resorting to sandwiches bought at stops along the way. It was not a happy trip, for I sat hour after hour, passing through a monotonous landscape, thinking always of my father and wondering if my language preparation would be adequate for the program that lay ahead of me.

I reached Montreal in the evening, asked a taxi driver to find me a hotel, and was taken to a rooming house near the McGill campus. There I spent the night, exhausted by tension and worry and the countless new and unfamiliar situations in which I found myself at every turn.

The next morning I went to the law school. Mrs. Phyllis O'Neil, secretary to the dean, welcomed me, and was most kind. Our friendship has continued now for twenty years, but I shall not forget her kindness on that day. The school sessions would not begin for another month, and it was obvious that the rooming house in which I stayed the first night would not do. She found me temporary lodging in the home of a Canadian-Japanese family named Yamashita, and then in the next few weeks I finally settled down in the home of a charming elderly French couple living on Beaconsfield Street. It was a small room, but cheap and comfortable, and I enjoyed my hosts and their son. They were a quiet family.

I was desperately homesick and for a time deeply depressed. It was unfortunate that I had to wait a month for classes to begin. I had nothing to divert me except long walks through the city. There was no one with whom I could talk who would understand my background, nor the strength of our family ties. Night after night I wept in my room, thinking of my father, waiting for letters from home, and wondering what news they might contain. I now think of this as one of the saddest, dreariest periods in my life. Everyone was very kind, but I was an outsider.

At last Professor Cooper came to Montreal, students began to appear on the campus, and classes were organized in September. In this first year of the institute, about a dozen enrolled. It was a most cosmopolitan group, including three or four Canadians, an American Air Force officer, and an Egyptian representing the Civil Aviation Ministry at Cairo. Germany, Greece, England, and Hungary were represented. We were full of enthusiasm for this was a new field and we were quite aware that we were pioneers and confident of our future. Professor John Cobb Cooper was a self-made man, without a law degree, who had risen through the ranks to become a vice-president of Pan American. He had accepted an invitation to join the Institute for Advanced Studies at Princeton. He and his wife had charming, warm personalities which had helped him in seeking out unusual people and stimulating them to do their best. The faculty was limited in numbers but of high caliber, and under his leadership we quickly developed a remarkable "esprit de corps" and an exciting academic and social life together. We realized that as pioneers we were a rather exclusive group. In that sense I was reminded of my *San-San Kai* experience at *Taita;* otherwise the atmosphere of easy and lively discussion within a small group made this quite different from anything I had experienced before. I was the only Asian present that year, an oddity of sorts, for I was a Formosan of Chinese descent who spoke English with a French accent. My French at that time was much better than my English, and many local French-speaking Canadians assumed that I had come from France.

I requested and received permission to prepare my papers in French rather than in English. The first of these, written before *Sputnik* surprised the world, was concerned with the legal status of space beyond the normal confines of air operations in that day. The ideas presented impressed Cooper who arranged at once to have the paper published in *Revue du Barreau de la Provence de Quebec*, the journal of the Quebec Bar Association. It was then reprinted in the prestigious *Revue Française de Droit Aérien* at Paris. This was the only student paper published that year and one of the first in the world ever to touch on the subject. Now, in the days of actual space travel, it is often cited as a pioneering classic in the field.

A second of my papers was then published in Paris, in the *Revue Général de l'Air*. This traced the history of aerial bombardment from the earliest times to the end of the World War II. I had good reason to be especially interested in this subject. I had witnessed the second use of a nuclear bomb at Nagasaki, and every nation was concerned that it should be the last.

I also prepared an article on space law which appeared in

Journal of International Law and Diplomacy of the Tokyo University Law School, perhaps the first such article to be published in the Japanese language on this subject. It stirred great interest and roused much comment in academic and legal circles throughout Japan.

Thus in my first year at McGill my three published papers received international recognition. I was working very hard, but I was also now enjoying the social life of our group. My father was still living, and we exchanged letters very often. I was fortunate in my friendships, too. My close friend and cousin-in-law, Liu Chin-sui, was taking his master's degree in law at the University of Minnesota. By the end of the first year I had come to know and respect my classmate Ian McPherson who had lived in Hong Kong, and had been a bomber-pilot in the Canadian Air Force during World War II, flying in Europe. Hamilton DeSaussure, a Harvard Law School graduate and a pilot in the United States Air Force became another close friend. There were others in this small circle, and we continue our friendship to this day. Mrs. Cooper and Mrs. O'Neil, the dean's secretary, acted as very gracious hostesses and counselors to us all.

As the first year drew to a close I faced a problem. My Boxer Fund grant could not be renewed according to the regulations, and the Institute program required two years for the master's degree. In the first year we completed lecture course requirements, and in the second we devoted ourselves to preparing a thesis. Faced with this problem, I decided to write to Dr. Hu Shih in New York. I had never met him, but we had already had an exchange of correspondence, and he had let it be known to others that he was deeply impressed by my record at McGill. My earliest exchange with this eminent and kind-hearted man had been embarrassing to me but had amused him. At Christmas, 1951, my first Christmas abroad, I mailed out many Christmas cards and thought it my proper duty to send one to the acting director of the foundation giving me financial support. This I did, and soon thereafter received a most friendly note of thanks from Dr. Hu.

He added, however, that since he was considerably older than I, he would speak frankly and tell me that the card I had sent was one intended to be used in sending a gift of money. I had thought the perforations in the design were merely decoration!

Now, in the spring of 1952, Dr. Hu wrote noting that the rules forbade extensions of the Boxer Fund grant, but that he wished to consult with McGill University authorities and with others to find some means of supporting my studies for a second year. Dr. Hu Shih and Professor Cooper canvassed private sources and applied to several leading airline companies, including Pan American, but without success. Then came a letter from Hu Shih saying that at last he had found someone to finance my second year under exactly the same conditions and in the same amount as the Boxer Fund grant, but that the donor wished to remain anonymous. He then invited me to visit him during the summer holiday.

I took the train for New York. This was my first visit to an American city. I stayed at a Y.M.C.A. for several days and went to call on Dr. Hu, finding him in a modest apartment, surrounded by books. He was a warm and kindly man who made most flattering remarks about my progress at McGill. In passing conversation he mentioned his father's three-year assignment on government service to Formosa at the end of the nineteenth century. When I left him he gave me several books.

On returning to Montreal I began working on my thesis, a very technical study of the legal status of military aircraft in time of peace and war. This turned out to be a splendid year. To my great joy my father lived on. More than a dozen new students were registered, and again they came from all over the world. The summer weather was warm and humid and the winter was extremely cold, but I was comfortably housed and I was hard at work. At the end of the term I completed my dissertation in French, it was accepted, and I graduated *magna cum laude* with a master's degree in law.

Once again I had a problem. What next? My parents joined

with the faculty in urging me to go elsewhere for further study, now that I was so well embarked on this specialized career, but where should it be, in the United States or in Europe? Dr. Hu wrote that if I desired to go to the States, he would be glad to recommend me to Princeton. Princeton had no law school, but Dr. Hu thought well of the work being done there in political science. After much thought, I decided I would prefer to go to France, to my old center of interest. I had saved some money from my scholarships, and my father volunteered to put up some money to support my further stay abroad.

I sailed from Canada in July 1953, aboard a slow Italian ship. We had a rough crossing to Southampton, and I was as usual a poor sailor. Nevertheless it was a lively and delightful trip, for many students were aboard the old craft, and on deck one day I met two attractive Stanford University girls with whom I took my meals after that and went to evening shows. On reaching South-ampton we went together by train to London. An English friend had secured a hotel room for me, a rather dismal place, from which I set out each day on long sightseeing excursions with the two Stanford girls. On that visit I must admit that I was not very impressed by England, and after a week I flew on to Paris, leav-ing my friends to come along by channel boat. After staying for a few days in the *Maison japonaise* in University City, I moved into the Greek dormitory, the *Maison héllénique*, where half of the residents were from Greece and the other half from all over the world.

A few days after my arrival in Paris, its transportation system was plunged into the biggest strike since the end of the war. The entire city was paralyzed, and my first impression of this great capital was far from the romantic one I had been under since my college days in Japan.

The Stanford girls came from England, rented a room, and set about seeing Paris. I joined them and life was pleasant again. We toured the famous sights, visited the Latin Quarter, the restaurants, and the night clubs, including, of course, the Moulin Rouge. One day as I was strolling by myself in Montparnasse I came suddenly upon an Oriental in the street before me. He appeared to be a beggar, thin, shabby, and barefooted, which was then unusual, even in the Latin Quarter. As he moved along, he casually swung what appeared to be an empty Japanese soy-sauce bottle. As I came abreast of him, he glanced up and then cried out in Japanese, "Ho-kun! My friend Ho! I can't believe it!"

It was my *San-ko* classmate Tabuchi who had gone on from the Third Higher School to the Art Department in Kyoto University in 1943. Ten years had passed, the war had intervened, and he was the first and only *San-ko* classmate I had seen since graduation, and I have seen none other since. We had much to tell one another. He had married in Japan, produced four or five children, and then had abandoned his wife and children to come to Paris, the Mecca of every Japanese artist. He had been in France two or three years and was attempting to make a name for himself as an abstract painter. We went at once to his atelier, four flights up and without running water, where I met his companion, a Norwegian girl. In adjoining rooms was another Japanese, a sculptor.

Soon after that I took my two American friends to visit the atelier and to see a bit of the true bohemian life of the Left Bank. The Norwegian girl seemed to resent the intrusion of these smartly dressed Americans and assumed a bored and conde-scending attitude. "What are you studying at Stanford?" she asked, "Home economics?" Since these were exceptionally intelligent girls, well informed, and sophisticated, they had good reason to take the snide question as a personal affront.

I enrolled in the doctoral program at the University of Paris. I had a heavy schedule, nevertheless I began to enjoy the city tremendously. I met a French girl, a student of music, with whom I went to many concerts and to the theater, and there were other friends among the cosmopolitan student body. On one occasion my friend and colleague Liu appeared, homeward bound around the world after completing his work at the University of Minnesota. We had a splendid week together.

My course work went smoothly and so too did my dissertation, making it possible for me to finish nearly one year earlier than I had anticipated. By mid-summer, 1954, I had met all requirements for the degree of *Docteur en Droit*. When the last details were complete, I left for home. But I left Paris with regret and some sadness, thinking that there might never be another opportunity for me to visit Europe. A number of friends saw me off on the train for Italy. At Genoa I boarded a very new and comfortable Italian ship for the month-long journey to Hong Kong.

As usual, I was seasick most of the time, a prolonged misery relieved only by short trips ashore along the way, Port Said, Aden, Karachi, Bombay, Colombo, Singapore, and Hong Kong. I had been living in the Western world for three years. Each of these brief visits ashore gave me glimpses of people moving from colonial dependency toward independence and nationhood, Egypt, Pakistan, India, Ceylon, and Malaya. In passing through the Straits of Malacca into the South China Sea, I was made keenly aware that I had returned to the East.

Hong Kong brought a brief respite from the unkind sea. There the staff of my brother-in-law's trading company entertained me lavishly for five days as I waited to take passage to Keelung aboard an antiquated British ship. On this last short run across to Formosa I shared a first-class cabin with an old Chinese gentleman dressed in a simple Chinese gown who at first impressed me as a simple, traditional back-country type. To my surprise he turned out to be a rather distinguished old scholar named Chien Mu, later the first president of a new Chinese university in Hong Kong. For reasons unknown to me he was taken up by General Chiang Ching-kuo and after that treated with great distinction, courtesy, and consideration.

At last we reached Keelung. I was astonished and overjoyed to discover that my father had come from Kaohsiung to greet me, together with my mother, my wife, and my son, now nearly five years old. This was the happiest reunion and one of the most exciting moments of my life.

VI

Academic Life— Formosa and Abroad

My parents rested in Taipei for a time after the excitement of our reunion, but on Father's return to Kaohsiung his condition grew steadily worse. It was as if he had held on to life with an unshakable will until he had seen me again and then gave up. As autumn and winter passed, he entered a painful period in which his heart condition made it extremely difficult to breathe and impossible to move about. We visited him as often as possible.

Our trips back and forth between Taipei and Kaohsiung, through the principal towns, the rice-producing lowlands and the sugar plantations, gave me glimpses of the great change that had been overtaking Formosa's economy during my long absence. Hundreds of millions of American dollars' worth of subsidies were pouring into our small island each year. New industries had appeared, factories were springing up, and transportation and communications systems were returning to the prewar standards of operation we had known under the Japanese. Soon these standards would be surpassed. Perhaps a billion dollars' worth of U.S. aid to Chiang had been supplied, and the dominating influence of the military was evident everywhere. We were living under martial law.

We talked very little about these things with my father now, and little was said of politics. I had plunged into an extremely busy program at the university and could not visit the south as often as I wished. One day early in May 1955, a telephone call summoned my sister, my second brother, and me to Kaohsiung. We drove all the way in great haste. My father was still conscious, but his struggles to keep alive were unbearable to watch. Then suddenly on May 12 he exclaimed, "I feel fine!", insisted on getting up, and came to the table with us for the first time in many months. This was such a marked change that we thought it very strange. On the next day he died. He was sixty-five years old.

That academic year at the university had already been rather difficult. On my return from France I entered a complicated situation and was, in a sense, the victim of my own academic successes overseas. International praise for my highly specialized publications generated jealousy on my own campus. I had enjoyed a degree of preferential treatment at *Taita* from the days we students were inaugurating our own departmental programs. When I left the campus to study abroad, I was in the lowest faculty rank, and I had been absent for three years. Throughout that period my family had received full pay, causing critics to say, "The university is too kind to Peng."

In the normal course of university affairs, promotions led from the beginner's rank to a lectureship, and after three years of satisfactory scholastic achievement, to an associate professorship. I was only thirty-one, and therefore by traditional Chinese standards, much too young for my sudden elevation now to an associate professor's rank. This caused a local uproar. Continental refugees in my own department led the attack and were joined by others in the law school. Some who had no real interest in me used the appointment as an excuse to attack the dean and the president in a regrettable play of academic politics. The fact that I was a Formosan may have contributed something to the controversy the prejudices exposed. At the first formal faculty meeting after my appointment was made, Dean Sah introduced me with a show of pride and flattering comment, whereupon the retired diplomat Lei Sung-shen, a professor in the same field of international law, abruptly rose and left the room. This unnecessary display of professional jealousy created an awkward moment and a foretaste of others to follow. A question was raised in the Legislative Yuan, which controls appropriations for the university. There critics of the university administration used my promotion to charge favoritism, collusion, or worse.

The university president supported me in these embarrassing disputes, and Dean Sah took every opportunity to refute the critics, sometimes going so far as to declare boldly that the traditional Chinese university system could not have produced such a young scholar. Sometimes my advocates seemed to consider me a prodigy, and I now realize I was developing a degree of intellectual arrogance that cannot have pleased the older scholars on the *Taita* staff. After serving the usual three years as an associate professor, I became, at thirty-four years of age, the youngest full professor in the history of the postwar institution.

In these years politics as such held no interest for me. I was concerned only with my own career and my writing. My lecture course became one of the most popular in the entire university and continued to be until the day I was arrested in 1964. Slowly I was compelled to recognize that the immediate problems of Formosa's insecure international position were quite as important as academic theories and special case-studies drawn from the past and from elsewhere in the world. We were living in an era of complicated and confusing change in Formosa's relations with continental China and with China's friends and foes overseas. It was the era of John Foster Dulles, of the American confrontation with Communist China across the straits, and of Peking's angry claims to sovereignty in the island. Mr. Dulles' grandfather had come to Formosa in 1895 on Peking's behalf to assist in delivering the island to the Japanese, and Mr. Dulles himself had contrived to leave Formosa's sovereignty and international status undefined during and after the Japanese Peace Conference in 1951. He had excluded the Chinese, Nationalist and Communist alike, from the Conference at San Francisco, and although the San Francisco Treaty specified that Japan give up all claims to Formosa and the Pescadores, it did not provide for a transfer of sovereignty to China. The Generalissimo angrily declared that it was not binding upon the government of China, which he claimed to represent. Under Washington's pressure and Mr. Dulles' persuasive argument, Taipei then signed a separate bilateral treaty with Japan in 1952. Technically speaking, the international status of Formosa and its people was not defined. Even the United States-Nationalist Mutual Defense Treaty of December, 1954, avoided the issue.

Although for all students of international law Formosa's legal position was clearly one of first importance, it was soon apparent that I could not discuss the question freely in the classroom. I could not touch upon it at all. When we talked of elements constituting the essential character of the modern nation-state, I could only say,

The foundations are not formed on the basis of biologic origin, culture, religion, or language, but rather on a sense of common destiny and a belief in shared interests. These subjective feelings, which rise out of a common history, are not necessarily related to the objective criteria of biology, religion, and language. Modern history holds many examples in which peoples of similar background and heritage constitute separate political entities. For example, the Anglo-Saxon tradition has produced countries as diverse as the United States, Canada, Australia, and New Zealand; all share a common tradition of blood, language, religion, and in large part, of laws, but each exhibits a separate political constitution and forms a separate nation. On the other hand, there are cases in which peoples of different origin and background now constitute a single state based upon feelings of common interest.

Belgium and Switzerland are examples, and a hundred years ago
Italy was a peninsula crowded with diverse states and princi-
palities, warring among themselves, speaking diverse dialects, and
based on diverse economies.

Even as we considered these problems, Singapore moved from
a colonial status to independence as a self-governing member of
the British Commonwealth, an association of Indians, Malays,
and overseas Chinese, obliged and bound by common interest to
form a political union and a nation-state.

My lectures and comments at this time reflected my earlier interest in Ernest Renan's essay on the question, "What is a
nation?" Renan, touring Italy at the age of twenty-six, had traveled about among the warring Italian states, asking himself the
question I was now asking my students to consider. I quoted
him before Chinese and Formosan students alike. No Formosan
dared pursue the subject openly in the classroom, but some always smiled when I touched upon the topic.

My own intellectual interest in the subject grew steadily in
these years. In my grandfather's day Peking had ceded our island
to Japan in order to preserve China's interests on the continent
and to prevent a Japanese advance upon Peking. At that time,
perhaps for the first time, the factions and clans and villages
throughout Formosa began to be aware of themselves as an
island people. They were developing an identity of interest. For
fifty years thereafter Tokyo vigorously pursued a policy intended
to make Formosans over into good Japanese subjects. By reor-
ganizing the economy, binding the island together with a modern
communications system, and extending a common primary school
educational program into every community, the Japanese had
strengthened the sense of common interest without making us
over into the good Japanese they desired. On the contrary, our
younger Formosan leaders, representing an emergent middle
class, had sharpened our self-consciousness as Formosans
through the home rule movement. This developed during World
War I and grew steadily more important until 1945. Now, under

Chiang Kai-shek's administration, I saw myself, my contemporaries, and our children subjected to an extraordinary effort to make all Formosans over once again into good Chinese, Nationalist Chinese. Where in truth lay the "common interest" and what was our destiny?

This was a period of intense intellectual activity. I was publishing constantly and prepared a long textbook on international law, a volume of over 600 pages which is still considered one of the best on the subject to be found in the Chinese language and remains in use at Taipei. I do not know what its reception has been at the universities in Peking.

As my academic credentials grew stronger, my name was becoming known on every campus. Every college offering courses in international law asked me to lecture from time to time, and even some of the military schools near Taipei sought me out. This moonlighting was a practice to which a majority of professors had to resort in order to supplement meager salaries. I encountered envy and jealousy here and there, for I was monopolizing these extracurricular opportunities in the field of international law, and my colleagues were losing opportunities for outside engagements and additional income. Another cause for trouble within the *Taita* faculty was the evidence of my growing popularity with the students, reflected in requests that I become their counselor despite my rather strict grading in the classroom and on examinations. It was the student's privilege to select his faculty advisor, and soon the situation was grotesque and had to be corrected. Whereas most faculty members were counseling no more than ten students, nearly a hundred had applied to me and large numbers sought me out at my home as well as at my office. The situation was getting out of hand.

In 1956, Dr. Henry Kissinger invited me to attend the annual international seminar at the Center for International Affairs of Harvard University.

It was refreshing to be in the Western world again and once more a member of an intellectual, cosmopolitan group. Some

thirty or forty participants joined in this two-month session, a
varied group that included a British parliamentarian, a judge
from Ceylon, a German journalist, and an Indian writer. Of the
three Japanese present, one was a woman lawyer and one a
scientist. We worked together through the summer months under
Dr. Kissinger's overall direction, meeting in general conference
or in groups each morning, and making scheduled afternoon
visits to schools, prisons, courts, and institutions of many kinds.
The political discussion groups were chaired by Professor Earl
Latham of Amherst College who especially delighted us with an
extraordinary wit and humor. We heard distinguished speakers
and had opportunities to talk with them, although no conclusions
were drawn and no paper published. It was an opportunity to exchange ideas freely on current problems. Since we were passing
through a series of crises and military confrontations in the Formosan Straits, the threatened resumption of a general war in Asia
meant that the Formosan question was a frequent topic of conversation.

When these Harvard sessions ended, I flew to Paris. On this
brief visit I discovered that my friend and former classmate Tabuchi was becoming a success. One gallery was buying all the
pictures he produced, he had divorced his Japanese wife,
married his Norwegian girlfriend, and was settling down to rear
a second family in a small chateau in the French countryside. I
also managed to spend a few days with friends at Göteborg,
Sweden, before flying back to Formosa.

Soon after this, in 1957, my second child, a daughter whom I
adored and spoiled with attention, was born.

Teaching, lecturing off campus, advisory work with students,
and constant research crowded the years after my summer at
Harvard and the brief visit to Europe. I published papers in
professional journals, and in 1958 I published in French a volume
based principally upon my doctoral dissertation. I still did not
consider myself a man of action but only as a member of an aca-

demic elite, removed from active political affairs. This was the last such year of my life.

IN 1960 I WAS INVITED again by Dr. Kissinger to attend a conference in Tokyo at which he was the leading figure. Concurrently I was named one of Taipei's delegates to a "Sino-American Conference on Intellectual Cooperation" to be held at the Far Eastern Institute of the University of Washington in Seattle.

My presence at the Tokyo seminar was of little interest to the Taipei government. However, it attached great importance to the Seattle gathering. This was to be managed by Professor George Taylor, then director of the Far Eastern Institute. Several American institutions would be represented, affording opportunities for intensive lobbying within the American academic community and for securing funds from American foundations.

Dr. Hu Shih was made chief delegate, and there were about forty other academicians from Taipei. All were to travel on official passports, and as if to confirm beyond doubt the importance of the enterprise, the Generalissimo and Madame Chiang invited the entire group to a farewell party at their Shih-lin mansion. I was one of two Formosans in the group and the youngest member. When disgruntled colleagues demanded to know why I had been selected, Dr. Hu spoke out on my behalf and left no doubt that he considered me his protégé. Until this point in my career I am sure he had favored me because of my academic attainments at McGill and in Paris. I am convinced that he had been quite sincere in pressing the *Taita* administration to consider me and a few other Formosans as the men who should be cultivated and brought forward for the future interest of the university. Here, however, I believe his enthusiasm began to be exploited by party and government functionaries with other and less admirable ends in view. For the first time I had an intimation that perhaps I was being brought forward by the Nationalists to prove to the world that Formosans were being given their proper place in Nationalist Chinese affairs.

This farewell party brought me face to face with Generalissimo Chiang Kai-shek for the first time. When we were assembled in his presence, Dr. Hu himself seized me by the arm to conduct me to the president and leader of the party. I was detained for a prolonged conversation, rather longer than he usually permitted on first social introduction. My instinctive reaction was not good. His remarks were set phrases such as "How are your family?", "How many children have you?", "Have you any difficulties?", "What can I do to help you?" My answers and Dr. Hu's remarks were interspersed with the Generalissimo's dry and meaningless interjections *"Hao, hao, hao!"* ("Good, good, good!") There was no depth of feeling or genuine interest here, but rather the overtones of imperial condescension or a royal prompting for me to ask favors which, if granted, would place me under personal obligation to him. Madame Chiang appeared only at lunch.

With the Generalissimo's blessing we completed our preparations and flew to Seattle. Dr. Hu made the keynote speech. Some ardent traditionalists felt that he was too critical of traditional Chinese culture and showed himself too eager to modify ancient Chinese values. That debate was carried on later at Taipei and became a major issue.

At one session, one of the participants, Dr. Tsiang Ting-fu, then the Chinese Nationalist ambassador to the U.N., startled everyone by proposing a study on how to liberalize the Nationalist government. He had been noted as one of the most enlightened and liberal officers in the government, and once even openly advocated the formation of a genuine opposition party. However, no one expected him to make such a proposal at this conference. Dr. Hu Shih, visibly embarrassed, cut him off by suggesting that this conference was not an appropriate place to discuss this matter, and that it should be considered on another occasion.

At the conclusion of our five-day Seattle meeting, I went

briefly to Cambridge, Massachusetts, to see old friends before I returned to the Pacific and to Japan. I had some weeks to spare before taking my place at the conference to be held at the International House, and this interlude gave me opportunity for a sentimental journey to Western Japan, to Kyoto and Kobe, but not to Nagasaki. In Kyoto I went back to my old lodgings of high school days. Twenty years had passed since I had been cramming my rooms full of books, and my head full of thoughts of France. My surprised old landlord welcomed me with enthusiasm and assured me that he had always known I would be a professor some day. This was my longest stay in Japan after World War II, and what I saw deeply impressed me. Japan had been totally defeated and in ruins, and now, freed of the burden of arms, the nation was making spectacular progress. I thought of Formosa, where the defeated Generalissimo, after fleeing China, continued to maintain a huge army and a military program which absorbed eighty percent of our Formosan budget. What could we do if we were freed of that burden as Japan had been freed in 1945?

On my return to the Harvard-Tokyo conference, I was happy to renew my acquaintance with several participants who had also been with me at the Harvard seminar in 1956. Again for two months we met together each day, and the atmosphere was decidedly unlike that I had known at Seattle. Here was a genuine attempt to examine major problems of the day and to exchange ideas on a wide variety of subjects. Dr. Hu would have been happier here, for these participants were not necessarily interested in preserving the status quo and the classic past, but rather urgently seeking reasonable solutions to the developing complexities of international life. It was a genuine attempt to examine major issues.

During the conference I made a speech in which I developed a new line of political thought. For the first time I noted publicly that the legal status of Formosa had not yet been settled by formal action, and suggested that the Formosan people should have something to say about their future. It was a guarded statement, but the implications were clear. I was beginning to think about the real day-to-day problems of my own people and my home-land. Several scholars sought me out privately to raise the ques-tion of Formosa's status. I began to think in political terms and to come slowly down to earth from the realms of abstract theory and consideration of the past as merely a body of case histories. From time to time, Formosan residents in Tokyo came to see me, always with questions about the future. Sooner or later I would have to come to grips with the issue.

The summer of 1960 gave me much to reflect upon. In retro-spect we see that the end of an era of relative liberalism in For-mosa came then with a serious attack upon freedom of speech and of the press, and upon all Chinese and Formosans alike who had dared suggest that Chiang's reconquest of the mainland was a hopeless dream. After a decade of isolation from the continent, many thoughtful persons believed a more positive effort should be made to bring the exiled Chinese and the Formosans together. The aging refugees were dwindling in numbers and sending their children and money abroad. A majority of the armed forces were now Formosan conscripts. The Formosan population was rapidly increasing, outnumbering the refugees by five to one. The time had come for the refugees and the Formosans to learn to work together in the common interest.

A few days before I left for the Seattle conference, a journalist named Fu Chung-mei had come to see me privately and in great agitation. He had at one time been a secretary to Chiang Ching-kuo and was now associated with the influential liberal editor Lei Chen, publisher of *The Free China Fortnightly*. Lei had been urging the government to permit formation of a loyal opposition party, a liberalization of the Nationalist party program within Formosa, and a more realistic appraisal of Formosa's true mili-tary and political situation. He most particularly advocated gen-uine cooperation between the continental refugees and the Formosan people. According to Fu, Lei's journal was being subjected to increasing pressure by the Nationalist secret police. "Something may happen any day," he had said. Now it had happened. Word reached us in Tokyo that Lei Chen had been arrested, together with a number of associates. Among them was Fu Chung-mei. It was chilling news and marked the beginning of a drive to suppress all talk or thought of cooperation between Formosans and continental Chinese exiles interested in forming a new political party. Lei, an elderly man, was eventually sentenced to ten years' imprisonment. Some of his associates were sent off to Green Island, the Devil's Island of the Nationalist regime. One of my friends involved in this was placed in solitary confinement, and remained there cut off from the rest of the world for many years.

While in Tokyo I received a cablegram from Taipei notifying me that I had been appointed to a state chair by the National Committee for Scientific Development of which Dr. Hu Shih was chairman. This was a marked distinction, for there were no more than twelve men so honored at any time. The grant of 5000 Taiwan dollars per month was intended to supplement my regular monthly salary of 2000 dollars and to make it unnecessary for me to moonlight. I had been teaching for a year at the Tunghai University, a private institution near Taichung founded by mission funds. Each Thursday I made the hundred-mile trip southward and took the bus to the campus in the hills. I enjoyed these lectures, for the Tunghai campus, away from crowded Taipei, was less formal. The student body was more relaxed but no less serious. The school was not Americanized to any marked degree, but it undoubtedly reflected something of its wider international associations. The position paid very well and I was reluctant to give it up. The administration at Tunghai proposed that I take a year's leave of absence from *Taita,* join the Tunghai faculty full time, and move to Taichung. This I had to decline.

On returning from Tokyo I took up my new work as a National Research Fellow, proposing to make a study of "Technological Development and International Law," a subject of considerable

international interest. The Formosan press gave my new appointment great publicity. In retrospect I am certain that there
were no concerted actions behind the scene, although Dr. Hu
sometimes seemed to be associated somewhere with these appointments and distinctions. One could imagine, at least, that he
and his like-minded liberal associates were happy to have it dem-
onstrated that Formosans were quite capable of taking a place in
the island's intellectual life at the highest levels, and should therefore be cultivated in the national interest.

This appointment was a true academic distinction and I was
pleased to accept it, but soon there were other distinctions less to
my taste, favors and notices that placed me often in a false
position and gave me the appearance of being used by the regime not unlike the "Professional Formosans" so often the subject
of Formosan sarcasm.

At about this time a comparatively liberal group within the
Nationalist party promised to sponsor a large conference that
would bring together representatives of all noncommunist Chinese communities around the world. Pragmatic overseas Chinese
everywhere were beginning to assess Chiang's chances of survival, weighing them against evidence that Mao Tse-tung and his
men controlled the whole of mainland China and showed growing strength. Taipei had soon to offer some convincing evidence
that the Nationalist party and government still had vitality. The
plan for a great conference at Taipei was opposed by hard-core
reactionaries within the party elite. The Generalissimo was not
prepared to take the risks of an open international conference,
sponsored by the government, which might generate criticism of
the party and of his own leadership.

Out of this came a compromise, a consultative conference, in
which carefully selected representatives of overseas Chinese
communities were invited to participate. There would be meetings of an economics group and an education and culture group.
Participants would be shown Formosa's great progress under Nationalist leadership, although it was a foregone conclusion that

little would be said about the volume of American dollar subsidy, the extent of American technical and military assistance, or of the Japanese base firmly laid down in the fifty years preceding the Nationalist occupation. Economic statistics, graphs and charts, could be made to speak for themselves, and they were impressive. Any attempt to discuss education and culture must touch on very sensitive issues, however, for the current overseas propaganda and the local realities would be difficult to reconcile.

The conference would be held in the hot-spring resort area on nearby Yang Ming Mountain, and was therefore called the Yang Ming Shan Conference. An intensive publicity campaign was undertaken to persuade the public that this was the biggest event of the year. It was announced that the Generalissimo himself would attend the meeting and entertain the delegates at dinner, thereby giving the conference his blessing.

A majority of the overseas Chinese guests invited to attend the conference were older men, senior leaders in their respective businesses and professions. They were not likely to ask embarrassing questions or to misrepresent the party's interests on returning to their homes. The senior members of the Taipei government were scheduled to be present, cabinet members and party officials groomed to make reports. On the eve of the conference, I learned through the press that I was expected to attend. Long debate must have preceded the decision to include me as a member of the education and culture group. It came as the greater surprise because I was then merely a thirty-six-year-old professor, and hence very junior in the ranks represented here.

All the reports made by the senior government and party officers strictly followed the party line. They predicted the inevitable collapse of the Communist regime in Peking and speedy recovery of China by the Nationalist government. The participants were supposed to accept this line. If questions were asked by the audience, they were concerned with trivialities. The basic position and policy of the government could not be questioned. Chiang received one small group at a time for lunch. The conference ended with a formal dinner to which all participants and government officials were invited.

Soon after this the Ministry of Education sponsored a National Education Conference to examine policies and the structure of the educational system. The president and deans of the National Taiwan University were conference members *ex officio*. I was also invited. Both the university president and the deans took pains to introduce me at the meetings although this was hardly necessary. Thanks to attentions given me in the press, I had become something of a celebrity within Formosa's small academic world.

The Taiwan Junior Chamber of Commerce, patterned after the American organization, decided to elect the "Ten Outstanding Young Men of Taiwan." Local branches of the Junior Chamber of Commerce sent in nominations, and less than twenty-four hours before the choices were made public, and too late to forgo the "honor," I learned that I was one of the ten young men chosen. I was nearly forty years old at that time.

The whole matter was a commercial promotion enterprise throughout. There was radio and television coverage and also interviews and articles in the press. To cap it all, an elaborate formal presentation took place, staged in Madame Chiang's noted commercial enterprise, the Grand Hotel. I was called upon to give a brief speech, and thereby the public image of a loyal Formosan was maintained.

These ten outstanding young men were invited to have tea with General Chiang Ching-kuo, acting in his role as head of the National Youth Corps. Undoubtedly a group picture would be taken, as is usual on such occasions, and this in turn would be used for youth corps publicity purposes. This was too much for me to stomach. I still considered myself a nonpolitical academician. I could not have my students see me in public association with the chief of the dreaded secret police who liked to consider himself a "Tutor of Youth." Too many students, their fathers, brothers, relatives, and friends were being imprisoned on his orders.

I sent a polite note to young Chiang's office saying that I had previous important engagements in Taichung and could not be present at the tea. When the inevitable group picture appeared in every island paper, my absence was conspicuous. At once there was lively speculation about why I boycotted a meeting with Chiang Ching-kuo.

VII

At
the United Nations:
A Personal Dilemma

The curious distinctions of appointment to various conferences and the absurd nomination as an outstanding "youth" at the age of forty all fell into the background soon after this. My university gave me new recognition by making me chairman of the political science department. Given the political situation within the island and Formosa's ambiguous status in international legal and political affairs, it was a daring move from an administrative point of view, an expression of official confidence made just at the moment when doubts were beginning to grow in my mind. Factions in the government were becoming more pronounced. Some of the aging party elite were becoming more and more reactionary with the passage of time in exile and others were becoming more liberal in an attempt to develop a viable island society and to meld all elements within it.

The appointment, which was a coup for the liberals, became effective on August 1, the beginning of the academic year. Lectures would begin in September. I was hard at work preparing for my new responsibilities when the president of the university sent his car one morning to bring me to his office on urgent business. With only a hint that he himself should be given certain credit, he astonished me by saying that I was about to be appointed officially to the post of advisor to the Chinese delegation to the United Nations Assembly in New York. A formal notification from the Foreign Ministry confirmed the news that afternoon.

The appointment could be explained, I thought, by the fact that the Taipei government was extremely nervous. The moratorium period for the China question had come to an end. Washington and Taipei decided that there must be a change of strategy since in the previous year support for the Nationalists had dropped to the lowest level in the annual vote on the question of seating Peking in the world body. Moreover, Taipei was proposing a complex counterplay involving voting on the admission of Outer Mongolia and of Mauritania. The intransigent Chiang Kai-shek claimed to represent Mongolia in his asserted role as "President of China." Russia sponsored the Mongolian bid. If Chiang vetoed Outer Mongolia, Russia would veto Mauritania. But the African nations wanted Mauritania in, and if Chiang blocked that admission by his proposed action, he would lose the African support he needed for his own position. I was told that Taipei needed someone in New York who could really work and had a knowledge of international law, someone vigorous who could command international respect.

My participation in government affairs now moved to a new level. On the day following notification from the Foreign Ministry I received a message from the Nationalist party headquarters inviting me to come in for a talk. There lay the true center of power exercised by the Generalissimo in his role as *Tsuntsai* ("Leader of the party"), the Chinese equivalent of *Der Führer*.

I was intensely busy for the next few days. Press announcements of my new appointment meant interviews, photographs, and statements. The appointment was discussed publicly at great length. A courtesy call at the Foreign Ministry gave me opportunity to talk with Shen Chan-huang, the foreign minister. My visit to party headquarters brought me face to face with T'ang Chung, the powerful secretary general. During this visit my personal and very private dilemma was clearly defined.

T'ang at once bluntly asked me to look into the Formosan Independence Movement in the United States. This seemed to me to lie somewhat apart from my appointed duties as advisor to the United Nations delegation in New York, and I replied carefully that this was a very complicated problem. The independence movement activists, I noted, had already completed army service and were postgraduate students. They were not simple farmers nor naïve children. I told him it was doubtful that I would be able to influence them against taking part in the independence movement because I felt even their own fathers would not have much influence in this matter.

T'ang dropped the subject but told me that another man at headquarters wanted to talk with me. This proved to be a rather sinister-looking party officer named Chang Yen-yuan, known to me later as one of the more notorious bosses of the secret police organization. He too asked me to investigate the independence movement in the United States and to use my influence to persuade them to abandon the issue. "Meet them and please tell them to come back," he said. "Let them see our prosperity now. We can guarantee their safety."

I came away from party headquarters deeply disturbed. Obviously the party bosses wanted to use me but was I also being exploited deliberately by the government, by the university, and by my sponsors? Within a day or two I paid a courtesy call at the Academia Sinica to take leave of Dr. Hu Shih. To him I remarked privately that I felt the appointment was merely window-dressing, to show a Formosan in New York. He was visibly startled at the idea.

My new colleagues, the professional diplomats, were leaving Taipei a few days ahead of me. My appointment had been unexpected, there were important matters to be arranged at the university, and my family had to be cared for. About two days after the public announcement was made, I received an invitation to

call on Vice-president General Chen Cheng at his home at four
P.M. I found him alone and in a mellow mood. He welcomed me
with courteous attention, tea and small dumplings were set before us, and we settled down in an easy and relaxed atmosphere.
To my surprise, however, my host remarked, "All your fellow
delegates had a dinner here yesterday. I so regretted that we
were unable to reach you to deliver the invitation." Obviously
this was a polite lie, for I had been available and the vice-
president could have reached me at any moment. I realized at
once that either General Chen had chosen this way to have a private conversation with me or, more likely, the other delegates
had wanted an opportunity to discuss Formosa's internal situation and China's U.N. position unembarrassed by the presence of
a Formosan.

The vice-president began to talk of his own recent visit to the
United States. He had been confronted by a Formosan Independence Movement demonstration in Washington, the first such public demonstration in the United States, and he obviously was
offended and angered. He had lost face. He felt the American authorities should have prevented such a rebellious gesture.

I assured him that there were demonstrations somewhere in
America every day, demonstrations on behalf of, or against, the
most unlikely causes. For example, there had even been demonstrations protesting the sending of a dog into outer space during
the early experiments with satellites and rockets. He accepted
this explanation without conviction and turned to general conversation. If he had thought to open a discussion of the Formosan Independence Movement in America, he put the thought
aside. After a polite interlude the teatime conversation ended,
and I came away sharply aware of the intense sensitivity of Nationalist leaders to all forms of criticism.

In the few days left to me I called upon my closest friend, Liu
Chin-sui, who was now an associate professor in the law faculty
and a specialist in constitutional law. He was dying of cancer,
but before entering the hospital for the last time he had begun to

draw up a constitution for Taiwan, a constitution for the future when Formosans would be independent and the continental refugees among us would be given their proper share in an island-wide administration and absorbed into the native island population. As we talked of my new assignment, I was reminded of a small incident that had occurred a few months earlier when Professor Edwin Reischauer of Harvard University had visited Formosa. Liu and I had been with him in a group of academic people about evenly divided between continental Chinese and Formosans. The American presidential campaign was then attracting world attention and Formosans had been excited to learn that the candidate John F. Kennedy had declared that the islets of Quemoy and Matsu were unimportant to the United States and should be given up in order to clarify the American commitment to defend Taiwan. This was mentioned, and Dr. Reischauer playfully said, "Let's take a poll now. Who do you wish to see elected?", whereupon all the continental Chinese present promptly said, "Nixon" and all the Formosans, "Kennedy."

I bid good-bye to my friend Liu for the last time. Ten days later I was in New York and he was dead. The sense of personal loss was great. My thoughts turned often to his dream of a proper and effective constitutional government for our island home.

There was ample time to reflect on this, for I was staying in a dreary hotel near the Empire State Building and was alone a great deal of the time. There were no fellow-Formosans on the delegation or its permanent staff who would understand Liu's aspirations and my loss. After paying a prompt courtesy call on Dr. Ting-fu Fuller Tsiang, Taipei's ambassador to the United Nations, I went dutifully to the office each day. There I shared a room with the naval attaché and was assigned to the Sixth Committee of the General Assembly, a committee dealing with legal matters.

Just a few days before the formal opening of the General Assembly, the U.N. had been plunged into a grave crisis. Secretary-General Hammarskjöld was tragically killed on an African mission. The Soviet Union insisted on adopting the so-called "troika system" by which instead of one, three secretaries-general would be appointed, representing Western, socialist, and nonaligned blocs. It was only at the last moment that U Thant was nominated as a compromise choice. The Nationalist delegation's task was especially complicated at this moment. The Generalissimo had made a public commitment to veto Outer Mongolia's application, and Russia had countered by saying that Moscow would therefore veto the Mauritanian bid. The Africans were blaming the Nationalist party leadership and the Chinese delegation was blaming Russia. Taipei resented strong pressures from Washington designed to prevent the veto and blamed the United States for providing insufficient support for Chiang's claim to represent Outer Mongolia in world affairs. After intensive consultations between our delegation and Taipei, the stubborn Generalissimo was persuaded to make the difficult decision to yield. Since Chiang himself stood to lose face before the world, someone would have to pay the price for the affront. Dr. Tsiang escaped, but the Generalissimo's extreme displeasure fell instead upon the *bon vivant* Ambassador George Yeh, Taipei's popular representative at Washington. This was a matter of behind-the-scenes court politics, suggesting the influence of Foreign Minister Shen Ching-huan who was known not to be one of Yeh's partisans. The Generalissimo summoned Ambassador Yeh, asked for an explanation, heard him out, and curtly said, "Stay in Taipei; you need not go back."

Thus Yeh lost the ambassadorship, but since he was one of General Chen Cheng's men, he was kept in the cabinet to mollify the vice-president and dull criticism among Yeh's influential friends in America. He was considered too liberal, and kept thereafter under close surveillance, followed everywhere by secret agents assigned to note his associates and report on his daily activities. By now even Dr. Hu Shih's relations with the Generalissimo were deteriorating, and he had good reason to be conscious of his vulnerability. He had become suspect.

One morning Ambassador Tsiang's secretary asked me if I had time to lunch privately with the ambassador in his suburban home. We drove out of the city together in his official car, and after a brief greeting by his young wife, the two of us sat down alone for lunch and a long informal talk, which took a strange direction. Dr. Tsiang, then sixty-six years old, began to recall his days as ambassador to Moscow in the years from 1936 to 1938, and soon came around to the subject of Chiang Ching-kuo. I sensed that we had come to the real purpose of the luncheon invitation.

In his youth it was well-known that young Ching-kuo had quarrelled bitterly with his father, allegedly because of the elder Chiang's harsh treatment of the wife of his youth, Ching-kuo's mother. The young man had gone off to Russia about the time the rising Nationalist general, then forty years of age, had cast aside Ching-kuo's mother in order to marry Soong Mei-ling, youngest daughter in the wealthy and influential Soong family, based in Shanghai. Ching-kuo attended the Sun Yat-sen Labor University in Moscow, but his movements within Russia after that are obscure. Ambassador Tsiang began his story by saying that one day he received a cable from the Generalissimo saying, "Please find my son and send him back."

The ambassador had promptly gone to the Soviet authorities, and a few days later he was notified that Ching-kuo had been found. Dr. Tsiang invited young Chiang to come to the embassy, and then told him of his father's cabled request. Ching-kuo, who was then about twenty-seven years old, replied, "I have a problem; I have married a Russian girl and I married for love." Dr. Tsiang invited him to bring his wife to the embassy. According to the ambassador, she proved to be a simple country girl who "didn't even know how to use a knife and fork properly." "I told Ching-kuo that he must return to China in any case, and must take his wife with him," said Tsiang. "He agreed. I then prepared appropriate gifts for them to present to his father." A few years later Ambassador Tsiang returned to China and was amazed to meet a Russian girl who had been, in his words, transformed into a "gracious Chinese lady" and had adopted a Chinese name.

Since then Ching-kuo had found in him a father-teacher figure, an older man to whom he could look for the friendship missing in his relations with the formidable Generalissimo. After that, he said, each time he returned to Formosa Ching-kuo met him personally at the airport and treated him with special courtesy.

In his conversation with me Dr. Tsiang enlarged on this relationship, saying that he did not consider Ching-kuo a "stupid person" but rather a victim of circumstance. "I told him bluntly on one occasion," said Dr. Tsiang, "that he seemed always to be surrounded by inferior people and that he should recruit good men, and he said to me, in effect, 'Do you think good people would associate with me? None of the able men want to be with me, so the only men around me are men nobody else wants.'" Tsiang thought this was proof that Chiang Ching-kuo was not stupid, and noted that he seemed to be comfortable with students and men of lower rank, but lost assurance when with men of superior education.

Dr. Tsiang then said he found occasion to tell the Generalissimo himself quite frankly that he should give his son more respectable and more appropriate jobs. He should not seem to be only a police boss. The response was ambiguous: "What can he do?", which might be interpreted "Is he capable of doing anything?" or as "What do you recommend?"

The ambassador then remarked to me that "He (Ching-kuo) is not a bad man, and he knows his own limitations. He needs able men about him," and as he reminisced in this fashion, I began to wonder why he was confiding in me.

Our strange, private talk, unattended and probably unrecorded, continued until four o'clock in the afternoon when at last I was sent back to my shabby hotel in the ambassador's car. During the long drive into the city I reflected on Dr. Tsiang's candor in speaking of the Generalissimo and his boldness. For example, he had said that he once advised Chiang to cut the size of his army because it was absorbing too great a share of the budget, and the Generalissimo characteristically had brushed this aside with the comment, "You probably know something about diplomacy and politics, but you don't understand military matters."

My only private conversation with the ambassador thus ended on a curious note. Between September and December the Chinese delegation lobbied intensively to gain support in the next crucial vote on the China question. Strategy was changing; from then on it was to be considered "an important question" requiring a two-thirds vote in the General Assembly for a decision. In addition to my light duties on the Sixth Committee, I was asked to analyze every speech made in the General Assembly that touched on the subject of China's representation in the world body. Thus as these texts came over my desk, I began to see the problem in a new perspective. When the voting took place at last, Taipei retained its seat by a narrow margin.

International interest in the China question was soon dulled by annual repetition. The fate of the Nationalist regime was at stake, but so too was the fate of the Formosan people. They were seldom mentioned in the debates. Our delegation refused to admit that these were separate interests, and my presence as a Formosan member implied a consensus in support of Chiang's government that did not exist.

Some Formosans questioned my integrity. Why was I willing to serve as a Nationalist representative at the U.N.? Several men who were active in the Formosan Independence Movement in New York came to me and proposed that I find an occasion to speak on the floor of the General Assembly on behalf of the Nationalist Chinese delegation and then suddenly and dramatically present the case for independence together with an appeal for U.N. action. At the same time, they thought, I should appeal for political asylum in the United States. This was entirely impractical; there would be no occasion for me to make a speech as that was not my role in the delegation, and I was not ready for such a dramatic gesture. The ground had not been properly prepared to capitalize upon the momentary sensation such an incident would generate.

It was apparent to all that the Chinese delegation had no interest in United Nations business other than the problem of keeping its own seat in the world organization. Before the session ended I requested and received permission to return to Taipei and to my new duties as chairman of the political science department at the university.

On my return to Formosa I found myself a center of attention among Formosan students and leaders in every field. I was at the peak of my career in a highly specialized field, the new technological aspects of international law in which I was a recognized pioneer. My brief assignment to the U.N. delegation had added nothing to the modest professional reputation I enjoyed abroad, but in Formosa it was taken as a demonstration of what a Formosan might and could accomplish if given opportunity. There was an overwhelming flood of invitations to speak of my experience in New York. Associations of every kind pressed for speaking dates, and students sought me out for conferences and advice. All this reflected their sense of isolation and a starved interest in international affairs that could not be satisfied under the Chiangs' restrictive control.

There was now little time to spend with my family or to indulge my hobbies. However, I went as often as possible to visit them in Kaohsiung. My son was doing well in his studies, and my little daughter, now five years old, was about to enter school.

We all shared an interest in dogs and tropical fishes. I was breeding guppies and maintained tanks of colorful imported freshwater fish. Sometimes we had as many as ten dogs in our home, and over the years we kept many breeds, shepherd, collie, Great Dane, dachshund, dalamation, Pekingese, terrier, and bulldog. For a brief time we bred poodles, and I was vice-president of the Dog-lovers' Association. My son began early to enter his dogs in competition.

My new administrative duties as chairman of the department of political science filled my days; nevertheless I accepted some public speaking engagements. On each occasion, I attempted to make clear the place of the China problem among many complex world questions. These public meetings were much less interesting than the discussions held in my own home and privately elsewhere about town. Students came with their friends in ever-increasing numbers, and discussions of Formosa's own future were often vivid and sometimes bitter. I have no doubt that among those present were agents reporting to the secret police.

Soon after coming back from New York I was again invited to visit Nationalist party headquarters, this time meeting with representatives of about ten security agencies, to present my impressions of the U.N. sessions or any other subject I might choose.

It was a revealing experience; my questioners returned again and again to the position, thoughts, and activities of Formosan students in the United States and to the character of the Independence Movement. I told my audience frankly and rather bluntly what students abroad think and talk about. Their advocacy of independence, I said, was not a matter of personal or isolated experience and belief, but a general reaction to the basic policies of government in Formosa. They objected to the *structure* of government in Formosa. They were not content to take part only in a provincial organization while being excluded from an effective place in the national administration that absorbed provincial taxes and made decisions binding on the provincial administration.

My listeners expressed a keen desire to change the views and thinking of students overseas, and I in turn gave them a rather pessimistic estimate of any attempt to alter the situation unless a basic change of government policy took place at Taipei. This was an extremely delicate subject. Everyone present knew very well that government policy meant Chiang's policy, the will of the party leader. I did not attempt to spell out the changes nor did I need to. These men were not fools, and they had called me before them as chairman of the political science department in a national university, presumably an objective observer. At the conclusion of our meeting many expressed thanks for a "most enlightening and useful session." They seemed to have genuinely appreciated my frankness. Thereafter from time to time I was invited to speak informally at party meetings.

One evening I was invited by a law professor to dinner at his home. Just after we left the dinner table an urgent message came. Dr. Hu Shih had had a stroke and collapsed at a meeting of Academia Sinica. I rushed back and took a taxi to Nang-Kang. When I reached there he was already dead, lying on the floor covered by a white sheet. I looked at his face whose expression was exactly the same as when he talked with intense concentration. It was then that I was told by one of his closest friends that the anonymous financial supporter who made possible my second year's study at McGill University was none other than Dr. Hu Shih. This most kind-hearted and thoughtful scholar had characteristically concealed from me, during our association of nearly ten years, the fact that he himself was the one who helped me finish my advanced study in Canada. In him I had lost a most understanding and unselfish friend and supporter.

Sometime after eight o'clock on a chilly January evening in 1962, a jeep pulled up before the house, there was a loud pounding at the door and when my wife answered, the driver rudely asked for "Peng," handing her a message. It was an invitation to present myself for a private audience with Chiang Kai-shek at ten o'clock the following morning.

The Generalissimo's office lay at the heart of the towered Government General Building at the center of Taipei. Like a beached hermit crab, he had appropriated someone else's shell for his own. After his flight from the continent Chiang had taken over the imposing building erected during World War I to accommodate the Japanese governors of Formosa. It was of vice-regal proportions, but had been gutted by fire in 1945, and was now rehabilitated to provide a temporary headquarters from which the Generalissimo proposed to direct "recovery of the mainland." It was a stronghold in itself, and on the plaza before it he satisfied some delusions of grandeur by staging grand military reviews.

As I rode by cab from the university to this towered red brick building, I was nervous and with good reason. I took my artificial left arm and hand out of my coat pocket, where I normally carry it, to let it dangle by my side. It was well known that Chiang's guards had orders to shoot instantly if anyone in his presence made a suspicious or very sudden move. Some guard, not knowing of my loss, might think I was concealing a weapon in that pocket. I recalled too many stories and allegations such as the one that on the occasion of a military academy graduation a young man who stepped forward to receive his diploma from the Generalissimo, nervously reached for his handkerchief to wipe his sweating forehead and was shot on the spot. And there was the story that as the Generalissimo's cavalcade rushed along a narrow country road near Kaohsiung, it came upon a farmer relieving himself on the roadbank. When the poor fellow hastily moved to cover himself, he was shot and killed by the passing guards. He had moved too suddenly just as the Generalissimo's limousine swept by.

On reaching the great building I was taken quickly to an ante-chamber in which I was briefed at length on visiting protocol, when and where to bow and how many times. I was told to sit if invited to do so, and to be sharply aware of the moment the Generalissimo desired to end the audience. He would make this clear by a gesture, and upon withdrawing from his presence, I was to bow, and at the door turn and bow again and then promptly depart. It was the protocol of a royal audience.

My name was called, the door opened, and I stepped forward into a huge room. There sat the small Generalissimo before a desk at the far end. Beside him sat someone taking notes, perhaps a bodyguard doubling as a secretary. Chiang himself held a folder or filing envelope on his lap and was glancing through it. I assumed it was my dossier and that he was belatedly doing his homework.

When I had bowed and had walked slowly to a position before his desk, he looked up and in his usual abrupt manner gestured as he invited me to "Sit! Sit!" Then followed some comment and questions. "You are just back from the United Nations. We thank you for what you have done. How are your family? How are your children? Have you any difficulties? If you have any problems, please come to see me."

My replies to these conventional questions were punctuated by frequent interjections of *Hao! Hao!* ("Good! Good!") which serve him in lieu of genuine or meaningful conversation on many ceremonial occasions. In less than ten minutes he indicated an end to the audience, I rose, bowed as prescribed, and withdrew.

What had prompted this curious interview? I had been presented to the Generalissimo on other occasions, and he had asked the same trite questions and had received the same answers. It was common knowledge that he insisted on seeing every person nominated for appointment by him, and that in considering promotions and appointments affecting the armed forces, he carried this to an extreme degree. In early years on the continent he had insisted upon interviewing general officers and men of ministerial rank; now he called in many more men of decidedly lower rank, creating the impression that he put little trust in the recommendations and judgments of his closest advisors. Inconsequential details were known to affect his decisions, and the story was then current that an important appointment had been denied to one unfortunate officer who, being hopelessly nearsighted, chanced to bow toward the wrong person in Chiang's presence.

This interview strengthened my impression that he expected to create or to heighten an individual's sense of personal and direct obligation to him by granting such personal attention. Chiang

Kai-shek had risen to power and held it through an extraordinarily shrewd manipulation of factions, playing off one against another within army, party, family, and government. My friends and I probed for the significance of this latest attention. We knew that powerful members of the party and army elite objected to concessions to Formosans that might help them advance from positions in the provincial administration to important or influential positions at the national level. We also knew that some relatively liberal and more realistic advisors urged the development of a wider base of support in the island population. Soon after this, various officers of party and government found occasion to have conversations with me. Some still talked about the "return to China," and others hinted that when a reshuffle took place in the government I would be considered for a high-level appointment. They implied that it was merely a matter of time and of my intention.

My inner thoughts were in turmoil. The government and party bosses had made a great mistake in sending me to New York. This experience finally politicized me, and I was to lead a dual life thereafter, for many months, until I made a final commitment to challenge the dictatorship with a public demand for reform.

VIII

My Arrest

While I was attracting the attention of party and government functionaries after my return from abroad, I was steadily broadening my contacts far beyond the campus. It may be that I was becoming less of an arrogant intellectual. Word seemed to spread that I was approachable, and that I welcomed anyone who wished to come around for our evening discussions. Our large house was often crowded with students from the university and from other schools in the region. Occasionally city councilors and local politicians came to join in the conversations.

No one believed in the "reconquest" of continental China. Taipei's claim that it represented the mainland provinces was absurd. The Generalissimo's pronouncements concerning Sinkiang, Outer Mongolia, and Tibet were ridiculous. So too were the attempts to keep alive some semblance of a claim upon Okinawa and the Ryukyu Islands. We were not much concerned with all of these. Our interest lay in the unrealistic claims made on behalf of Formosa itself, that it represented China and the "Free World," and that the island population gave undivided support to the recovery of China. There was no open talk of independence, but in discussing Nationalist China's position in the United Nations, we felt that someday Chiang's government would be voted out. The fundamental problem was reform and reorganization in order to create a government tailored to reality.

It was no longer possible for me to be a detached observer, and it was embarrassing to continue to give the public impression that I was one of Chiang's men. Public prominence had brought in its train great personal difficulties. The ordinary petty academic jealousies generated by faculty politics within my department were compounded by Chinese dislike of administrative subordination to a younger man who was a Formosan. Campus politics were uninteresting and a waste of time. I began to have troubles with a new dean whose family assumed that since he was my superior within the academic hierarchy, my entire family was indebted to him and subordinate to them. When the woman who lived with the dean attempted to meddle directly in our private family affairs, I was compelled to make an issue of it, and this affected our relations upon the campus. At the end of the academic year, July 1962, I resigned the department chairmanship with great relief.

I was free to accept an invitation to undertake a special research project requested of me by the deputy foreign minister, Yang Hsi-kun. Under a one-year contract I agreed to prepare a paper on Africa. Taipei was seeking to counter Peking's expanding programs of aid to Africa. The project was funded by an Asia Foundation grant. This project was not so far removed from the situation in Formosa as it might first appear. Part of my report entitled "The Sentimental Basis for Pan-Africanism" was soon published in the Taipei literary magazine *Wen-Hsin* (*Apollo*), creating a local sensation. I had commented at length on the African struggle to attain identity, nationhood, and independence. I called attention to the diverse peoples who had been cut off from their own past by colonial rule, and were now seeking to control their own destinies. I had not intended to write a political tract, but when the editor's prefacing note declared, "That article makes us think of Formosa," the reading public saw it as an allusion to the local situation and Formosa's history. It could not have been well received at party headquarters.

Soon after this I attended a cocktail party given by one of my Chinese colleagues, and there I met an American diplomat who laughingly remarked to me that I would be astonished by the thickness of my "Who's Who" folder in the American embassy files. We had a lively general discussion of the China question and of local politics. Other social occasions led to a dinner at which I met a number of embassy staff members. Several later came to my home where a typically frank American "bull session" took place, ranging over many aspects of the current international political situation. There were other occasions to talk with Americans, and at a public concert I was presented to the ambassador, Admiral William J. Kirk. He knew something of my career and invited me to call upon him at his office for a long talk. Before this could be arranged, he was suddenly recalled to Washington.

I was now often asked to talk to church groups. Hitherto I had been too preoccupied with academic affairs and had not shown much interest in the local Christian community although members of my family were extremely active in it. My late father, my mother, and my sister were officers in the Presbyterian church, an uncle was a pastor, and a cousin would soon become president of the Taipei Theological Seminary. Given my academic background and connections, my appearance at church-sponsored meetings usually drew a considerable audience.

At one of these public meetings, early in 1962, I addressed an audience at the Tainan Theological College. This is the only school in Formosa where all instruction is carried on in the local Formosan dialect. I therefore chose to speak in Formosan rather than in the official Mandarin Chinese, and I found myself discussing the problem of Formosan self-determination, speaking more bluntly than ever before in an open meeting.

About this time the deputy secretary general of the Nationalist party, Hsu Ching-chung, had been instructed to found a Japanese-language magazine. It was to be financed by the party and edited on Formosa for distribution in Japan, and it was to be called *The Free China Monthly*. My friend Hsu asked me to recommend someone for the editorial work at Taipei, someone who could speak and write well in both Chinese and Japanese. Knowing full well that it was a party enterprise, I recommended a young man who for two years had been coming to my house quite regularly to participate in discussions of Formosa's future.

Hsieh Tsung-min had been brought to my attention by my late friend and colleague Liu. He was the son of a well-to-do family living in central Formosa. Although he had not been at the top of his class as an undergraduate in the law school, he had presented an outstanding graduate thesis in constitutional law under Liu's guidance. From our law school he had gone on to the only graduate school in political science at that time, the Cheng-chi University. There he made a very favorable impression upon the Chinese faculty who in turn had recommended him for employment as an instructor at the Feng-shan Military Academy in south Formosa. But far from the capital and his stimulating friends, among very dull Nationalist Chinese military instructors, he soon became profoundly unhappy. His deep dissatisfaction was known, and he was about to be fired when I took the opportunity to recommend him to Hsu for this more congenial editorial employment at Taipei.

Among Hsieh's friends who also came regularly to my home was a young man of Hakka descent, Wei Ting-chao, a farmer's son of brave and solid personality. He was a competent student who had graduated from our law school. But he then refused to take a job commensurate with his academic training until after he had worked in a coal mine for several months "to gain experience of real life," after which he became a research assistant at the prestigious Academia Sinica. As the months passed, these two young friends often took the lead in defining and clarifying Formosan problems under Nationalist occupation, often expressing regret that many more people could not share in our discussions. Is seemed to us so reasonable and so easy to make people see the absurdities and injustice of the situation.

We had become tired of talking only among friends who shared a common point of view, going over and over the same ground without moving toward a solution of the Formosa question. That solution could only be found in a reorganization and thorough reform of government and the admission of Formosans to effective participation at every level.

In essence we were reviewing the following principal issues, policies, actions, and institutions:

1. That the administration at Taipei represented a "government of China" was an absurd fiction which amounted to a gigantic hoax.
2. This fiction enabled the Nationalist party government to maintain two levels of organization, the so-called "national government" in which all positions of effective power were reserved for continental Chinese who had come into the island in recent years, and a subordinate provincial administration partially open to Formosan participation.
3. It was advertised to the world that the national government was a "constitutional democracy" with elective participation in the Legislative Yuan, although the legislative membership had been elected in 1947, on the continent, in rigged elections. The constitutional provisions requiring quadrennial elections had been suspended in order to keep these refugee mainland Chinese members in office indefinitely.
4. The governing elite, continental Chinese, justified this political discrimination by taking the position that Formosans are backward, tainted by fifty years of Japanese rule, and in need of a long period of political "tutelage" before becoming qualified to enjoy full representational rights at all levels of the government.
5. By suspending elections after 1947, the government was able to maintain the well-advertised but illegal "elective National Legislature" in which less than three percent of the island's actual population was represented.
6. By holding on to Quemoy and Matsu, and making a show of military action there, the government maintained the fiction of "national emergency" and a "state of war," thus justifying the suspension of civil rights

under continuing martial law. The "emergency" was artificially and indefinitely prolonged in order to curtail Formosan participation in normal constitutional democracy.

7. Over eighty percent of the national budget was spent on military affairs, including elaborate secret police organizations. This was the highest national per capita rate of military expenditure in the world, higher even than the rates in Vietnam, Israel, or Korea. The armed forces numbering more than 600,000 men was too small to invade the mainland or effectively challenge the huge Communist Chinese military organization, separated from us by 100 miles of open sea, but it was far too large to be supported by the island economy. Only massive foreign aid kept it going on this scale.

8. No genuine opposition party was allowed to come into being. The Nationalist party did not dare to face the challenge that a genuine political opposition party might produce.

9. Corruption and inefficiency marked every office of government, party, and army, creating a burden which the Formosan people should not have been asked to bear.

10. From kindergarten to college the party and the Government carried on an intensive political indoctrination that was warping the minds of the rising generation, and was designed only to produce blind support for the one party and its leader.

11. The Youth Corps was a para-military agency of the party and government in which membership was compulsory. Its function was similar to the "Hitler Youth" of Nazi Germany and other totalitarian regimes.

12. Any unconventional behavior or creative thinking, any critical mind or independent spirit is not only limited, and frowned upon, but punished. The effort to return the Formosan people to the narrow, xenophobic traditions of ancient China must be resisted.

13. No genuinely effective labor unions were permitted and labor was exploited under the "emergency" provisions of the law.

14. As in continental China before World War II, the working class farmer and landless agricultural laborer were being exploited by the government through compulsory exchange of farm produce for fertilizer and by heavy taxation. The abuses of the masses that brought about the Nationalist government's downfall on the continent in 1949 had been carried over into Formosa and cannot be disguised by the widely advertised "Land Reform Program."

15. In public it was compulsory to show outward signs of loyalty to the party. Loyalty to the Generalissimo was the only criterion of patriotism. The basic requirement for success in all tests was a profession of un-

wavering loyalty to the "Party Leader, and the Founding Father, Sun Yat-sen, and his *San min chu-i* ("Three Principles')." Even the application for a barber's license or a driver's license required a written pledge to these loyalties.

At last in the early months of 1964 we decided to draw up a summary of our ideas and a statement of our position and problems, something that could be distributed not only to Formosans but to the continental Chinese who were also chafing under party dictatorship and fearful of the future. Hsieh volunteered to draft a statement and Wei agreed to help.

One evening Hsieh appeared at my house with a bulging *furoshiki* ("wrapping-cloth") out of which tumbled about 100 pages of manuscript, an exposition of the Rights of Man, beginning with the American Declaration of Independence and the French Revolution. We convinced him at once that we needed something brief, not a dissertation such as this. We needed a concise statement, written in manifesto form.

After intense discussion and many revisions, with Wei's help we prepared a new draft, a text in good Chinese, that would fit into broadside format about the size of a newspaper page. The principal credit for this document must go to Hsieh. Here were Formosa's problems set forth in unmistakable terms.

We proposed to call our manifesto *Taiwan Tzu-chiu Yun-Tung Hsuan-yen* ("A Declaration of Formosan Self-salvation"). A brief preamble noted that the people of the island of Formosa wanted to be governed by neither the Nationalists nor the Communists, but by themselves, and that in self-interest and self-preservation the twelve million people must replace Chiang Kai-shek's regime by a government freely elected and responsive to the public welfare. We then made eight points which can be summarized here:

1. The world must recognize that there is one China and one Formosa. The Chiang regime has been able to survive only because of American support; nevertheless American policy is moving toward recognition of Communist China, and uses the Formosa issue as a bargaining point.
2. Return to the mainland is not even remotely possible. The military

forces under Chiang's control are a defensive force, entirely dependent upon the United States for supplies. It is too small to conquer the mainland, and much too large for peacetime purposes, consuming eighty percent of the budget. While preaching freedom and democracy Chiang Kai-shek violates basic human rights at will, monopolizes political power, and through use of secret police imposes dictatorial rule. The political commissar system weakens the military organization and reduces its efficiency. Formosan conscripts drafted to replace aging continental Chinese soldiers must wear the Nationalist uniform, but they remain Chiang Kai-shek's silent enemy.

3. The slogan "Return to the Mainland" enhances the position of the Chiang regime externally by exploiting an American neurosis concerning communism and Communist China, and as an excuse internally for martial law, enables the Chiangs to enforce dictatorial rule.

4. The Nationalist government represents neither the people of continental China nor those on Formosa. The Generalissimo's regime was driven from the continent only two years after the elections of 1947. The Formosans who constitute eighty-five percent of the population have less than three percent representation in the national legislature. Although for external propaganda purposes, the government says that the continental Chinese and the Formosans must cooperate, in practice it employs every means possible to divide them and set them against one another in order that they will not unite in overthrowing the dictatorship. Chiang's manipulation of factions within the ruling party is here extended to the general population.

5. A top-heavy military expenditure and a high birthrate are the two greatest internal problems. Chiang's own statistics in this year (1964) showed that military expenditures account for more than eighty percent of the budget, but this does not include many hidden or indirect costs. Unemployment daily grows worse. Advocates of birth control are considered as defeatists, and a high birthrate is encouraged only to produce conscript soldier's for Chiang's armies twenty years hence.

6. The army and party elite, under Chiang's direction, pursue policies designed to eliminate opposition leadership by destroying the economic base of the middle class. When community leaders everywhere rose in 1947 to protest economic exploitation after the first eighteen months of Nationalist rule, about 20,000 were killed or imprisoned on Chiang's order. This was followed, in 1950, by the so-called land reform, manipulated to impoverish the well-educated middle class.

7. Economic policy is irrational, designed to support the huge military establishment rather than to develop a healthy agricultural and industrial life

suited to Formosa's resources and manpower. The farmer, heavily taxed in an artificial price system, produces principally to feed the army rather than the productive laborers. Genuine tax reform would necessitate a reduction in the military budget. Social instability is growing acute as a few collaborators become very rich and the farmers and laborers remain impoverished and driven to meet the tax burden.

8. Can Formosa be an independent country? Since 1949 the island has in fact been independent. On the basis of population Formosa ranks thirtieth among the members of the United Nations. We must cease imagining ourselves to be a big power and face reality, establishing a small but democratic and prosperous society. Some say that Chiang has become an emperor, and we must only wait until he dies. But we must not overlook the possibility of a desperate young Chiang handing Formosa over to Communist China, nor should we even for a moment forget that Formosa may become again the victim of international power politics. We cannot wait passively for "progressive reform"; the history of the Nationalist party and government clearly shows that any form of compromise with Chiang is either an illusion or a deception designed to trap the intellectual appeasers who hope that the passage of time will bring an ultimately peaceful transfer of government to Formosan hands. Formosans who collaborate with the party government for economic gain must be warned that they may pay a heavy penalty one day at the hands of an angry people.

After elaborating upon these several themes, we summarized our three principal objectives:

1. To affirm that return to the mainland is absolutely impossible, and by unifying the island population, regardless of place of origin, to bring about the overthrow of the Chiang regime, establishing a new country and a new government.
2. To rewrite the constitution, guaranteeing basic human rights and obtaining true democracy by establishing an efficient administration responsible to the people.
3. To participate in the U.N. as a new member, establishing diplomatic relations with other countries striving together for world peace.

In the heart of our manifesto we spelled out our principles, and in doing so effectively defined the shortcomings of the Chiang administration. For example we emphasized the necessity of the principle of democracy and the popular election of the head of state who should not be an idol to be worshipped, nor invested with absolute power nor immune from criticism. He should be a public servant dedicated to public service and subject to control of popular representatives. There must be guaranteed freedoms of assembly, organization, and expression, and opposition parties must be guaranteed legal status. Graft and corruption in government must be eliminated insofar as possible and the treatment of soldiers, teachers, and public employees must be improved. The efficiency of government must be increased, and healthy civil service must be established. The independence of the judiciary must be guaranteed, and all laws that encroach upon basic human rights must be abolished. Illegal arrest, interrogation, and punishment must be prevented hereafter.

We said that the secret police system must be abolished, and the positions and functions of police officers regulated according to democratic principles, and that a law-abiding spirit among the people must be actively cultivated. Every man should have the right to unrestricted communication, freedom of movement, and travel at home and abroad. The burden of armaments must be reduced to fit needs of self-defense only, and the position and livelihood of retired soldiers must be guaranteed.

We were concerned first with problems of individual freedom and of orderly and just government. Given these we could properly address ourselves to the problems of a distorted economy, unjustly managed for the benefit of the party and army elite, their families, and their friends. By greatly reducing military expenditures, we could develop a budget for long-range planning. Our material resources and manpower were being grossly mismanaged. We proposed to increase national productivity, reduce unemployment, and raise the general standard of living with a view to reducing the gap between the very rich and the very poor. The Chiang regime had managed confiscated Japanese properties and foreign aid subsidies only to benefit itself and its friends, supplying low-wage labor to favored industries and depriving the farmers of a just share of their harvest through the enforced "fertilizer-crop exchange" program. The public was overburdened with heavy indirect taxes.

We concluded our manifesto by declaring that we wanted neither the program of the extreme Right, the Nationalist party program, nor that of the extreme Left, the Communist party program. We appealed for support for a Formosan self-determination movement that would break the hold of the Nationalist party dictatorship, and unite all the people on Formosa in a constructive democratic program. We asked that our manifesto be circulated, reproduced, and quoted at every opportunity.

HAVING AGREED on the final draft after so many months of discussion and indirect debate, we were exhilarated, flushed with a sense of success, but conscious that now we were on a dangerous path. Life seemed to have taken on a new meaning. The obstacles in our path were dwarfed by the magnitude of the effect we hoped this manifesto might have upon the lives of ten million Formosans and upon the refugees living among us. Every thoughtful man and woman on the island was aware of some of these problems. We sought now to bring the picture into sharp focus. We would define the issues for them or at least help the individual clarify his problems by defining them. If our manifesto generated debate in every community, it would prepare the way for popular support for any overt attempt to break up the party dictatorship and destroy the stranglehold of the secret police system.

Up to this point our achievement was an intellectual exercise. We had a well-polished text, written in excellent Chinese, but from here on we had to come to grips with the daily reality of a police state, of back-alley spies and secret agents, of the controlled press and radio, intimidation through economic pressures, and all the other devices used by a dictatorship to keep the masses in line. We proposed distribution of the declaration to Formosans and Chinese alike, to all local leaders, businessmen, doctors, teachers, councilors of all ranks and at all levels of the administration, all members of the Legislative Yuan, and military men. If we could suddenly blanket the island with our manifesto, Chiang's party and secret police would be unable to locate all copies and unable to suppress the ideas we had set forth. It would prove impossible to arrest everyone found to be in possession of our sheet, and those arrested could prove that they had received them without their foreknowledge or consent. The government would be thrown on the defensive as never before. So we thought.

We decided that we needed 10,000 copies to begin with. The next question was where and how could we reproduce this document.

Mimeographing was technically impractical. Moreover, the manifesto had to look substantial, not like a fly-by-night advertising throw-away. After weeks of discussion we decided that we must print it. Hsieh's father had recently sent him about 1000 dollars for miscellaneous business investments, and we considered buying a press with this. But we were not skilled printers ourselves, and a press would be very difficult to conceal in a private home. We would have to have the work done in some obscure back-alley establishment.

Hsieh very carefully prepared a "working copy" which we could place in an unsuspecting typesetter's hands. He removed words and phrases alluding to the Chiang regime, substituting references to Mao Tse-tung and Peking which made it superficially appear to be an attack upon the Communists. While this was being done we compiled distribution lists by drawing upon membership rosters of the Teachers Association, the Doctors Association, and similar business and professional lists. Hsieh then asked his typist to prepare mailing labels, ostensibly for the party magazine of which he was now the editor.

Hsieh found a small family business that specialized in typesetting and arranged with the proprietor to set up the text of our "decoy version" of the manifesto. While this was being done he searched about other shops for individual type faces he would need to bring the finished text back to its correct form.

This took some weeks. When everything was ready, Hsieh, a bachelor, rented a room in an obscure hotel in the old and somewhat disreputable Manka section of the city. It was not unusual for men to take rooms such as this for romantic meetings, but no women came to this one. Hsieh's only visitors were our friend Wei and me. Hsieh wrapped up the heavy boxes of set type and carried them there in a pedicab. Someone on the hotel staff may have noticed his bringing them into his hotel room, for the manager soon found an opportunity to burst in unannounced. The boxes were out of sight, under the bed, and since he saw nothing unusual in the three men talking together, he mumbled an excuse and withdrew. This should have alerted us to take greater precaution; we were on the edges of the Manka underworld here and were ourselves too innocent to realize that every alley had its spies and every hotel its paid informants. A secret police spy network was perhaps the only efficient organization that had come over to Formosa from the continent.

In that hotel room, we completed the substitutions necessary to restore the text to its original form. The next requirement was a supply of paper, an order easily taken care of. Hsieh then found a very small, family-owned and unlicensed shop that was furtively printing pornography and hence cautious and vulnerable. The owner agreed to run off our sheets, if we supplied the paper.

Wei and Hsieh took the heavy blocks of type to the shop and saw them locked into place on the printing bed. Leaving Wei to stand guard, Hsieh then hurried across town to bring the paper supply. A very long time passed, the printer became impatient and restless and Wei became worried. At last he left the shop and went to the main street nearby, just in time to meet Hsieh and help him bring in the bulky paper from two pedicabs.

They were astonished, then, when the printer abruptly said

that he had decided not to do the job after all. There was a brief angry exchange, but there was nothing to do but to return the paper temporarily to the paper-shop and to carry the set type back to Hsieh's rooms.

No further moves were made for about ten days. Friends who scouted the neighborhood learned that the printer's neighbors were saying that some Communists had attempted to print up an attack on the Generalissimo; nevertheless Hsieh continued his search for a press that might take the job. At last he found an old machine with a single owner-operator. This was located in the northeastern part of town, near a small Presbyterian church to which I was expected to go in the following week to discuss the subject of "human rights." After the usual haggling, the old man agreed to do the job on the following Sunday, the date of the autumn full-moon festival.

On that day Wei helped Hsieh carry type and paper to the printing shop. He wore his military uniform and spoke only in Mandarin Chinese. The two represented themselves as members of a military school faculty who desired to run off copies of an examination paper which must not be allowed to fall into students' hands. This was not an uncommon practice in Formosa and seemed to rouse no special interest or questions on the part of the old printer.

He was slow, working without an assistant, and the machine was old. It was a long, tedious job, continuing from about nine o'clock in the morning until the middle of the afternoon. Wei stood by watching carefully until noon when he was relieved for a time by Hsieh. A first few imperfect copies were destroyed, but in the end 10,000 acceptable copies were ready. Each sheet, properly handled, could become a stick of political dynamite. After quickly checking through a finished copy and finding it in good order, Hsieh crossed the city by cab to tell me that we were ready for the next move.

Hsieh and Wei paid off the printer, bundled the heavy sheets into two pedicabs, and went to a shabby hotel nearby in which a room had been engaged. Two big empty trunks were carried in, and we stuffed the printed sheets into them. Then leaving Hsieh to rest awhile, Wei and I transported the trunks by pedicab to the home of a student who lived nearby, in the heart of the city not far from the Generalissimo's high-towered offices. This student-custodian was a girl who did not ask what was in the trunks. We stored them in a fourth-floor storeroom until we could prepare address labels, and mail them all over the island.

Our work done, Wei and I returned to Hsieh's hotel room to rest. It was early evening. Hsieh napped on the bed while Wei and I sipped tea. I was thinking of leaving soon for an appointment at a Japanese restaurant.

Suddenly there was a pounding at the door. Before I could open it, eight plainclothes police agents burst in, brandishing revolvers and shouting, "Hands up!"

As Hsieh rose from the bed he was knocked to the floor and beaten. We were then made to stand by while the room was thoroughly searched. It seemed an interminable search, and while it was progressing, one of the agents pulled a crumpled copy of our manifesto from his pocket. It was not printed on our good paper. I assumed at once that it had been run off quickly at the first printing shop during that ill-timed moment when Wei had stepped into the street to look for Hsieh.

During the excitement of these first moments of our arrest, we had a last brief chance to speak to one another, agreeing that since everything seemed to be known, we would tell only the truth concerning our activities. We were ordered to be silent, and had no choice but to obey.

Paradoxically we had been trapped by our own underestimation of the police-state organization under which we lived and against which we were in protest. As campus intellectuals we had not truly realized to what extent Formosan life had been corrupted to serve the Chiangs' purposes. Every petty informer knew he would be rewarded, all printers had been warned to report any unusual job orders, and every hotel-keeper had orders to call police attention to unusual events and behavior. Worst of all, we had assumed the printers to be too dull to take an interest in our secretive operation and not clever enough to see that they could earn something by reporting our activities.

I found myself thinking "How many years must I spend in jail?" Curiously, "seven years" came again and again to mind. I thought of my family—of my wife, my children, and my mother. I thought too of my friends in Formosa and abroad. I later learned that Wei expected torture and death, and that during the course of later interrogations he demanded to be shot at once. I do not know what Hsieh was thinking at that time. He had been roughly beaten, and I doubted if we would see each other again.

At last we were ordered to march out. As we passed down through the hotel lobby we saw the hotel clerk shrink back and a thin woman of twenty-five or thirty years of age hiding her face. I guessed at once that it was she who had reported our presence in the hotel, and our coming and going with our unusual luggage.

The alleyway and street before the hotel were filled with a crowd eager to see who and what the police were after. They fell back a little to open the way to the police car and a jeep drawn up nearby. Into these we were hustled and quickly driven away.

A short ride through the evening streets brought us to a police substation at Round Park, site of the notorious incident that had sparked the uprising of 1947. It was the evening of the Moon Festival, and the moon hung in the eastern sky, round and glowing. There was to be no happy celebration for our friends and our families this night, and for us the future was very dark.

IX

Interrogation

I saw the last of my friends Hsieh and Wei at the police station door, where I was taken at once to a harshly lighted third-floor room and seated at a desk, with my right wrist chained to the desk leg. A young, uniformed policeman silently took his place in a chair beside me. The windows were shut and the room was oppressively hot.

We had all heard stories of the treatment of political prisoners. I expected to be beaten and then subjected to many kinds of torment and was only a little relieved when a low-ranking, elderly, uniformed officer came in, looked at me briefly and then said, "If this were ten years ago you would be shot. Now, however, I don't think you will be." He did not elaborate and soon left the room. I sat for perhaps an hour, asking again and again for water. Since I could not lift my hand, the silent young policeman had to hold the cup to my lip, but after three or four such requests he became irritated, and by gesture and expression he let me know that he did not want to be bothered again.

The suspense was broken when a short, middle-aged, and undistinguished Chinese plainclothesman appeared who introduced himself simply as a section chief of the Special Investigative Police. His first remarks led me to believe that he had already

talked with Hsieh, for he seemed less concerned with the content
of our manifesto than with the technique we had used in preparing it. "What you have done was extremely professional, it could
not be improved upon," he said.

On learning that I had not yet had supper he sent out to a
nearby street foodstall for soup, rice, vegetables, and pork. My
handcuff was removed for a few minutes, but since I had no ap-
petite I left most of the food untouched. I was trying to steel
myself to face torture, or at least a beating. The handcuff had
just been replaced when a tall, self-assured man who did not
bother to introduce himself came in. He was coatless and cool,
and his behavior suggested that he was of higher rank. I had the
impression that he had come in merely to look me over. His stay
was brief, and his comments limited but rather curious: "This is
a political case," he said. "Don't worry too much, it is not too serious. Certainly everyone has different political opinions, and this
is not a crime. Not only that, criticism of the administration will
serve to improve the government." He seemed to be soothing me,
trying to ease my fears.

As he withdrew, the short, middle-aged man returned with
paper and a pencil, and asked me to write my personal biogra-
phy, starting with my grandfather and recording every detail I
could think of. I was instructed to name all my friends and to
record everything I could about them. It was a preposterous assignment, but I started to write slowly.

It was midnight or thereafter when I began. I had written only
two or three pages when three very large men came in and
brusquely told me not to bother, but to go with them. We went
down to the street, dark and deserted, and climbed into an Amer-
ican-made military vehicle, with two guards beside me on the
back seat and two squeezed in front beside the driver. All were
heavily armed. Driving northward we left the quiet city, drove
through Shilin suburb, and turned to enter an area known as a
training camp for special agents. This forbidding compound is
regarded by the public with fear and apprehension. The barracks

gave the impression of a military camp and I saw many people moving about. I was taken at once into a small, bare room with concrete walls, a space measuring about twelve feet square, holding only a desk with two chairs placed to face one another. There were two stones about the size of a melon laying in the corner, and they made a strange impression on me.

I was told to sit down but was not handcuffed this time. The second man who had spoken to me at the police station came in. He took his place across from me, again saying that no crime of violence had been committed, and that no matter of personal honor or integrity was involved. We were concerned here, he said, with a matter of political opinion. Another man who seemed to be of even higher rank stepped into the room. He stood behind me and repeated exactly the same comment, adding, "You must cooperate with this man, and everything will be all right." He then left.

My interrogator settled himself to his work. He was not sinister looking, but was entirely without emotion, machine-like, without sympathy and without hatred. Placing a pad of paper before him, he began a monotonous formal enquiry, name, birthplace, birthdate, father's name, family condition, employment, and so forth. He asked all this in a flat, mechanical tone. At last he came to the heart of it. "Explain what you have done," he said.

We sat facing one another in that bare comfortless interrogation chamber for at least four hours. Dawn came. I heard the roll call in the barracks area. My interrogator went out briefly and returned with tea and bread. "Eat whatever you want," he said, and with that he left the room. I guessed that it was about eight or nine o'clock in the morning. I was not handcuffed, but there were guards on duty at my door. I was totally exhausted but could not manage to sleep sitting upright in that hard chair. I was aware of great activity outside as the hours passed until at midday, tea and a bowl of rice and vegetables were brought in. I simply sat with my head buried in my arm on the table too tired to eat. There was only one interruption during the afternoon. A huge man whose coarse fat face filled me with aversion came in. He was exceedingly ugly and sinister. To my astonishment he said that we had met at one time, soon after my return from France. I had never seen him before, to the best of my knowledge, and said so, but he insisted, saying that he had heard that I was there and had "just dropped in." Then he went away. I wondered if he too had come to have a look at someone with whom he might have to deal later on.

Thus I sat alone throughout the afternoon, going only once or twice to a toilet in the next room. As dusk came I again heard great activity in the barracks-yard. I could not sleep, though I tried. I learned later that Wei and Hsieh were being interrogated nearby, and that the girl who had taken in our trunks also had been brought in for interrogation.

Someone then came and without identifying himself obliged me to sign a formal printed pledge, a standard document, saying, "I am willing to be punished if I tell anyone of what I have seen here or of what happened here." This done, I was escorted to a waiting jeep, and with plainclothes guards seated on each side of me, was driven back into the heart of the city and past the Taipei railway station. Not a word was spoken by my guards or the driver. I was exhausted and near the breaking point, and as we rode along the familiar streets, I worried about my family, worried about my classes, and about test questions for some pending examinations.

Suddenly, after passing the railway station, I was aware that we were nearing the most dreaded spot in the capital, the Security Section Building of the Garrison Command. This massive stone building had been a Japanese Buddhist temple before 1945. The crypt beneath it, once an ossuary, had been cleared of bones and ashes and made over into a jail with interrogation chambers from which few sounds could reach the outside world. Here many persons were questioned and tortured, before being sent off to imprisonment or to death. Such was its reputation. It was surrounded by a complex of military buildings in a walled compound at the heart of the city. Here, I felt sure, the decision would be made about my future.

We drove directly into the enclosure, without a gate-check, obviously by prearrangement, and stopped before a building adjacent to the temple, looming up in the dark beside us. My silent escorts gestured for me to get down from the jeep. I was met at the door by a uniformed officer, a lieutenant, who addressed me with extreme politeness, almost as a guest, as Professor Peng, with apologies for having to trouble me to come here. His greeting *Chao tai p'u chou* ("Please forgive our inability to make you more comfortable") was scarcely appropriate under the circumstances, and despite my tension I was tempted to laugh.

As we entered the building he introduced himself as "Staff Officer Wei," speaking in the accent of a Fukienese and with the utmost deference. We moved to an inner room which, he said, would be mine. The contrast with the twelve by twelve concrete interrogation cell in which I had been confined could not have been more surprising. The room was air-conditioned; a bare round table surrounded by five upholstered chairs stood at the center, and at the side, in a corner, stood a neat single cot, ready with pillow and blanket. Lieutenant Wei apologized for its simplicity, saying that he would be in charge of my living arrangements here, and emphasized the fact that he was not an investigator but merely my custodian. He told me, "This is a political thing and not serious. All you should do is to tell all quite frankly to the investigators who are coming soon. If you have any personal need, ask the guard for Staff Officer Wei."

A soldier came in and searched me again in routine fashion, and took away my shoestrings, belt, and wallet. Something happens to a man's self-assurance, he feels helpless and defenseless, when he must shuffle about in unlaced shoes and must clutch at his trousers to keep them on. Dinner was then brought in, a standard officer's meal, and after eating I asked a young man who looked in at the door, "May I have a bath?" I hadn't had one in two days and was sticky with sweat and dust. He looked startled, disappeared for a few minutes, and returned to say very formally, "You are allowed to wash."

A guard escorted me to a nearby room, instructing me to leave the door ajar. In this bare cubicle with toilet and a box-like water sink and faucet, I took a quick sponge bath. There was a small window, and beyond it a wall, about three feet away. Beyond that, in turn, was the public street and the free world in which I could hear the sounds of lively evening traffic.

Soon after I returned to my room five persons came, including the young man who had arranged the bath. They were all expressionless, showing no emotion of any kind, and one very short man said not a word throughout the long hours that followed. These five did not introduce or identify themselves in any way. One led off by saying, "We want you to tell everything. Even if Mao Tse-tung came into this place, he would have to tell all. You have no way to escape or to hide anything."

There was in this an implied threat that I would be forced to talk if need be. Thus began the true interrogation.

FOR ABOUT SEVENTY-TWO HOURS I was questioned endlessly. The same questions were repeated over and over again. No record was being made in my presence, but I soon assumed that the Celotex ceiling above us was bugged, and that the questions and answers were being recorded or at least being transmitted to another room for others to overhear. At about two-hour intervals the interrogation team was replaced, with the one silent member reappearing again and again. After a time a middle-aged man with a doctor's kit began to come in at intervals of about thirty minutes to check my heart and blood pressure. The questioning was suspended while he performed his duties and was resumed when he nodded assent and withdrew. There were mealtime interruptions of about one hour. I ate very little and tried to sleep in these periods, but always the five-man team returned to resume the questioning.

As the hours dragged on a pattern began to appear in these interminable questions. The interrogators seemed convinced that our action in preparing the manifesto was only part of a huge plot with powerful backing. "Who is behind you?" "How many?" "What foreign organization?" "This is only the first step; what is your next plan?" "You have foreign financial support. The American government must be behind this!" "We know the American government has special units in all countries to overthrow governments they don't like. Syngman Rhee, Diem, for example, and now the Generalissimo?"

We had been arrested on September 20, 1964. They assumed that we had been plotting for a general rising against the government, or at least a massive demonstration, on October 10, the Double Ten celebration of the founding of the Republic, when many foreigners would be present at the grand reviews and would witness the protest against Chiang Kai-shek. As we learned later, the security forces had expected a big case and had cleared several prisons to prepare for hundreds of arrests. Our manifesto had boasted that we had popular backing, and a large and growing secret organization with branches in every part of Formosa. Unfortunately this was not quite true; in an attempt at psychological warfare, we had overreached ourselves. We had sympathetic supporters throughout the island, but as yet we had no formal organization. The purpose of our manifesto was to arouse interest and confidence and to win support for an ultimate islandwide protest against the Chiang regime. Apparently the security officers actually believed our boast, and demanded to know the details. In a rather backhanded compliment, they insisted that mainland Chinese must be involved, because no Formosan could write such excellent prose. They suspected that at least two prominent mainland Chinese had assisted us. One was Professor Yin Hai-kuan of the Philosophy Department of *Taita*, and the other the historian Li Ao. Both were my good friends.

Now I realized that after two or three days of such interrogation it would not often be necessary to resort to physical torture.

The prisoner is so exhausted mentally and physically that the application of the slightest degree of torture would cause a man to yield, to confess anything, to sign anything. He will cry: "Just let me alone! Just let me sleep. I'll say or sign or confess anything you want me to. Just let me alone!"

My interrogators repeatedly said that many people accused the garrison command of frightful physical tortures, and again and again they asked me to note and admit that I was not being tortured. The hint was always there that if they chose to go further, they would, to obtain the confession they were sure I should make. They could not believe that the three of us had acted as we did quite on our own, but after about three days of such intensive questioning the pace slackened, there were longer intervals, until at last a general officer appeared, a cold, hard character in a white civilian suit, to whom the others showed great deference. He made it very clear that he did not believe my statement that there had been no big plot behind our action, that we were only proposing a beginning, and not preparing for an imminent mass uprising. After listening to the questioning and my answers for a brief while he said, "You are hiding something; this is not so simple as you say." Before leaving the room he said, with a note of contempt, "You see, politics is the dirtiest thing in the world!"

The interrogations were suspended after about one week. Life settled down into a boring routine. There were no newspapers, no books, no writing materials. The monotony was broken only occasionally when older Chinese guards dropped in to talk of the homes they had left behind. One tall, thin guard was particularly outspoken in telling how he had been brought over to Formosa in 1949, believing as his comrades did, that they would soon return. He was married and had a daughter. One day he had been shanghaied in the street, forced into military service, and taken far from home, from province to province, and finally had been shipped to Formosa. "If I had known I was going to stay here forever," he said, "I would have deserted." He had been on the island fourteen years or more, his daughter would now be twenty years old and married, and he probably would never see her again. He said that he couldn't often bear to think of this sort of thing, and that with other old soldiers he sometimes took a bottle of wine out to the hills on Moon Festival night and they would sit together and weep from homesickness.

He came several times and then suddenly one day he disappeared. I assumed that his outspoken complaints had been monitored on one of these occasions. Four or five other guards dropped in occasionally to chat, bringing little gifts, toothpicks, pickled vegetables, and the like, and one even brought his own supper to eat with me at my desk. These were older men, always talking of their past, nostalgic, homesick, complaining of their meager pay. One amused me by venturing to say cautiously, "You don't really look like a sinister person!" One day a man wearing a cook's apron brought in my dinner, and as he placed it before me, he whispered cautiously, "I know who you are. One of my nephews was your student. Don't tell anyone."

I received a bundle of shirts and underwear from my family, but there were no messages. Lieutenant Wei arranged for me to have a hot bath occasionally, and I was physically not uncomfortable. I had some money in my pocket at the time of my arrest; it was being kept for me by my custodians, and with it I was able to pay for the laundry sent out by an orderly. Once the grueling interrogation had ended I could complain of little except extreme boredom. This was relieved to a degree when after repeated requests, Wei brought me pencil and paper with which to prepare questions for the impending examinations at *Taita*. He promised earnestly that they would be delivered to the university, but, as I discovered later, this was never done.

It was only much later that I was to learn what was taking place elsewhere with regard to my arrest and its aftermath. All who had played some part in our capture were well rewarded. Substantial monetary rewards went to the maid at the hotel and the printer who surreptitiously struck off a copy of the manifesto, then refused to print, and reported us as Communists. The second printer who did the actual work had gone at once to report our suspicious enterprise to the police. It was said that after he received his reward, he became so fearful of "Communist" revenge he installed a telephone near his bed so that he could call the police in an emergency. Those who had dealt with us in the line of duty were promoted. The officer who led the arresting squad was jumped two ranks and made head of a police substation, and Staff Officer Wei was promoted and given a medal. I have been told that many others were given substantial recognition.

President Chiang Kai-shek had not been informed at once of my arrest, and this led to an odd and awkward moment for the president of my university. It had become an annual custom for the Generalissimo to invite a select group of scholars and teachers to dine with him on Teacher's Day, usually in the last week of September. A day or two after my unannounced arrest, a formal invitation to attend the dinner reached my house. When I did not appear at the gathering Chiang asked the president of *Taita*, "Where's Peng?" Although Professor Chien already knew that I was arrested, he dared not be the first to inform the Generalissimo, so in great embarrassment he contrived an excuse for me. When at last the fact of my arrest and the reasons for it had to be revealed to the aging party leader and president, he was enraged.

My friends Hsieh and Wei had been kept separately in the dreaded basement nearby and were being interrogated as I was. They were not subjected to systematic torture, but were slapped and choked from time to time in the effort to make them confess to a nonexistent larger plot. Each of us was told that the other two had made full confession, and that details of our stories must coincide, or else our individual punishments would be more severe. Obviously Hsieh and Wei were receiving rougher treatment than I, and the reason now seems to be that I was known to have prominent foreign friends. I learned too that the silent agent who sat as an observer at every questioning session was a special representative of the political section of the garrison command, keeping check on the men who handled the case. The man most often present was Staff Officer Wang whose wife, I learned later, had been one of my students at Taiwan University. Wang was to remain close to the case from beginning to end.

My family knew that I had been arrested, for I had left home with Hsieh on Sunday afternoon, had not come back, and the police had swarmed in to make a search of the house at midnight. Although the garrison command kept quiet, someone in the police force leaked the news and the rumor spread instantly through the city. A *New York Times* correspondent promptly went to garrison headquarters to make an inquiry but was turned away with the statement, "We have no such person in our custody."

It was obvious that I had vanished. The university term began, and I did not appear. I was supposed to fly to Korea to attend a meeting being held at a university in Seoul, and I was also scheduled to go to Bangkok to another international conference held under the auspices of the American Friends Service Committee. The garrison command continued to deny any knowledge of my whereabouts. About repeated queries, *The New York Times* man warned them that he had definite knowledge that I was being held by them, and that the American papers would announce it if the garrison command failed to do so. This forced their hand. One month and four days after the arrest, a brief official notice stated that the three of us had been arrested and would be tried for "destructive activity."

The English-language newspapers at Taipei were allowed to publish their own brief versions of our arrest only after prior censorship by an officer of the garrison command. In its issue of October 24, buried on page six, the *China Post* carried a news item captioned, "Professor, Two Students Nabbed on Charges of High Treason." I was described as an "outstanding youth, aged forty-one." The text offered little more than that "The Taiwan

Garrison Command said in a brief press release last night that Peng Ming-min, Hsieh Tsung-ming, and Wei Ting-chao were caught red-handed while committing an act of sabotage in Taipei last month. . . . In this country, now on a war-footing, persons involved in cases of treason or subversion are to be tried by a military court."

All Chinese language papers throughout Formosa carried a short text, without variation or exception, issued to them by the garrison command. Neither elaboration nor comment were permitted.

All our friends received the news of our arrest with disbelief and great shock. Some of them privately scorned us for what they thought was our extreme naïveté in attempting to print and distribute criticism of the government. Thinking back today, I believe that what we tried to do was certainly no more fanatic than any antigovernment activity in totalitarian countries or than what many American civil rights leaders or antiwar activists have tried to do. This includes such activities as demonstrations, picketing, destruction of draft files, or kidnapping of government officials. Our only mistake was that we did not succeed. If we had succeeded, I believe no one would have criticized us for being too naïve. I feel the same about my later attempt to flee Formosa. If I had failed I am sure I would have been accused by some people of being naïve and reckless.

At once every agency of the party began a campaign to misrepresent what we had done and said in our manifesto. True to form, there was a consistent attempt to blacken our characters as "immoral criminals, betraying the Fatherland" coupled with an extraordinary effort to obscure the true nature of our act and the substance of our critical manifesto. The reform issues we had raised were ignored. The party spread a version that was the exact reverse of our arguments and statements. For example, we had clearly advocated a sensible cooperation between Formosans and Chinese exiles in an endeavor to strengthen and develop Formosa. The party's interpretation had it that we had urged that all Chinese be killed or thrown into the sea, or that they should be used as guinea pigs for medical research.

Other points were taken up, twisted, and misrepresented in like fashion. The party forged proof to be exhibited and discussed at party meetings at all levels.

Rumor-planting was a prime device, using party cells in the military units, in the schools, and in every other possible outlet, but not in the newspapers. These rumors and baseless fictions were always introduced as clarifying discussions of the Peng case and as explanations of what really happened. These intensive efforts to discredit us in the eyes of Formosan youth seemed also designed to frighten the continental Chinese. The line of argument ran that "our government is not perfect, but if we let the Formosans take over, you will all be killed." It could only be interpreted as a campaign to unite the faltering Chinese exiles against the island people. Behind it lay the government's very real fear that if the majority of exiles cooperated with a majority of the Formosans, the one-party system would be destroyed and the Generalissimo would be unseated.

I found it hard to believe, but it was true that some of my university colleagues succumbed to this propaganda, expressing surprise that Peng was such a vicious person. Some quite honestly and boldly said, "It cannot be true." Formosan students were shocked by the arrests and the subsequent derogatory attacks. In many cases, I have been told, we became popular "hero-martyrs." The party was defeating its own purpose with such grotesque propaganda.

At the time of our arrests, or during the investigation thereafter, an undetermined number of copies of our manifesto reached private hands. The formal indictment read out at our subsequent trial mentioned only 9800 copies when in fact we had printed 10,000 copies. We could only assume that some agents taking part in the arrest or handling our case had quietly set aside some interesting and possibly vendable souvenirs.

A copy reached a certain nonparty member of the Assembly,

and he in turn gave a copy to a friend in the Japanese embassy at Taipei. This was sent on to Tokyo, where it was reported to have been put away in a safe in the Foreign Ministry. Nevertheless, soon after my release a foreign ministry official made a copy available to friends in Tokyo, and soon enough the text was published and distributed in Tokyo. We had not yet printed a title at the head of our manifesto, and we had left space for some sort of symbol at the end. The Tokyo copies appeared with an accurate text, but with a title "Declaration of Independence of the Formosan People" and a decorative symbol at the end.

This was embarrassing, for we had not intended it to be a "Declaration of Independence" but rather a summary of Formosa's problems and an expression of our views. We had thought to call it "Self-salvation of the Formosan People," nothing more ambitious. The garrison command thought I had somehow instigated this release abroad, as it was also published in Hong Kong soon afterward, but unfortunately I could not take credit.

The government made no public formal reference to my case from October 24, the day of the brief press announcement, until my trial, April 7, 1964. Nevertheless, it was extremely sensitive to foreign comment and criticism. Professor John K. Fairbank's letter published in *The New York Times* expressed concern and someone wrote to Amnesty International in London, prompting its staff to begin an enquiry into my case. Dr. Kissinger of Harvard called the Chinese embassy at Washington and the dean of the Law School at McGill University called the Nationalist Chinese embassy at Ottawa. Formosan students staged a demonstration before the embassy gates. The Chinese vice-minister of justice, Cha Liang-chien, happened to be in Ottawa on business at the time, and had much explaining to do. The Canadian Association of International Law wrote to its counterpart, the Chinese Association at Taipei and to the Ottawa embassy. My former professors in Paris protested to the Chinese embassy in France. Formosan publications abroad carried many articles concerning our arrest. Dr. Tsiang Tien-fu cabled from New York, warning the government to be extremely careful in handling the situation. All this shock and uproar abroad impressed Taipei when it suddenly realized the international interest in the case. Seen from abroad, it would become a test of Taipei's good faith in claiming to be "Free China." The American embassy at Taipei preserved a discreet silence.

My two colleagues, being unknown abroad, had no such influential foreign friends, and no such publicity to inhibit and restrain Taipei. Hsieh Tsung-ming's younger brother, an outstanding graduate student in economics at *Taita* at the time of our arrest, immediately prepared and mimeographed a brief protest and managed to give it fairly wide distribution. For unknown reasons he got away with it without investigation or arrest. Tempting fate, he resorted again to the mimeograph machine to prepare a sharp criticism of the regime, following along general lines the criticisms we had set forth in our manifesto. Two Chinese friends collaborated in the project.

The trio were seized by agents of the Investigation Bureau. They were tortured and, crazed by pain and fear, young Hsieh broke down completely. He was sent under guard to the university's mental hospital, where he was heard screaming at night and lapsing into violent periods in which he smashed everything he could lay hands on. At one point he eluded his guards and was gone from the hospital for a day, but returned on his own volition. After some months of treatment in the mental ward, he was remanded to jail. Then came court martial and a comparatively light sentence of three and a half years. One of his Chinese companions was sentenced to four years. I believe the third man was sent off to one of the Thought Reform camps. The worst of these is the *Lu Tao* ("Green Island") camp, on a small, rocky islet lying in the sea east of Taitung. Here most of the inmates were serving fifteen- or twenty-year sentences, many of them too obscure and too poor to attract notice or rouse public interest. Under the Chinese system if a man is arrested but found innocent, he must find a guarantor before he is released. If he is convicted and serves a full term, he must also find a guarantor, and this is very difficult, for who dares stand security for a man he has not seen for fifteen years? Green Island holds many people too poor or friendless to find a guarantor. This is especially true of poor Chinese who came alone to Formosa in 1949. After serving long sentences they have no one to speak up for them or to guarantee their good behavior.

After our manifesto affair, and the affair of the younger Hsieh, the government issued written instructions to all schools, offices, factories, army agencies and the like, and to any organization possessing mimeographing equipment. Such equipment, said the government, must be handled very carefully, especially in the evenings; it must be locked up when not in use by authorized persons, and must never be used by unauthorized persons or illegal groups.

But as so often happens in such cases, the situation became grotesque when the garrison command issued an order that telephone books must show the name and number only, and must not show an address. This was a "security measure" to deny access to mailing lists for subversive literature. Even the usually docile newspapers protested this new order, and it was soon revoked.

I was living in boredom. A month had passed when in late fall a soldier suddenly appeared, said, "You are to move," and immediately escorted me to another American military staff car. I was handcuffed to the car itself this time, and two armed guards accompanied me. We drove eastward through the city and passed very near my house. We went through the suburbs to another military camp at San Chang Li. Here on a small hill, in the midst of a rice paddy, was a walled compound. I was taken to a long, low wooden barracks building and to a small room with a table in the center, and two cots, one on each side, that served in lieu of chairs. On the walls were printed signs: "No noise," and a strange one saying "You must not sit together on one bed!"

As I entered a young stranger returned from a bath nearby.

We introduced ourselves. He was a young chemistry student from Tunghai University named Wu Chung-hui, of Taichung city, a Formosan, who in his second year had been arrested with 200 students for participating in what was known as "a big plot case." There had been an incident involving students from nearly every university, and one or two military academies. Hundreds had been questioned, and some shot. Wu knew my name. His reaction was a curious mixture of shock and pleasure that a person like me had come to share his plight. He had been held two years, tortured at times, and shifted about from one agency to another without being brought to trial and without formal sentence. He was one of the regime's lost prisoners, but only one among very many. I wondered if I were to become one of them.

The atmosphere of this camp was dreary, gloomy, and hopeless in the extreme. The guards and soldiers moving about appeared to be a select lot, hard and cruel. A tunnel led into the side of the hill within the camp confines, the deep interior a well-known site for tortures. The guards assigned to us were excessively rude, and the prisoners were treated more like animals than humans. Even the food doled out was unbelievably bad. The door to our room was always locked, and if we wished to go to the toilet, we were obliged to shout for the guards to escort us there and back, standing by us at all times. Sometimes in the night we found it almost impossible to rouse them to this duty.

Wu proved to be one of the most idealistic youths I have ever met. We talked of everything, of our families, society, history, and of the future of Formosa. He had his own scheme for the romanizing of the Formosan dialect for use on a typewriter and in print, so that we could cut ourselves off from traditional Chinese writing. His hatred of the Chiangs was extraordinary. He expected to be shot, but if not he would be happy to survive if only to see the end of the Nationalist government and party.

Occasionally we sat side by side on one cot or attempted to communicate in whispers, but instantly a guard would come to the door to shout and curse us. It was clear that our quarters were bugged, and we had to presume that we had been brought together in the expectation that we would reveal to one another information that our captors wished to have. No one appeared to resume our interrogation.

I was beginning to lose the sense of time, but discovered that Wu had devised a means of recording passage of days on the bars of soap we were permitted to buy. We were required to wash our own clothes, and young Wu insisted upon doing mine for me. Once a large package was delivered to me from my family. It contained shirts, a Bible, and food, but the fried chicken was altogether spoiled and the fruits were dry and inedible. For want of anything else to do I read the Bible from beginning to end for the first time in my life.

We became depressed, miserable, and angry. We learned that Hsieh and Wei were somewhere in the same compound, and so one day I began to sing a Christian hymn at the top of my voice. We heard an answer from a distance. Then I shouted in Japanese, *"Gambare!"* ("Fight on!"), and this created an uproar as four or five guards rushed to our room, followed by the furious prison commandant. When he cursed me, I answered, "The rules don't forbid singing!" He retorted, "But they do forbid noise! You are trying to communicate with someone!" I was reckless, for I realize now that I had given them a good excuse to punish me with solitary confinement or worse.

After two weeks with Wu and no interrogation, I was suddenly told that I would be moved again. With sadness we said good-bye to one another and I was taken out to an American jeep, chained to it, and under guard driven back to the city. On passing near my house I saw a neighbor in the street and wondered if he saw me. To my surprise I found myself returning to my comparatively comfortable air-conditioned room at the center of town. I was given a meal, but no one came to see me.

The next morning a prosecutor came in with his aides. Placing a sheaf of papers on the desk before him, he began to ask questions based upon a record of my conversations with Wu during the preceding weeks. There was no effort to hide the fact that our room had been bugged and our rambling conversations fully recorded. This interrogation was routine, a point-by-point examination, machine-like and thorough. I was asked to identify and confirm quotations from our exchanges and to elaborate on my remarks to Wu wherever I had quoted or cited someone else commenting on the situation in Formosa. I now tried to evade revealing the sources for some of my own remarks.

After this session I sat for many days in almost unbearable idleness. Occasionally someone would look in to ask about specific people, some of whom I knew and many of whom I had never heard. Many were foreigners. On one occasion I was asked to comment on Henry Kao, the mayor of Taipei, and on another I was asked to describe my relationship with John Fairbank of Harvard. Sheets of paper were brought from time to time, always carefully counted before and after I had made notes, and the pencil was always taken away at once.

It was now late November. During this long interval I could look from my window onto the court between my place of detention and the main administrative building, the old temple. Very often I saw the university's personnel officer coming and going. We all knew of course that he was the Nationalist party's security officer and that he was supplying information concerning university staff and student body.

Although from this time on my family were occasionally allowed to send in fruits and other foods, I was now quite cut off from human society. Even the guards ceased coming to the door to chat. It was a comfortable solitary confinement, but it was solitary confinement nevertheless. I was not even allowed to see a barber and was soon shaggy and bearded.

Then one day Lieutenant Wei appeared to say, "You are going to see an important person today and you must have a haircut." A girl barber came in to give me a shave and a trim, and my belt and shoelaces were returned to me. After dark Wei came again carefully dressed, and took me out to a dark sedan waiting at the door. This time I was not handcuffed and there were no armed guards. I wondered what the occasion could be.

As we drove a short distance to an office near the Government Building, Wei said to me nervously but with an air of importance, "You are going to see the head of the Political Warfare Section of the Garrison Command, General Ning."

General Ning, who proved most polite and courteous, began by saying, "We are sorry for this incident. It is a misfortune. Have you been badly treated? Please let me know. I myself am a university graduate. I studied agriculture before I entered the military service. You know much more than I. I can't argue with you on any point. It is our duty to do this sort of thing."

I later discovered that General Ning had just been elevated to this position, and that he wanted to demonstrate his capacity by handling my case well. He was not very bright, but he seemed simple and sincere in doing his duty. As a high-ranking military man he was really trying, and seemed better than the average officer. Mr. Wang who had attended the long sessions of my earlier interrogation was his protégé, almost his personal secretary.

I was with General Ning about thirty minutes. He was most courteous, treating me almost as a guest. He said that he wanted me to meet with some important officers who could give me the true picture of the situation in Taiwan. I gained the impression that thus far they had decided it was no use to kill me, but rather better to reeducate me and exploit me in an attempt to handle the Formosan people who do not trust the government.

Lieutenant Wei was waiting outside in the corridor. General Ning in a fatherly manner said, "Don't despair. You have had a distinguished career. People think well of you, and I am sorry that this has happened."

As he closed the interview and summoned Wei from the corridor outside, he referred again to his desire to have me meet with some important officers, concluding with the astonishing remark, "Do you mind if I show them part of your manifesto?"

On the ride back to quarters Wei nervously kept repeating, "What did he say? What did he say?" Ning headed the Political Commissars, the most feared agency in the entire garrison command, and Wei was awed by the thought that I had been called in and might air criticism of the way his section was handling my case. A few days later it was announced that General Ning was coming to see me in my quarters. There was great excitement within the compound. I was shaved again and my room was carefully cleaned, and the principal prison officers appeared in full uniform. The visit by the general and his aides was stiff and formal. He asked me if everything was all right and desired to know what kind of food I was getting. An officer hurriedly interjected that I received the very best, the same food as the officers received in their mess. After less than fifteen minutes General Ning withdrew, saying as he left, "The government will still need you someday."

Some days later I was notified that I again had to prepare to meet some important people. The next morning I was taken to a military clubhouse. About ten persons were gathered about a conference table and General Ning who had set this up, presided. Dean Sah of the university was there, together with a representative of the Defense Ministry. Two or three professors from a military academy were also present. Perhaps the most influential man present was General Wang Shen, chief of the Political Warfare Section of the Defense Ministry, who was considered Chiang Ching-kuo's right-hand man; he had been commandant of the military school at which I had taught. To my surprise I found a certain Ho in this group. Ho was a graduate in economics from the University of Wisconsin who had later become a senior official in China. From there he had managed to be sent to the United Nations, but when Chiang fled to Formosa, Ho thought the end had come for the Nationalists. He proposed to Ambassador Tsiang that they make off with the funds then banked for the delegation in New York. An indignant Dr. Tsiang reported this to the Generalissimo and for a long time thereafter

Ho was unable to come to Formosa. Then, for reasons obscure to all, he was taken up by a former minister of education, Chang Chi-yun, who managed at last to obtain clearance for him to go to Taipei. Although no decent position could be found for him, he continued operating in Formosa in one shadowy capacity or another. It developed that he fancied himself a specialist on the Taiwan Independence Movement in the United States, and now was about to extend his range to become an authority on my case.

One by one the men around the conference table made speeches that reflected, inadvertently, the sting of the manifesto and the hope that I could be reeducated. We had criticized the military and military incapacity, and it may be that some of the issues we raised were clearly defined for them for the first time. Apparently General Ning in his new position desired to show a new style of operation. Both he and General Wang assured me that they, too, had been revolutionary as youths, and had determined to override or correct the bureaucrats and politicians that so weakened China. Both spoke with evident sincerity. General Wang Shen said with deep feeling that the military also "hate those members of the Legislative Yuan. You do not know how much we hate them." On a more personal note he went on to say, "We thought that you were a good scholar. I invited you to the (military) school when I was commandant there, and just a few days before you were arrested the school had formally passed upon an appointment for you to become head of the political department. When I was notified of your arrest, I was deeply embarrassed. Indeed I had a red face! I was promoting you within the military establishment."

One young general from the Defense Ministry was formal, nervous, and awkward. "I am so honored today to come here to report on the military situation," he said, forgetting that he had been merely called on to help reeducate a prisoner. He stressed the fact that the military were so busy preparing the counter-attack upon the continent that they had little time for political affairs.

One speaker took up the issue of discrimination, rather lamely observing that "of course there are very few Formosans in the government. Don't you know that there are so very few jobs available that we even fight among ourselves (Chinese refugees) for the jobs? How then can we find enough places for Formosans? What are you going to do with persons displaced by Taiwanese?"

Dean Sah shrewdly remained silent throughout this reeducation session, but the talkative Ho frequently offered unsolicited comment. At one time, in an aside in English, he remarked that "you must know Chiang Kai-shek is a necessary evil; we cannot get on without him." I was tempted to translate this back into Mandarin for the benefit of these military officers. I was not asked for comment. This gathering of relatively liberal men had been convened to give me food for moral reflection, and at the end of two hours I was sent back to my room.

Hsieh and Wei were exposed to similar reeducation conferences at the military clubhouse. Wei is said to have burst out "Shoot me! But all of you present here deserve also to be shot!" whereupon General Wang Shen, director of the Political Warfare Section of the Defense Ministry, made the gesture of taking off his coat, saying, "Come on, let's fight!"

The attempt to reeducate me did not end there. Several days later I was notified to be ready to go out for the evening, and at about eight o'clock Lieutenant Wei escorted me in a sedan to the big building of the new Military Historical Museum at the heart of the city. This had been created to show the world the glorious achievements of the Nationalist military establishment. The director, a general officer, was one of Chiang Ching-kuo's men. We arrived to find the building lighted throughout, and were greeted at the door by the director-general himself who then with utmost courtesy took the two of us on a guided tour. We saw docu-

ments, maps, pictures, and a collection of objects said to have be-
longed to the National Father, Sun Yat-sen. We were obliged to
listen to an indoctrination lecture lasting an hour and a half. I
was treated like a VIP rather than a prisoner subject to reeducation and a true captive audience. The assumption throughout
seemed to be that I was totally ignorant of events of the past fifty
years in China. As we moved about from floor to floor and exhibit to exhibit the general spoke some English now and then in
trying to impress me. At last we were escorted to the door, and
with the greatest politeness the last comment was "Any time you
want to see this again, please let us know." With this I was sent
back to my prison.

The next step in my reeducation came in the form of visits
from two highly placed civilians attached to the Political Warfare Section of the Defense Ministry. One, an elderly man who
said that he was formerly a professor in international law in
China, told me that they had been directed to explain to me how
great were the difficulties faced by the government in preparing
for the return to the mainland. These proved to be rather one-
sided conversations, for we were men living in different worlds.

For a brief period after these signs of favor there seemed to be
a marked improvement in my daily treatment. Lieutenant Wei
came in to chat occasionally, sometimes bringing cookies and
candies after dinner. "I believe you will be released very soon,"
he said, "for the government needs you. We recommend it. But
you understand of course that the decision will be made at the
highest level."

Occasionally prosecutors or interrogators dropped in after dinner. They too wanted to chat, and in the course of their
conversations made it clear that they all knew what Formosans
are thinking. They apologized for the government, and voiced
complaints of the lower officer ranks and the enlisted men. They
said, "The Moon Festival bonuses are merely a moon-cake!"
When they touched obliquely on the February 28 uprising of
1947 and the wrongs of the Chen Yi period they recognized that

the Formosans had a legitimate complaint and never said to me that it was a "Communist plot." They described, with an air of resignation, the poverty of the common soldier, especially at the time of Japan's surrender, saying it required "rotating pants for the victory parades" in order to cover up the threadbare condition of the army.

I was later to learn that throughout this period serious discussions were going on within an *ad hoc* committee formed to consider my case. The five principal members were (1) the chief of the garrision command, representing the army, (2) the secretary-general of the Kuo Ming Tang (K.M.T., the nationalist party) representing the party, (3) the secretary-general of the president's office, (4) a senior advisor to the Generalissimo, Tao Hsi-shen, whose official title was chairman of the Board of Directors of the Central Daily News, and (5) the deputy premier.

Pressure upon the committee was great for these men were aware of my popularity and influence with students and the younger generation as a whole. They wanted to use me to avert any violence or an upheaval that might destroy their grip upon the island, and could not afford to make more of a martyr of me than I already appeared to be in student eyes. They seemed to be baffled upon discovering that someone so well placed as I, and so often favored, could have become so disgruntled. In their world of relationships based on personal loyalties and enmities, there was no room for individual dedication to abstract causes as ephemeral as democracy and human rights. Their third great concern was for world opinion, especially that of America, whose tax-dollars and arms kept them in power, and for the Formosans overseas who were striving to draw international attention to the injustices of the dictatorship.

Throughout all the interrogations and public comment, members of government, party, and army loaded their criticism and rebukes to me with words that more properly should be addressed to a disloyal son, an immoral reprobate, who has brought disgrace on the family. I was "ungrateful," my criticisms were a "betrayal." All serious criticism of the government or of the Generalissimo was taken as a personal affront to Chiang. This attitude was not limited to my case, but to all challenges to his absolute authority and judgment. Every political offense must be reported to him and, as a personal offense, must be judged by him. He was the father of the nation-family. As the all-powerful father, he must exercise the power of life and death over every member; he may choose to be lenient and forgiving or he may be extremely harsh. Without hesitation he can overturn court verdicts or modify them. Even his closest advisors found it extremely dangerous to contradict him. Opinions may be given if he asks for them, but may not be offered without solicitation. He governs capriciously in the style of a feudal lord.

A majority of the men serving in the hierarchy under Chiang reflected in greater or lesser degree this moralistic approach to political criticism. They were shocked that I should have criticized the leadership after so many personal favors had been shown to me. It was useless to point out that I wanted only to criticize and expose and correct the abuses of a government.

In mid-December a little man dressed in a shabby suit came to call on me. He looked like a petty clerk. Without identifying himself, he opened his little bag, took out a sheaf of blank paper, and forthwith began very formally to ask me once again all the routine questions I had already answered a score of times. I felt very strange, as if I were repeating a bad dream. "What is your name?" "What is your profession?" and so forth. This interrogation was carried over into a second day, at the end of which I was asked to sign the record as a formal statement. Then followed about ten days in which I was left entirely alone. I learned later that all the formalities had been completed, and all these investigators and committees and advisors were now waiting for the final decision to be made at the highest level.

By this time I had fairly well convinced myself that I was about to be released, and it was therefore a great shock one morning when Officer Wei came in to say that an order had come down directing my immediate removal to prison to prepare for a court martial. He too seemed nonplussed, repeatedly assuring me, "It is necessary to go through all this procedure" as a formality, insinuating vaguely that I was then to be released.

After I had gathered up my few things, and again signed a pledge of silence, I was taken from my air-conditioned quarters and moved to a military court detainment compound not far from the law school.

X

Court Martial and Prison

To my surprise I was received at this new detention center by the mysterious and rather shabby little clerk who ten days earlier had asked so many repetitious questions, taken note of my answers, and obtained my signature to verify a record of them. He was to be my prosecutor. Now he produced a clean copy, typed up in legal form, and we sat together for another three hours going very meticulously through his record of questions and answers. Once again I was obliged to attach my signature.

Dusk had fallen and supper time was approaching when I was taken in to Room 2 in the prison cell-blocks. There were two beds in the room, a water tap and a toilet, but no chairs and no desk. I found a Chinese military officer already there, waiting trial on charges of corruption. I became aware that the room next to ours held several women.

Supper was brought in. We were obliged to place our trays on our beds and to sit on the floor. There was a window over my bed but we were forbidden to close it, and since it was December it soon became very cold. While we were at supper, the warden appeared at the barred window which separated us from the corridor. He was an army lieutenant, fat, crafty looking, and too talkative.

It was December 24, Christmas Eve. After supper the women in the next room began to sing Christmas carols. This was too much for me. I nearly wept, thinking of my devout mother and my Christian family.

During the next six weeks I awaited formal indictment. I could not receive or write letters until the formal charges had been made, nor could I see members of my family or engage a lawyer in my own defense. My sole diversion was the spectacle of prison-life around me which I was seeing in a new dimension. I learned much concerning the character of the scores of prisons maintained throughout Formosa. Terror of these prisons keeps the Formosan people in subjection. Abstract ideals of democracy and human rights seldom occur to the common man. The rigors of these prisons were far more immediate.

I was being detained in one of the several cells known as patients' rooms intended to be used as a hospital bay. I learned that Lei Chen and Su Tung-chi had both been held in Room 2. The prisoner had to purchase necessary things, toothbrushes, soap, chopsticks, the wash basin, toilet paper, and rice bowls, and if he wished to prepare notes for his trial, he might purchase a pencil and a pad of paper. Our rooms looked into the prison yard, but when certain prisoners were allowed to exercise there, all windows looking into the area had to be closed to prevent any communication. Room by room the prisoners were allowed to walk in the open for ten minutes, four days a week.

Across the yard from our cells were larger barred cells like animal cages. Each held ten to twenty prisoners who were required to sleep on the floor and were subject to sudden unannounced inspections, night or day. Originally this compound was supposed only to hold pretrial prisoners, but now it was a mixed group. Some were under sentence for more than ten years, some for life, and some were awaiting execution. There was no dining room. These prisoners and those serving long sentences were obliged to seat themselves in circles on the ground around big food bowls. When it rained they squeezed themselves into the corridors.

These were working prisoners. Some worked in the kitchens and were obliged to bring food to other prisoners, and others were employed in a laundry that took in the uniforms of low-ranking government personnel, bedding from railway sleeping cars, and the like. Some were employed in a clothes-making factory, producing military uniforms, and other uniforms for minor government employees. Some were engaged in handicrafts. There was a construction team, sent out under guard from time to time to work on public and private projects. The profits from this forced labor were huge, and were shared, not by the prisoners, but by the officers in charge and by the prison staff.

Later, after my release, I met a Chinese who had been a university instructor, had been arrested as a Communist, and had spent thirteen years in this and various other prisons. Conditions as he described them for the period 1949-50 were incredible. Chiang Ching-kuo was then cleaning up the island to make it secure for his father's retreat. According to this man in earlier years the big cells were so overcrowded there was no room for all the prisoners to lie down at one time. They were compelled to take turns sleeping. The courts did not bother with trials in political cases then, but simply consigned the victims to detention until one day the sentences were read off at a roll-call, six years, ten years, fifteen years, from which there was no appeal.

For me the most chilling experience was the sight of prisoners condemned to death. It is Chinese tradition that on sentencing, and while still in the courtroom, iron shackles are welded on the prisoners' ankles, and are not removed until the execution. We saw condemned men in the prison yard from time to time, and the sound of clanking shackle-chains outside our window was heartrending. Sometimes men wore these chains for two or three years while awaiting decisions upon appeal. Appeals are automatic, but if the final one is rejected, the wardens come before dawn, the cell-door is opened, and the prisoner knows his fate. Execution takes place at once. All prisoners know that if the prison office lights go on before four A.M., someone is about to be taken out to death. The dreadful sound of pounding follows as a hammer is used to break the leg-chains, and this sometimes takes nearly ten minutes. The entire prison awakes and that sound pierces the heart. I saw several men taken away. On one occasion, as a huge Chinese was taken out, we heard him trying to sing, then screaming "Long live Mao Tse-tung!" before he was gagged with a towel, beaten, and dragged away screaming like a pig carried to slaughter. After every execution all the prisoners are subdued, there is an atmosphere of mourning, but if a prisoner betrays his feelings too openly, if he fails to eat, or weeps at the prospect of his own fate, the guards may curse him, shouting, "What? You sympathize with him?"

All of Formosa knows the story of Thomas Liao's sister-in-law who was over seventy years old and suffering from high blood pressure while being held in the cells next to mine. Her son, under sentence of death, was taken out and paraded back and forth in the exercise yard within her sight, four times a week, until an act of clemency released them both, an act of clemency produced by Liao's decision to abandon the Independence Movement in Tokyo to return to Formosa.

So the month of January passed. At the Lunar New Year, February 1965, Hsieh, Wei, and I each received a present from General Ning, a packet of eggs and dried shredded pork. The general was continuing to cultivate us in his effort to win us around to the government's cause. The formal charge was brought against me in February. It was lengthy and I found myself charged with "an attempt to overthrow the government by illegal means." This formality made a change in my prison life. I could now communicate with my family, sending and receiving one letter per week, each not exceeding 200 Chinese characters in length. One could not say much in 200 characters, but then there was very little that we were allowed to say in any case. Now, too, members of my family could come to see me for ten minutes once each week on Thursday. We had not been in direct communication for more than four months.

On the night before my mother and wife came to see me, the warden appeared to be very nervous. Too often, he said, unpleasant scenes take place at these first meetings. Sometimes two or three years have passed since the prisoner last saw his family. Women cry and scream. He begged me to control my emotions. I sensed that he feared I might report some incident of bad treatment.

When the family came they were registered at the outer offices, check-slips were brought in, and a guard conducted me to the small meeting room, panelled on one side by heavy glass. I could see my wife and mother but could not touch them. We were to communicate through a speaking-tube arrangement. I knew that in a case such as mine there would be a recording made, in addition, a clerk took notes beside me. We were not alone at the long counters running beneath the glass panel, for other prisoners were also greeting families on this Thursday afternoon.

We had been strictly forbidden to discuss my case. There could be only small talk about health and the children. My mother, nearly seventy at the time, begged me to read the Bible and to pray.

At this first brief meeting she raised the question of engaging lawyers. Since my confession was signed and the government had developed its case against me, there seemed really no need to go to this expense. Nevertheless, she was worried and felt that it would be better. A few weeks later I agreed.

I had already begun to prepare my defense. Clearly it was useless to argue the legality of the government that had imprisoned me, and I decided to base my defense on the ground of "freedom of opinion," pointing out that there had been no attempt on our part to use violence.

My family decided to engage the services of Liang Shu-jung, a Chinese member of the liberal wing of the Nationalist party and a member of the Legislative Yuan elected on the mainland in 1947. He was relatively young, had been trained in Japan, enjoyed a good reputation, and was very ambitious. He had good personal relations with many important figures in the government. My family had no illusions, for Liang had served as the editor Lei Chen's lawyer, and Lei was then in prison serving out a ten-year sentence, principally for having urged the Generalissimo to permit formation of an opposition party that would attract Formosan support to the Nationalist regime.

Liang was surprised and seemed to be pleased with the request that he represent me. On consulting with liberal members of the party and official friends, he was told that from their point of view it was a good sign that a Formosan would ask a Chinese to take on the case. He should by all means take it, for in doing so he would become one more intermediary between the Formosan people and the government. He would of course have to be extremely cautious not to incur the wrath of the Generalissimo who had ordered the prosecution to begin.

In these circumstances a prisoner's defense lawyer is permitted to visit him for consultation, and so when Liang appeared, I was taken out to a small room. The prosecutor himself was present and had with him a recording-machine. Under the circumstances, what could we do or say?

Although I was not so informed, the trial date had been set for late March. In the interim several small changes took place. Staff Officer Wang of the garrison command now began to come in quite often "to be sure that my stay was as comfortable as possible." At the time of my family's first visit I had complained that I had not been able to bathe for more than one month. My conversation and my complaints of course had been recorded. Soon after that the communal bath was reactivated, and we were each allowed one bath per week. Wang began to see my family often, assuring them that I was well and assuring me that they were fine. "The authorities will be very careful," he said, and from his conversations I drew the conclusion that in some quarters there was fear that I might be outspokenly critical of the prison administration when I appeared in court. It was a bit of psychological warfare designed to soothe me.

During this period I was taken before a judge three times for brief preliminary hearings. These meetings were informal and private, with only one recording clerk present; the questions were simple and each session lasted no more than one hour.

Two days before the trial I was notified and my family was asked to supply my best suit. The barber came to tidy up my appearance. For the first time since September 20 I felt somewhat restored to an outward appearance of respectability. The authorities too seemed to think this was an occasion of great importance. The courtroom itself was repainted by a team of prisoners, and Wang came in several times a day. There was a sense of tension in the camp and he was worried about what might happen. I learned later that the government feared that there might be a student demonstration on the day of my trial or that there might be riots in the city. On March 27, the morning of the trial, the entire district was heavily patrolled, military units were mobilized nearby, and traffic was cleared from the streets. Thus the whole city was alerted to the importance attached to the event.

A car was sent to bring my mother, my wife, and my brother to the court. They were received with great courtesy and shown around the camp which was on dress parade, as it were, for this occasion. Again and again they were assured that this would be an "open trial."

According to the standards set by the inner core of hard reactionaries around Chiang, we should have been shot out of hand on the night of September 20. That we were permitted to appear in any court was an overindulgent concession. But the trial was not to be conducted by the traditions of Anglo-Saxon law, but by a Chinese adaptation of the forms of Western legal practice. From one point of view, China had come a long way in the past fifty years. From another point of view such a performance was a travesty of justice.

An "open trial" was a figure of speech. Tickets had been issued to fill the seats, and the spectators were a carefully selected group. The Chamber of Commerce was represented and members of the Legislative Yuan were present. Journalists' organizations sent observers, and student representatives were given seats. Since the United States was so often and so inaccurately accused of promoting the Independence Movement, the American embassy had requested and been given two tickets, but since the embassy apparently wished to dissociate itself from this accusation, only one man came, briefly toured the camp and left before the trial session opened. There were no foreigners present.

All spectators, lawyers, and the three judges were seated; the proceedings began sharply at 9:00 A.M. To my astonishment, everyone present stood up when I entered the room. I remained standing, everyone resumed his seat, and the trial began. It was brief, for the guilty verdict had long since been agreed upon. This was a *pro forma* legal gesture to satisfy public opinion. I was rather surprised to find that the shabby old prosecutor had stayed behind the scenes, and that a more presentable man had taken his place.

The morning was taken up with the prosecutor's statement. He quoted our manifesto, asserting vigorously that we three had said that recovery of the mainland was impossible. He spoke with fervor, as if this in itself were high treason. Perhaps in their eyes it was. We had severely condemned the government and had used the words "overthrow the government." We had said that we had to obtain our objective by whatever means was needed, even by "sweat and blood." (This, we argued later, was an old Chinese expression, a literary figure of speech not necessarily meaning violence.)

And so on and on, issue by issue, as we had outlined them in our text. The judges leaned forward to ask questions, point by point, and thus before the morning session had ended, somewhere between eighty and 100 spectators had become familiar with our criticisms.

I was returned to my cell, and Hsieh and Wei in turn were brought in for a similar examination and review of the charges.

Arguments on behalf of the defendants began about four

o'clock in the afternoon. This time we were all brought into the court at one time. It was the first time we were together since our arrest, and while we looked eagerly at one another, nodded, and stood side by side, we were not permitted to talk. Both my friends looked well.

Our defense took the line that the question was one of freedom of opinion, that patriotism was not merely the shouting of slogans and cheers for the head of state, but that criticism too was a form of patriotism. My lawyer, Liang, was hesitant and timid, merely repeating in perfunctory fashion the arguments I had rehearsed with him. Hsieh's lawyer was both witty and forceful and made the sharper arguments. At one point, he said that the heart of the whole case seemed to be the "crime" of criticizing Chiang Kai-shek, and that under the law this was nothing more than a libel case. At this, some spectators burst into laughter. The prosecutor and the judges looked embarrassed.

Although we felt the audience on the whole was with us, neither we nor our lawyers shouted or made dramatic appeals. We were earnest and firm and made no excuses for our behavior. We made no attempt to act as martyred heroes. We tried to show that we were reasonable men ready to take great risks to alter and improve the Formosan situation if this could be achieved. We were not fanatics.

We learned later that this position had created a favorable impression on many in the handpicked audience, but that the military were unhappy. Indeed some of them were very angry since they had expected us to make the traditional Chinese confessions of culpability and to plead for clemency and forgiveness.

When the defense had completed its arguments and we three had been heard, the judges invited members of our families to say something, if they wished. Perhaps they expected at least to hear the traditional appeals for mercy made on our behalf. My two elder brothers were there, with my mother and my wife, but they all declined to speak. Hsieh's sister and brother likewise preferred to remain silent. We had felt that protest was useless, that the outcome had been decided upon by higher authority, and that the trial was no more than a façade. It was a legal technicality gone through to sustain the appearance of "modern justice" on Formosa.

In contrast, Wei's brother shocked the court by rising to begin an angry denunciation of the whole proceeding, saying that it was illegal, that the government itself was illegal, that martial law was illegal, and that the three of us should not be tried at all. We were led out of the chamber, and the trial came to a close.

By now it was about seven o'clock in the evening and we found that all operations in the camp had been suspended. The prisoners were not fed until 7:30, but I was too keyed up and exhausted to take my supper.

Early the next morning Staff Officer Wang came to me in excitement to say that after the trial one of the reporters present at the trial, probably an American-Chinese recently assigned to Taipei, had gone at once to the garrison command headquarters to ask if I had been tortured. He had noticed my left arm hanging immobile at my side throughout the day's session. Spokesmen for the headquarters hastened publicly to explain the true cause. I had been severely wounded by an American bomb.

On that day every Chinese-language newspaper on the island, without exception, carried the same story of the trial, word for word, saying in part that the three defendants had all admitted guilt in questioning the government policy and the plan to return to China. We had all "repented" in court and we had all "begged for clemency."

My strong-hearted old mother was furious. At the first opportunity she attacked Staff Officer Wang, saying, "Look at this! You are all lying!"

The garrison command dispatched an officer to the editorial rooms of the two English-language papers in Taipei, demanding to know what they were going to print and insisted upon prior censorship. Their stories were brief and, on the whole, accurate, omitting the face-saving story about a "clemency appeal."

It was widely noted that the trial had been conducted with unusual speed, three men tried in one day, and we presumed this had been arranged to minimize publicity and tension. We did not expect delivery of an early sentence, hence we were amazed when within the week we were ordered to prepare ourselves for the final appearance. Such speed suggested that the outcome had been determined well before the trial took place.

On April 2 we were taken into court once more. On entering we again had the opportunity to nod to one another but no more. The entire audience this time numbered no more than ten persons in addition to our families, and included five or six Chinese newsmen.

Again we stood together before the three judges. The presiding judge stood to read the sentences. Wei and I were sentenced to eight years' imprisonment, and Hsieh to ten.

The newsmen openly showed their surprise at the severity of these sentences, shaking their heads and showing sympathy in their faces. Even the talkative prison warden later confided to me that he was amazed. Our families were shocked at this severity.

Later we were led to believe that our failure to beg for clemency was taken for arrogance, that it had originally been planned to sentence us all to five years only, but that higher authority was enraged by our failure to repent.

We immediately initiated a formal appeal. This would be presented in writing. There would be no further hearings or appearances in court. My lawyer and I drafted a text, reflecting the arguments put forward in the courtroom, and the appeal was filed. According to law, the court must respond within sixty days, and thirty days is the usual time, but no answer came to my appeal. July, August, September, and October went by. We thought that perhaps this was a good sign, that there was disagreement at the highest level, and that the highest authority could not or had not made up his mind.

The routine of prison life was somewhat modified and permission was now granted for me to have reading material. The prison rules said that there could be no novels and no newspapers, but these rules were breached for me. My family was allowed to bring in popular fiction magazines, hardly what I wanted, and in time I acquired a complete set of Sherlock Holmes, of Winston Churchill's memoirs of World War II, and three volumes of DeGaulle's *Memoirs,* a paperback edition in French. International law treatises were admitted both in French and English texts, together with law dictionaries. At last I was permitted to see *Newsweek, Time* magazine, and *Reader's Digest* after they had been slowly and carefully censored by political officers attached to the prison. I also had some French grammar and conversation books sent in, and spent a couple of hours every morning reading and practicing conversation. It was a good mental exercise in the solitude of my cell.

In an issue of the English edition of *Reader's Digest* I found an article concerning Amnesty International, a nonpolitical organization that undertakes the difficult task of helping political prisoners, wherever they may be. To my surprise, not long after that, I received a letter from Mrs. Karin Gawell, a member of the Swedish Section of Amnesty International. Someone had informed the organization of my case.

This was the first letter from abroad delivered to me. The second came from my McGill University classmate, Ian McPherson, who had become general counsel for Air Canada. On the occasion of a visit to Canada by the Nationalist Chinese Vice-minister of Justice, Cha Liang-chen, McPherson asked him to deliver the letter to me at Taipei, and it was done. I have since learned that these were only two of many letters addressed to me from abroad. The others I did not see, but these alone deeply moved me; they were convincing evidence that my friends abroad were deeply concerned.

The spring and summer months were exceedingly hot and murky, almost unbearable during the hours when windows had to be closed because of the presence of certain prisoners in the exercise yard. Petty incidents would either entertain us or deepen our inevitable periods of depression. I was tense and irritable much of the time, and found myself constantly making an issue of the language question with the prison officials. The deputy director was a repulsive character, shifty-eyed, devious, and mean at heart. He began to insist that all conversation during visits with my family be in the official Mandarin Chinese. I pointed out that there was no prison rule forbidding the use of the Formosan language, and it was up to him to employ a clerk who could understand it. When I wrote a long letter addressed to the garrison commander, complaining on this point, he tried to calm me down, for he knew that my letters received attention high in the hierarchy. He coupled his soothing remarks with a veiled threat, reminding me that the editor Lei Chen, who had occupied my Room 2, had had trouble and had been punished like a child for noncooperation. He probably lied, but he intended to intimidate me.

I had learned of a young military cadet who had been involved in the same case as Wu had been. He always had to have his left hand bandaged, for it had been totally wrecked during a period of torture. Some of his companions had been shot and of three brothers arrested with him, one had "fallen from the train and been killed while trying to escape" on the journey, under guard, from Tainan to Taipei. The second brother was in my prison, still awaiting trial after more than two years. He often wakened us all, shouting and screaming. He was chained, and after this went on for several months, he disappeared.

Another prisoner, a Chinese, became deranged during the exhausting examinations, and tried again and again to commit suicide by striking his head against the wall. From time to time in the evenings he was brought to Room 3, the cell adjoining mine, where he was chained to a bed. He did not scream, but we could hear the struggle as he fought to destroy himself.

An impersonal excitement swept over the camp on the occasion of a heavy typhoon. Sometimes the lights went out throughout our district in the city. Normally we had to bear the light from a naked bulb shining in our cells through the night, but on these occasions, when the prison plunged into darkness, the camp guard was instantly alerted, all doors were locked, and candles were lighted in the corridors.

One day I was told that as a favor my room would be repainted. My cellmate and I were moved to Room 4 for three days. When we returned, the painter found occasion to come back for a forgotten brush. He was one of Wei's uncles, serving a ten-year sentence, and waiting until the guard was a little distant, he suddenly whispered to me that "They have installed a bug in the ceiling."

I continued to occupy Room 2. Hsieh had been brought to Room 4, and Wei was in Room 6. Wei used sometimes to sing folk songs after supper, and very occasionally we shouted meaningless non-words, just to let one another know we were still present. This invariably brought guards to our doors. For a time Hsieh was cleverly able to pass notes back and forth. We were obliged to clean our rooms each morning before a working prisoner appeared, moving from cell to cell with a trash scoop or dustpan. Hsieh had bribed our man by giving him fruit, and he managed to sweep up and then deposit crumpled bits of paper upon which we had written a few characters.

Wei and Hsieh risked retaliation for bold and outspoken criticism of the prison administration. Hsieh undertook to sue the policeman who had beaten him up when we were arrested in the hotel room, and both men sued investigators who had mistreated them. Their papers were sent up through the prison offices, the garrison command sent in some agents for investigation but no action followed. Wei was always quarreling on the issue of censorship. When the wording of a letter to his family was altered by the prison censors, he undertook to sue them too, saying that they could have returned the letter to him or could have destroyed it, but they had no right to alter it in passage. This made the deputy director furious, and one day when I was walking back and forth in the exercise pen, I saw this man standing outside Wei's window, talking to him through the bars. Soon I heard the sounds of a violent argument. The director shouted that Wei was "nothing but a traitor," and Wei retorted that the deputy director was "nothing but a pig, a running dog of the K.M.T." I was alarmed, and could not resist shouting to Wei, "Stop it! It's of no use!" I was fearful of the consequences for Wei, but nothing came of it. We were still being treated carefully, and our case handled cautiously, but no decision came down in response to our appeals.

The monotony of prison routine was relieved one day by notification of the impending visit of an important person. Everyone was required to clean his cell thoroughly and white cot covers were issued, just for the day. At the appointed hour our windows were all shut, and at the moment of the visitor's arrival, strings of congratulatory firecrackers were shot off at the gate, the strange sounds echoing in prison compound walls. I heard people moving about in the courtyard and on peering through cracks and flaked-off spaces, I was astonished to see Chiang Ching-kuo dressed in a neat dark suit and highly polished shoes, smiling and nodding as he inspected the exercise yard, the corridors, and the general layout of the camp. This visit had nothing to do with our case, and Ching-kuo did not approach our cells. His inspection tour lasted perhaps an hour.

He came twice during the months I was there. The reception and his tour of the camp was the same on each occasion. Why did this very busy man take time for such a gesture? I could not understand. I did not know if he visited other prisons, but here every inmate had been seized and was confined by his garrison command. Was this sadism or was this a manifestation of that curious characteristic noted by Ambassador Tsiang, a desire to present an appearance of concern for the underdog? One could understand his frequent visits to army camps and barracks as an obvious attempt at camaraderie, but visits to military internment camps such as ours could not be so easily explained.

In the early autumn, when the reply to my appeal was long

and illegally overdue, my mother and lawyer, after long discussions and consultations with relatives and close friends, reached a conclusion. The matter of prime importance now was to get me out of prison by any means. Under Chiang's regime any thought of my becoming a martyr would be totally futile, a wasteful expense of spirit bordering on insanity. Any means available had to be used to secure my safe release. People, especially those who were familiar with Chinese politics and mentality, would understand that the regime had to save face, and any attempt on our part to bring about my release would be understood as well. Once I left prison, there would be ample opportunities for us to repudiate whatever the government could say about the circumstances.

I noted with great interest much later that this same approach, not uncommon in Asian domestic politics, was adopted even by the United States government in Asian international politics. In order to secure the freedom of the *Pueblo*'s crew, captured by the North Korean government, the United States government agreed to admit its "guilt" in violating North Korean sovereignty, even though throughout the whole incident the United States maintained that it had never done so. Immediately after the return of the prisoners, the U.S. repudiated its confessions of gulit and declared any admissions were for the sole purpose of obtaining the release of the crew.

Although it was intensely distasteful to her, my mother agreed that I must appeal in person. It would be done under duress and the world would surely understand. We did not talk about it during our brief conversations at the prison meeting-room. A secret note on the subject was placed among my papers, something for me to find and contemplate without discussion.

The appeal was sent to the Generalissimo. I began to sense an impending change, perhaps my release, when my family sent in clothes, necktie, a white shirt, and a gift of flowers. This last prompted an amazed guard to mutter, "How strange for anyone to send flowers to a prisoner who has no place to put them." On

November 3 I had supper at five o'clock and at about six o'clock, as it was getting dark, the prison director summoned me to his office upstairs. He sat alone, with papers lying on the desk before him. Picking up one, he said solemnly, "The decision on your appeal is here. It has been rejected. You are sentenced to eight years in prison." There was a long moment of silence. He then said, "There is another document here. At the President's special order you have been granted amnesty. You will be freed."

"What of Hsieh and Wei?" I asked.

"I really don't know. Nothing about them has been said."

"When can I go home?"

The director was obviously savoring this last moment of authority. He preferred to be vague. "Maybe tonight . . . perhaps tomorrow. Go pack and be ready. There may be some further business to finish."

This was not true. Everything had been prearranged with military precision, even to the minute that I was to step through the prison gate.

I returned to my cell. My roommate congratulated me. Staff Officer Wang came in to say nervously, "Now surely you are not going to make a parade or have a big celebration? You will not shoot off firecrackers to celebrate?" I assured him, "No, I am not interested in firecrackers."

Soldiers came in, packed my many books, and with them in hand escorted me to the prison office. To my surprise I was not asked to sign documents or to produce a guarantor for good behavior. In my presence and in the presence of the director of the prison and his staff, my effects were carefully inspected. It was a moment of suspense for me, for I was smuggling out several papers I had written in prison, records of my experiences and observations, which I later published.

At precisely 9:45 P.M. on November 3 we stepped out of the prison gate. My release was timed too late for publication in the evening papers, but just in time for a television news announcement on the last evening broadcast. By then I would be already in my home, and there would be no crowd waiting there to welcome me.

The prison director and Staff Officer Wang of the Political Warfare Section of the Garrison Command escorted me to a chauffeured car and rode with me across town. I noticed a military jeep standing by as we entered the small lane leading into the university housing area. One block further on we drew up before my gate, and I left the car. I was at home.

XI

Surveillance

I was received by an excited, joyful, and tearful family. My mother, wife, children, and my brother in Taipei were all there, together with my lawyer who tactfully took his leave after a few minutes. The house was filled with flowers. The family had been notified late that afternoon, with strict instruction not to advertise the fact that I would be released.

We talked throughout the night. My brave and able mother told me of how the deal was made, the drawing up of the humiliating statement of repentance and the conclusion of the agreement that led to my release.

All the morning papers announced that I was home. My lawyer released a statement saying that I had "repented" and received clemency. Every government and party propaganda organ announced with great pride that I had "confessed" to my misdeeds and had been pardoned. Implicit in much of this was the idea that Chiang's critics, the intellectuals and the Formosan malcontents, had at last seen the virtues of the Leader. Clearly the regime thought it had won a great victory.

Because of its basic insecurity the regime felt the need to humiliate and punish the Generalissimo's critics, and thus confessions and repentance became an important part of the policing technique. It did not seem to realize that confessions signed under any form of physical or psychological duress are not only worthless but damage the regime that extorts them. For example, Taipei would not be able to understand why, of late, the leading leftist intellectuals in Europe and America have condemned the Castro regime for extorting a blatantly false "confession" from the Cuban poet Herberto Bodilla Lorenzo. In this "confession" he was made to describe himself as "ignoble, unjust, cowardly, treacherous, and lying."

A few days after my release from prison, the Canadian Broadcasting Company called from Montreal and tried to do a telephone interview as a part of its program, "This Hour Has Seven Days." Since I was aware that all our conversations were being recorded by the security agents in Taipei, I did not feel free to talk.

What should I do with my life now? I soon discovered that I was under surveillance. My house was watched and I was followed wherever I went. I had received no reply to my letter to the university president asking to be kept on the staff. There was not even an acknowledgment that the letter had been received. My contract was not renewed and my relationship with the university had come to an end. Nevertheless we were still living in a university faculty house and no move was made so far to evict us.

Two or three days after my release my wife and I paid a courtesy call upon President Chien of *Taita*. At the door I began by saying at once, "Thank you for your concern," but his reply was chilly and evasive. We quickly took our leave and that was the last I saw of him.

I was anxious to learn how my family had fared throughout the months I was in jail. A jeep had been stationed nearby for a time and police watched the house, noting who entered; but after two months it had been withdrawn. Investigators called on my wife now and again, but my family had not been harassed in any way. Fortunately my son and daughter experienced little trouble once the initial shocks had faded. They were lonely, however, for friends, who had normally come to the house, decided that it was wise to stay away.

For me and for my family those next few months provided a test that sorted out the true friends from the false. The jeep always stationed near our gateway cast a chilling shadow over our lives.

On the city streets some of our acquaintances ignored us or turned away to avoid an encounter. My Formosan university colleagues stayed away. Of the students, some who had come often to our home, who had flattered me and boasted of our acquaintance before my arrest, now began to deny that they had been associated with me off campus. Some even went so far as to ask the school to strike my name from their records as an advisor or teacher.

All this hurt. I felt isolated and lonely, but fortunately this frustration was offset to a degree by my admiration for those who dared come to visit, who risked possible danger to their own lives and careers. Some students quietly found occasions to meet my wife and ask for details and to express friendship and concern. Some boldly came with gifts of books and fruit. The true friends soon became apparent. I made no move to resume old associations, leaving others to take the initiative.

Soon after my release from prison, General Ning held an elaborate banquet for me, to which General Wang Shen and other high officers close to Chiang Ching-kuo in the military establishment were invited. Nothing serious was discussed during the evening. They simply congratulated me on my release and wished me the best in my "new life."

Although I was now technically free to travel within the island without permission, it was at once evident that I would be under surveillance at all times. If I went out by taxi, a jeep followed; if we dined in a hotel or restaurant in town, agents took tables nearby and dined there, too. If I went by train to Kaohsiung to see my family, plainclothesmen were nearby.

For some weeks I remained quietly at home, reading all the

periodicals and books I had missed during the prison months, and recording some of the thoughts I had mulled over during enforced idleness. For a time I clung to the illusion that I would be recalled to the university, where I really wished to be. One day, Staff Officer Wang appeared bringing with him a Mr. Kao, an ex-Communist who was now the deputy chief of the Sixth Section at party headquarters. They had come, they said, to discuss my future, and proposed that I accept a job as a research associate in an institute for study of Chinese Communist affairs. I would be reasonably well paid, and I would receive a good house as part of the salary.

I rejected the idea. Perhaps they assumed that I had been willing to buy my way out of prison by a "confession of guilt" designed to appease the Generalissimo, and that I would seize this opportunity to gain security by working for the party. I made it very clear that I would not consider it. Nevertheless, they lingered on in my house for nearly two hours, advancing every argument to overcome my objections. At last, to end the irritating discussion, I observed with some heat that I would rather peddle my books in the street than work for them. They took their leave. The deputy chief then wrote an official report complaining that I had been most uncooperative and rude.

In the following months I became aware of the predicament in which the Presbyterian church of Formosa found itself. Before 1945 the number of Christians in Formosa, although comparatively small, formed an important minority, almost an elite leadership group, exercising an influence far exceeding their numbers in the total population. Through the churches, the schools, and the mission medical services, Formosan attention had been drawn to the Western world for a century. Late in the Japanese era the Presbyterians came under heavy pressure, for they continued to use the Formosan dialect in the mission schools and church services, and resisted attempts to impose emperor-worship and the Japanese state religion, Shinto, upon Christian converts. From 1945 until 1949 the Christian community was relatively undisturbed, but from 1950 to 1965 the situation was altered. On the one hand everything was being done by the government to revive extravagant traditional Chinese folk-customs, so long condemned by the missionaries and discouraged by the Japanese. This was done in an attempt to recover and strengthen popular ties with continental China. On the other hand many missionaries and diverse Christian sects were brought into Formosa under quasi-official encouragement. Karl Rankin, the first American ambassador to serve at Taipei, boasts in his memoirs that during his ambassadorship the number of missionaries and their family members rose from a mere thirty in 1950 to more than 700 in 1957.

By 1965 a great change was taking place. Nationalist policy clearly suggested that local Christians, especially the long-established and well-organized Presbyterians, were now considered a liability. The government proposed to obliterate all sense of Formosan identity. It demanded that Mandarin Chinese be used in the schools, and it required the introduction of the cult of Sun Yat-sen worship with its elaborate associated demonstrations of respect for Sun's successor, the Generalissimo.

For some time the Presbyterian church in Formosa had been a member of the World Council of Churches, with headquarters in Geneva. When certain members of the World Council began to advocate recognition of Peking, the Nationalist leaders were furious. When the government demanded that the Formosan church sever its connections with the world organization, the Presbyterians stubbornly refused. The moderator of the Formosan synod was summoned to the garrison command and told that he must work for withdrawal. Church officers and members were continually harassed. Several Japanese pastors visited Formosa and upon returning to Japan published a volume of essays in Japanese, giving impressions of the island and of the church organization and programs. At their invitation a moderator of the Formosan church synod prepared a brief introduction. Soon after the book was published in Japan, he was arrested and on being taken to Security Headquarters was shown a copy of the book. One of the visiting Japanese clergymen had written some unflattering remarks about the local situation in which the church found itself. The frightened pastor, under threat, signed a "confession of guilt." He was then told that the government henceforth could prosecute and imprison him at any time on the basis of this signed document. He must now campaign to force the Presbyterian church in Formosa to withdraw from the World Council of Churches. My cousin, the president of the Taipei Theological College, was called upon by agents of the Investigation Bureau and given similar orders. When five Formosan ministers accepted an invitation to visit Japan, their passports were picked up and canceled as they were about to board the plane at Taipei.

During this time the church leadership was deeply embarrassed by the presence of a visiting fundamentalist preacher from the United States, the Reverend Carl McIntire. This guest attended church meetings at which the World Council membership was being discussed and at each of these he loudly prayed for the "speedy recovery of China by Chiang Kai-shek" and urged the Generalissimo to begin the invasion.

Under such diverse pressures the Formosan church was forced to yield, and at last, with great reluctance, voted to withdraw from the World Council of Churches.

My sister, Peng Hsu-yuan, had been president of a church-sponsored college at Tamsui. She has never been a political activist, but during the months of my enforced idleness and of pressure upon the church in the World Council membership affair, her school was also subjected to government concern. One day two groups of garrison security agents appeared at the Tamsui campus. While one group waited outside, the other slipped in quietly to tack up posters that read "Down with President Chiang Kai-shek! Up with the College President!" Then the second security squad rushed in with a great tumult, to tear down "subversive posters" which were then used as evidence to discredit the school and my sister.

Surveillance continued but followed an erratic course, sometimes severe and close, and sometimes lax. I could only guess
that this reflected in some degree the attitudes of the officers giving directions to the subordinate agents who were always near
my gates.

One day in early 1966 a car drew up at the gate and a man
came to the door to hand in a card identifying him as "Secretary
of the Youth Corps." He had come at Chiang Ching-kuo's order
he said. Although General Chiang was very busy, he happened
to be free at three o'clock that afternoon, and wondered if I were
free too. He would like to invite me to his office to "hear my
advice."

This surprising invitation was couched in the most polite
terms. I instinctively felt some danger; I had learned that my earlier refusal to accept an invitation from Chiang Ching-kuo had
generated prolonged discussion on the university campuses. Now
was this stranger with the printed name-card actually presenting
a genuine request? Or would I disappear if I once entered the
car he offered to send for me? I felt that I should not refuse a
second invitation, so I told him that I would not need a car, but
would present myself at the Youth Corps offices at three o'clock.

I told my wife where I was going and at the appropriate time
called a cab and crossed the city. I was received by Chiang's secretary, Li Huang, a smooth talker, who asked me to be seated
but made no move to take me on in to his employer. For an
hour he carefully briefed me on all Youth Corps activities, making a great effort to demonstrate how liberal the corps and its
officers were, and how eager to help students. I had little to say.
Again I was amazed at the ease with which they thought that,
after a taste of prison, I might now be brought around to sympathize with their party program and perhaps even be persuaded to
a degree of collaboration. At last he rose and said, "I will see if
the general is ready."

He went into an adjoining room, returned, and said, "Yes, he is
awaiting you."

By this time I had glimpsed young Chiang sitting at his desk and in the seconds before I actually entered his office I saw him rising, carefully adjusting his collar and coat. He stepped forward from behind his desk, smiling cordially and bidding me be seated. I had never met him, and a hint of surprise may have crossed my face when his first words were, "I haven't seen you in a long time." "How are you?" he said. "How is your health? And how is your mother?" He had never met her, but by now the story of her effort to have me released and her vigorous protests were certainly well known in all government offices involved in my case. He even asked about my sister, the president of the Tamsui Institute of Business Administration, who was in trouble just then.

After a moment or two of small talk he remarked gravely, "Many persons have been deeply concerned about you." I was tempted to remark that he was in an excellent position to know, when he said, "Have you any difficulty? Can we help you?" I promptly said, "Yes. I haven't started to work again. Frankly, I want to return to Taiwan University to teach."

There was a flicker of embarrassment before he turned to Li Huang to ask, "Does President Chien know of this?" It was Li's turn to be embarrassed; he gave a noncommittal answer, saying, "We'll discuss this with him."

I came away from this rather easy and informal twenty-minute conversation with quite mixed reactions. Chiang Ching-kuo seemed much less gross in appearance than the impression conveyed in his photographs. There was a warmth in his questions that had been altogether missing in his father's clipped, conventional remarks. The pattern was the same: "What can we do for you?" but he conveyed more sincerity. It was hard to reconcile the public image with the private one, or to believe his show of humane concern for students when I knew so well what was going on in scores of prisons throughout the island, all of them under the jurisdiction of this man.

I knew that there were continuing discussions of my future, for

an old and influential party man named Tao Hsi-shen talked with
my lawyer from time to time. I had been warned that Tao was an
indirect and crafty man, a manipulator employed as go-between
in many of the factional disputes that Chiang Kai-shek exploited
with such a masterly hand. On one occasion Tao came to see me.
After an hour's rambling talk he came around to the point. In the
United States and England Mr. George Kerr had published a
book entitled *Formosa Betrayed,* a detailed eyewitness account
of the manner in which our island had been handed over to
Chiang Kai-shek's control pending a treaty transfer of sovereignty and then exploited ruinously by the Generalissimo's government and his family. This American consular officer described
the Formosan demands for reform in 1946 and 1947, the incident
of February 28, 1947, and the bloody reprisals that followed
when the Generalissimo sent in 50,000 Chinese troops. The book
was banned in Formosa, but copies were circulating privately,
and were to be found in the American servicemen's libraries of
the USO, the air force, and the army. He complained, "That
book attacks our government. Someone must write a refutation.
The truth must be published." I had read it and thought it a re-
markably accurate record of what happened in Formosa during
the period 1945 to 1947, but I pretended now not to know what
Tao was talking about. He dropped the subject, and I learned
later that the best the government could do was to compel
Thomas Liao to write a letter protesting Robert Turnbull's favorable review of the book that had appeared in *The New York
Times.*

A little later, Tao proposed through my lawyer that I join the
Institute of International Affairs. This had once been a division
of the Defense Ministry, but had been technically detached and
made, in name, an independent corporation. The board chairman
and principal officers were high party officials, and it was almost
exclusively subsidized by the government. This was Chiang
Ching-kuo's "think tank" devoted to the study of communist

affairs and to analyses of the international situations. Now they wanted to make me a member.

The director of the institute, Professor Wu Chung-tsai, came to visit me one morning. He was exquisitely polite, and after some desultory conversation, he handed me the formal appointment to the institute. A matter of face was involved; I could not toss it back to him then and there, and so I merely said very earnestly that he must understand I know nothing about Communist affairs. Both of us knew that my acceptance would be a public relations triumph for the party. When he had sipped the last cup of tea and bid me good-bye, he left the appointment paper lying on a table.

I allowed some weeks to go by and then called on him one evening at his home, returning the document together with a letter formally declining the appointment. The matter ended there.

About this time I discovered that my arrest had made me taboo at the American embassy. Formosans have always been baffled by Washington's relations with Taipei and by the extraordinary concern shown for the sensibilities of the Generalissimo while appearing to ignore the demands and aspirations of the Formosans. No American official living in Formosa can be unaware of the suppression of civil liberties. Before my arrest I knew several embassy officers and often had occasion to see them. Ambassador Kirk had asked me to come in to talk with him. Now, after my release, I discovered that I was altogether cut off. In 1966 a number of prominent Formosans and Chinese, including members of the Legislative Yuan, invited the current ambassador to dine with them to discuss the general situation. The ambassador accepted and the date was fixed. Then the embassy sent a secretary to request a list of the persons to be present. There were about ten names in all, mine among them. On the next day the secretary appeared again to say, awkwardly, that the ambassador would be embarrassed if I were present. I therefore had to withdraw so the party could be held as planned.

The problem of employment was becoming critical. I was thoroughly unhappy with my prolonged and enforced idleness. I finally had to accept the fact that I would not be able to go back to the university. My mother laughed at me, saying, "How can you expect them to allow you to corrupt youths there again?" When the suggestion arose that it might be arranged for me to do research at the Academia Sinica I agreed to accept it. What then took place is obscure. The *ad hoc* committee on my case was involved and also some security organs. They appear to have written formally to the Generalissimo asking if it were all right for me to work at the Academia Sinica. Apparently his answer was no, for nothing came of it.

During the same period, the Canadian Association of International Law, through its president, commissioned me to write a legal paper. I knew all my former colleagues and associates in Canada were apprehensive about my professional and personal life. By this kind gesture they wanted to boost my morale and gave me some financial support. I was deeply moved by the concern and thoughtfulness extended to me by those friends in Canada, whose memory had remained so dear to me.

I was kept under light surveillance during late 1965, but in 1966 a drastic change took place. My case was transferred from the garrison command in the Ministry of Defense to the Investigation Bureau (I.B.) of the Ministry of Justice. The I.B. organization may be compared with the Gestapo in Nazi Germany. It is quasi-independent and very powerful. Every member of government knows that his I.B. dossier is on file if the president should want it, and every private citizen who draws attention upon himself may be sure that the I.B. takes careful note. The lines of authority come directly from the Generalissimo, and the allegiance of every agent must be to him without question. Through the I.B., Chiang keeps check on every branch of his civil government. It is the most hated and feared agency in the dictatorship.

The rivalry between the garrison command investigative agencies and the I.B. is old and keen. Chiang exploits this skillfully.

As I have noted, there were men in high government positions who thought I should be destroyed, that I should have been summarily shot soon after my arrest. Other influential persons argued that this might provoke deep resentment among Formosans and that I should be reeducated, won over, and used to strengthen the regime within the island. My rude rejection of every offer from the party proved that the lenient policy had failed. I had said that I'd rather be a peddler in the streets than serve in the party. Now the reactionaries in the apparatus could argue that the garrison command had failed in handling my case.

The directors of all security organizations, about ten in number, met regularly to coordinate their work. The meetings were chaired by the Generalissimo, and final decisions were made by him. I assume that the decision to transfer my case from one agency to the other was made at one of these meetings.

A senior official in the Investigation Bureau, Wang Kan, a section chief, invited me for dinner through my friend the historian Li Ao, and at dinner he opened the conversation with the remark, "We are sorry the garrison command handled your case so badly and were unable to find you a place. When Dr. Hu Shih was alive, I was assigned to protect him (i.e., to watch his every movement), and as you know, these military men are awkward persons. From now on we are going to look after you."

My contact with the garrison command completely ceased thereafter. General Ning, Staff Officers Wang and Wei, and all the others had lost face. As the months passed I observed a marked contrast between the personnel and general character of the two rival organizations. Men like Ning reflected something of the old Chinese tradition of military men employed by and subordinate to, the scholar-bureaucrat in the imperial system. They were straightforward, doing their duty sincerely, holding the literary man and the literary tradition in great respect. They might consider the cultivated literary man somewhat eccentric, complicated, and difficult to understand, but he represented China's literary tradition and the great Chinese past. In contrast, I came to feel that the I.B. was staffed by the worst elements in the government. The agency that did Chiang's dirty work attracted the most unsavory types, crafty, extremely devious, overly clever, and never to be trusted.

Wang Kan of the I.B. office came to see me very often, for he was now working with Tao Hsi-shen on the problem of placing me. The director of the I.B., a legendary person named Shen Chih-yeh, invited me to dinner. He was perhaps the most feared man in Formosa, and the one most trusted by Chiang Ching-kuo. He is reputed to have been trained to infiltrate Communist organizations, and to have spent more than ten years in the Communist apparatus, enjoying Mao's confidence and rising to high levels before returning to the Generalissimo.

The I.B. had converted a Japanese-style house into a clubhouse. A car was sent for me, and as we drew near, I noticed a plainclothes agent idling at the corner and others attempting to conceal themselves behind telephone poles along the street. I was greeted with elaborate courtesy by Shen, a short, thin, nervous, but not particularly impressive man. My friend Li Ao was also there as a guest, and with obvious flattery Director Shen repeated that he was honored by our presence. After polite conversation and tea we were ushered into the dining room for an elaborate dinner. I noticed at once that the conventional ceiling had been replaced by panels of perforated bagasse-composition board that had become so familiar to me in my several prison cells. I looked at Li Ao, looked up at the ceiling, and laughed to myself, when Director Shen began urging us to speak frankly. "Please talk freely . . . any criticism of the government. It must be improved . . . ," and so on. Our hosts made an obvious attempt to convince us that the I.B. was not political but concerned principally in detecting and eliminating corruption, no matter how highly placed the investigated person might be. When the dinner ended, we were returned to our homes. Not much of substance had been said by either host or guests. On leaving the club, I again noticed a plainclothes agent hiding behind the telephone pole near the gate.

People began to be more relaxed in meeting us, as the months passed, and many came to talk with me about the current situation. The Chinese who filled every significant office and controlled the government were becoming fewer year by year. Their sons and daughters were going abroad, principally to the United States, and it was well known that their parents were carefully investing funds overseas in the family's interest. Time seemed to be on the Formosan side.

Political activists came to my home quite openly. These were principally university graduates, city councilors, and school teachers, who wanted to run for elective offices and to work toward reform within the system. The government was criticized, of course, and the more vicious officeholders and practices were often cursed, but these men did not talk of violent revolution. They wanted to alter the government step by step, through legal means, and sought the most effective way to run as nonparty candidates. They discussed how to form a solid opposition front when campaigning for office.

A nephew of Su Tung-chi, Mr. Wu, was one of the most admired and highly respected members of this group. One day he brought with him Chen Kuang-yin, introducing him as one of his best friends. Chen came from a small place in central Formosa and was unknown to any of the Taipei men. We noticed that he was very quiet, and assumed that this was because he was only a high school graduate, of limited background. One day he came alone to tell me that he was going to Japan to see some of the political activists there. I wished him a good journey.

He returned about one month later, and said that he had met some exiled Formosans in Tokyo, including Su Ben, the author of the book, *Four Hundred Years of Taiwanese History*. He brought greetings from the men in Tokyo, he said, and delivered to me copies of various Independence Movement publications. He laughed when I said it was remarkable that he had managed to smuggle them in. He then pulled out of his pocket and handed to me a device which I knew actually to be a toy then sold in many Japanese department stores for only 450 yen (about $1.60). It was a tiny battery-operated radio which enabled one to broadcast to one's wife in another room, or to the neighbors across the fence. He then handed me 200,000 Japanese yen, saying that my friends in Tokyo wanted me to accept it as a gift. I handed it back to him, saying that I had no need of it. When he left that day, he took the money with him but left the publications and the toy.

A few days later he returned, saying that he was going to Japan, this time to investigate the manufacture of certain types of vinyl bags which he desired to produce in Formosa. He asked if I would like to write a letter of introduction to Su Ben. I observed that I had never met Mr. Su and he had, and therefore he needed no introduction from me, but he replied that a letter would nevertheless be helpful, since he had met Su only in a superficial way. Since Su had many contacts in Japanese business circles, a letter from me would give Su a better reason for introducing him to men who might be helpful in the business he proposed to undertake. Su and I were well known to one another by name. With some reluctance, I wrote a note in Japanese in which I said briefly something to the effect that "The bearer is a serious young Formosan. Please help him in any way you can." In signing I used the name Makiyama and asked the bearer to explain to Su Ben that it was from me.

One morning in early March 1967, Chen rushed into my house, apparently in great fright. He said that our friend Wu had been arrested. "On the evening of February 27," he said, "I spent the whole night in Wu's home helping him mimeograph a leaflet to be distributed next day (the anniversary of the 1947 uprising). On the next morning we filled our pockets with these and took the train southward. I got off at a station near Taichung and Wu went on. It is the last I have heard of him."

In the next few days all of us were intensely worried. I was aware that my every movement was being watched, and that the house was under renewed close surveillance. Members of our group came to me to ask, "What shall we do?" One by one they were being picked up. Some were being followed wherever they went, and all were being watched. Chen came again and again, saying that he must do something for Wu's family. Wu had left some debts, so he went about collecting money from various friends who were eager to help Wu's wife. One day he came to say that one of our friends wondered if they should not run to the American embassy to seek asylum. I said, "That is of no use. They'll push you out, for they are not interested in our problems. Tell them all not to be frightened, and not to show fright by acting unnaturally, for that might incriminate them." When he came yet again that evening, I feared for his safety, and suggested that I should go out for a short walk. The agents watching the house would follow me, and he could slip out the back door and leave unnoticed, which he did.

About two weeks later Wu's family received a postal card from him, postmarked Hsinchu, saying, "Because of urgent business, I must go away for a while. Don't be worried." We had to assume that, under arrest, he had been compelled to write this, a deception, in order to lull his friends into a sense of security so they would not attempt to hide or to leave the island.

To our surprise nothing further happened until midsummer. Surveillance continued. Wherever I went, a jeep followed at a distance. Sometimes I was followed on foot, and if I turned back suddenly, the agents dodged and tried to hide. Sometimes agents posing as students, carrying books and notebooks, followed me on and off the buses, but if I stared at them hard, they turned aside or pretended to leave. Occasionally I was tempted to turn suddenly with my camera as if to take their pictures. They always dodged or hastened away.

One day I saw an American car draw up before my gate. As the watchful agents pushed forward, a huge man, carrying a bundle of papers, stepped out. He ignored the guards and came on to my door. It was Professor Mark Mancall of Stanford, an old acquaintance who had come to Formosa on earlier visits and now came to see me. We made a luncheon date for the following day. When I went into the city to the Ambassador Hotel on the following morning, the agents followed me. In the hotel dining room they stood at a distance, and we thought it possible that they carried recording devices to pick up our conversation. Professor Mancall left Formosa that afternoon, and soon thereafter he was notified that his visa had been canceled.

In midsummer 1967, the number of political arrests increased. Some of the victims tried to hide but were usually found and picked up. A rumor spread that an armed uprising was planned, and that there was written proof that I was involved. It was said that a document had been found, signed by me, concerning this alleged plot. I was baffled. It was absurd; what had I ever written that could possibly be interpreted in such a way?

By the end of the year most of my political friends had been arrested, and my own relatives were beginning to feel the pressure. My brother in Taipei, for example, was denied a business loan because of our relationship although he had always been entirely apolitical. Soon after Chiang Ching-kuo came back from a visit to Japan, the I.B. section chief, Wang Kan, called on me to say that Director Shen would like to invite me to dinner again, and in passing, dropped a hint that Chiang must have brought back some information concerning the Independence Movement activities at Tokyo. A week later he came again with a firm invitation, fixing a date and the time at five o'clock in the afternoon.

On the appointed day Wang Kan came to pick me up. Two rather sinister-looking I.B. officials greeted us at the I.B. clubhouse, apologized that Director Shen had an urgent meeting and sent his regrets that he could not welcome me, but added that he might be able to join us later in the evening. From the coarseness of their speech and manners, I assumed that neither of them had had much education. We were ushered into an anteroom in which stood a brightly decorated Christmas tree. I made some light remarks about it. After a few minutes of idle conversation one of these men suddenly became very serious and businesslike.

"Now, we have some questions to ask. Have you ever written a letter to the Independence people abroad?"

"No."

"Are you sure you have never done so?"

"I am sure."

"All right." Rising, he went into another room, quickly returned with a brown manila envelope, and took out a piece of paper. It was my note, written in Japanese, addressed to Su Ben and given to Chen. "Is this not your writing?"

"Yes, it is, but it was a note of introduction, not a letter."

"Do you know Su Ben?"

"I have never met him." I explained what had taken place, but my interrogator paid little attention.

"Did you not know that this man is a Communist who lived in Yenan? That he was a close friend of Liu Shao-chi? And that he is on the most wanted list of this government?"

"I knew nothing of these things."

"But haven't you received 200,000 yen from Chen together with a broadcasting device and some forbidden publications?" He named the precise date and hour at which Chen had called on me.

"Certainly, Chen brought these things to me, but I refused to accept the money, I destroyed the publications, and the device is a toy sold cheaply everywhere in Japan."

"You know that money was supposed to be for your political activity."

"I returned the money, which Chen said was a gift sent to me. The toy is something sold for 450 yen in every big store in Japan. I receive all sorts of unsolicited publications, and those I destroyed."

My interrogator made it plain that he did not accept my explanation. "You are in touch with the Japanese group. You know that we have arrested many of your friends in this past year. All of them have confessed that they have been plotting sabotage, bombings, and assassinations. And they have all confessed that you are the ringleader. Some of them now denounce you, saying that you led them into this trouble, and that it is unfair that they should be punished if you are not to be punished. They say they have only done what you told them to do. We know that you are the idol of youth on this island, but you are only corrupting youth. You are a demagogue. You are a source of evil!"

Throughout this tirade, growing shriller with each passage, Wang Kan remained quite silent, leaving us every now and then to go to a telephone somewhere nearby. He seemed to be reporting on the progress of this interrogation and the denunciations. The older of the two hosts was relatively moderate in his comments, leaving it to the one who seemed to be his subordinate to make these angry accusations and disparaging remarks.

The exchange, or more accurately this diatribe on their part, went on for at least two hours. At the beginning I tried to explain that these young men, now under arrest, had come to me to talk of legitimate political activity, that they wanted to run for elective office and to oppose the one-party system. I repeated again and again that I had never heard any talk of plots, bombings, sabotage, or assassinations. I lost my temper, and shouted, "You can make anyone confess anything you want them to. I know! I have seen it done!"

They had the last words, of course, and they were revealing. "We are not afraid of any foreigners," one shouted, "and do not forget that we can kill you. We can destroy you at any time, as you must know!"

During all of this Wang Kan went in and out; I assumed that he was asking for instructions. The scene seems to have gotten out of hand, and these rough agents were apparently carrying the interrogation and threats much farther than had been anticipated. At last Wang broke in to suggest that we go into the next room for dinner.

We took our seats and wine was served. The atmosphere was,

to say the least, chilly. I thought probably I was to be arrested on the spot. When the dinner came to an end, we returned to sit by the sparkling Christmas tree and to have a cup of tea marking the end of the evening. It was almost midnight when they decided to break it up.

Wang Kan rode with me in a strained silence for most of the way. As we neared my house I saw my wife hurrying along the street. She had become extremely worried, and had set out on foot to the I.B. clubhouse. I called to her from the car, we picked her up, and were soon at home. Despite the hour and the circumstance, Wang came in. He was embarrassed and obviously upset. He would be held to account if those rough characters had revealed too much of the agency's real attitude toward me. I was angry and reckless. It was possible that some of our group, under fearful pressure, may have repudiated me and even made up tales of plots and plans for violent action, but I also knew that others would be as steadfast and honest as Hsieh and Wei had been. I began to believe Chen had really been sent to trap me, to give the I.B. an excuse finally to eliminate me from the scene.

I turned on Wang rather harshly, saying, "You were present all the time. Are these reasonable men? They are like animals, yet they hold important places in your organization. I am prepared to be arrested again. Anything but this kind of treatment!"

He brushed this aside, embarrassed, and then after a few conventional remarks, he left.

I said to my wife, "We must be prepared, for I shall be arrested again," and in the light of what I had to tell her of the evening, she agreed. The next day I called on my lawyer, told him the story, and said that I was prepared to be picked up any day. I then wrote two long notes, one in Chinese and one in English, explaining what had happened. Giving them to my close friends, I asked them to make them public if I should be arrested.

As I have said, my lawyer was a member of the Legislative Yuan, and a few days later he encountered the I.B. Director Shen in the legislative offices. When an opportunity came to speak privately, the lawyer told Shen what I had told him of my experience and that I was extremely angry. Then, he remarked to Shen that even if the charges were true, it was no way to treat me, for the results would be precisely the opposite of the Investigation Bureau's and the government's desire.

On Christmas Day, a few days later, Wang Kan appeared at my door, bringing two huge packages of gifts, apples, coffee, and other rather expensive fruits and candies prepared appropriately for Christmas.

"These," he said, "are gifts from Director Shen, with apologies for the recent misunderstanding on the part of his subordinates. He had not intended that they should treat you in that way. He sends his apologies and regards." An acquaintance, seeing the gifts later in the day, laughingly said, "Do you suppose we dare eat these things?"

On the one hand, Director Shen had made an apologetic gesture, but on the other surveillance was increased. My guards made no effort to remain inconspicuous or to dodge behind trees or telephone posts, or into doorways. On the contrary, whenever I walked out, they surrounded me on all sides, crowding close. They were no longer following me, but were now escorting me whether in the street, on buses, or in the train. Once when I had taken a taxi from the station to my brother's home in Kaohsiung and had dismissed the cab, the driver returned to the house ten minutes later and asked to see me. He did not know me by sight or name, but had come back to warn me that I had been followed. He said he thought I must have a personal enemy, for he had been stopped as he left the house and had been asked questions he could not answer. He had not realized that he was talking with I.B. agents, and paled when I told him.

One day I tried to take pictures of one of the men, but instead of running away, he rushed forward, seized my camera, and threatened to hit me. He refused to return the camera, so my wife and I went to the police, reporting a robbery. That evening it was returned to us by an embarrassed policeman who explained that a "five-year-old child had found it in the street." The film had been removed.

One day a rather bold and brave American friend came to see me. The appearance of any foreigner nearby excited the guards. When he left, the guards began to follow him. He broke into a run and quickly outdistanced the agent who tried to catch him. On one occasion the Academia Sinica sponsored a Social Science Conference. About a dozen American scholars were invited to participate. As the day for the conference approached, my custodians became extremely uneasy. They feared that I might attempt to meet the Americans, or that some visiting scholars might attempt to look me up. Even the ordinary police were instructed to watch me closely, and Wang Kan of the I.B. made it a point to visit me daily to make sure that I was at home during the conference meetings. He told me one day that the American embassy proposed to entertain the visitors, and that the I.B. knew that I would be invited. He advised me firmly not to accept, but no invitation was forthcoming.

Friends who were teaching at the University of Michigan brought my name to the attention of the university's Center for Chinese Studies at Ann Arbor. Soon a Michigan professor visiting Formosa found occasion to discuss with me the possibility of my going to Michigan. In 1968 I received an invitation, issued jointly by the Center for Chinese Studies and the University of Michigan Law School. At about the same time I also received an invitation to return to McGill University Law School. These invitations were heartening to a man so long isolated from academic life.

Difficulties rose immediately when the government learned of these invitations. Through my lawyer, through Tao Hsi-shen, and through representatives of the party and Investigation Bureau I was pressed to decline them. In effect each agency politely but firmly urged me not to apply for a passport. There was no need to apply, they said, since I would not be permitted to leave Formosa. A request to do so would only embarrass the authorities.

There was a further difficulty. Every applicant for an exit permit must supply guarantors for one's "correct thoughts" and "good behavior" while abroad. Those guarantors may not be close relatives such as one's wife, brother, father, or cousin. They must agree in writing to be answerable for one's behavior and thought while abroad, and must "accept punishment" if one does not live up to the government's expectations. The terms are vague, but this pledge is exacted of every person applying for passport and exit permit. Under the circumstances I could ask no one for such guaranty and was obliged to reply to Michigan and McGill with expressions of thanks and regret, and a brief explanation that I could not even apply for permission to leave the island.

Upon issuing the invitation, Michigan had sent along a form to be filled out. Among other items of information it asked for a statement of the research subject I might propose to take up. I had suggested that I would like to make a comparative study of laws concerning political crimes. Obviously my letter enclosing this form had been intercepted and scrutinized, for soon thereafter, I am told, the Chinese embassy in Washington asked the University of Michigan what the invitation was all about.

In the face of this, I was doubly appreciative when the university renewed the invitation in 1969. By this time I was under closer surveillance, and I was again warned not to apply for a passport. Under the circumstances, however, I decided that I would apply in any case. There was little prospect of a change of government attitudes, but it seemed important to me to establish a record of the government's refusals. In smuggled letters I told friends overseas what I proposed to do, saying that this had to be my last attempt to leave Formosa legally. Meanwhile these friends abroad were attempting to bring some pressnre to bear upon Taipei. Ian McPherson in Canada arranged for the Canadian Association for International Law to cable Chiang Ching-kuo urging him to allow me to go abroad to pursue my profession. The Swedish section of Amnesty International likewise cabled, and other foreign friends used every means at their command to press the Nationalist authorities.

At last I found one brave man who was willing to become my guarantor and to sign and seal the written forms required of him on my behalf. Taking in hand my application for a passport and exit permit, together with the other necessary supporting documentation, I went to the proper government office. A clerk accepted the papers in routine fashion and said that I would have an answer in about two weeks' time, and although I left the office with no hope of success, I had a curious feeling of elation. At last I was putting the government on the defensive in this matter.

When after a fortnight I returned to that office, the clerk smiled knowingly and politely told me that my application was now being considered by a higher authority. A month later I received a formal letter saying simply that my request for an exit permit had not been granted. Before my application was formally rejected, the matter was discussed at a joint meeting of security organizations presided over by Chiang Kai-shek. When the negative decision was made on my request, Chiang reportedly remarked that attention should be paid to my daily life. My close friends were approached by security agents, and party officials began making inquiries about personal and financial aspects of my life. The instruction apparently went, through ubiquitous party organs, even to the primary school my daughter was attending. One day her teacher called her and asked how her father had been doing, and what his financial situation was. My friends and my ten-year-old daughter were perplexed by this sudden show of concern about my private life.

The surveillance continued. I protested and sometimes was very rude to Wang Kan on the telephone. I protested to my lawyer and I protested to Tao Hsi-shen. Now even visitors who came to the house were being questioned. This harassment even continued through the days of the Lunar New Year of 1969, when there is usually some relaxation. Under instruction, Wang continued to come to see me, though I was aware that he disliked doing so. On the New Year I said to him, "Even on Quemoy and Matsu Islands the Nationalist forces have ceased firing for five days at this time of the year, and the Communists have done likewise. Obviously your treatment of me shows that the Nationalist government and party consider the Formosans a greater threat than the Communists."

I still had some friends who had private contact with secret police sources. They warned me that I was now really insecure, and that anything might happen, arrest or an "accident" contrived by those who wished to be rid of me. On the other hand, it was recognized that such an "accident" or my arrest might deepen public animosity. I was told that the security agencies had determined that in the event of a public disturbance of any kind, three men would be destroyed at once. They were Henry Kao, the present mayor of Taipei, Kuo Yu-shin, an outspoken non-K.M.T. member of the Provincial Assembly elected by a solid constituency in I-lan, and me. The three of us were referred to in security documents by a coded sign, three concentric circles.

Surveillance agents were working three shifts around the clock. My wife was being followed more often and much more closely. In our neighborhood, as elsewhere throughout the city, there were dirty little vendor's shacks at the street corners. They had been put up illegally by ex-servicemen, but the government did not disturb them. One near our gate virtually became headquarters for the agents who were assigned to keep watch on me. The vendor's wife was also a prostitute, we learned. She had developed something like a clubhouse for these bored men. They borrowed chairs from her, and as they sat smoking and reading newspapers, she sometimes brought soup, tea, and towels for them.

After a few weeks had passed, I began to notice that the I.B. agents often were not there in the evenings for long periods of time. Occasionally I managed to slip out and away from home without being followed.

From time to time I was overcome by a feeling of desperation.

It was not human to live like this, unemployed, and aware that each week the circle of friends with whom I could meet became more limited. I felt suffocated in such isolation, with the threat of arrest hanging over me from day to day and hour to hour.

Wang Kan's obligatory visits became an irritation. The liberals in the party still hoped to make a deal, still hoped to persuade me to come over to them and identify myself with the party in the public eye. They continued to talk of finding me a position. Wang urged me to make a deal, pointing out again and again that I could have regular hours and duties on almost any terms. This would settle the problem, he said, and would mean an end to the surveillance that was causing me so much distress.

I decided, instead, that I had to escape.

XII

Escape
to Sweden

I was willing to take any risk, but I did not dare tell
my family that I had resolved to leave the island or die in the attempt. If they knew what I planned to do and did not report it
promptly, they would become accomplices in my crime and
would be punishable by law.

One night I managed to slip out unseen, and by appointment
met a small group of my most trusted friends. I told them I had
determined to leave the island and suggested a way in which I
thought it might be done. They were surprised at my suggestion,
aware of the danger it entailed, but thought we might be able to
bring it off. We began to review the problems that had to be
solved, step by step. The first of these was to determine to which
country I should go.

It could not be the United States, for this would embarrass
Washington. Taipei would instantly demand my extradition and
complications would result. Nor could it be Japan, for we had
had too many examples of Japanese police collaboration with the
Nationalists in returning Formosan expatriates to torture and
prison in exchange for favors Tokyo desired in Taipei. It had to
be a country with which Taipei had no diplomatic ties. I would
not and could not go to a Communist country, for Peking was

just as eager as Taipei to crush the Formosan Independence Movement. I suggested Sweden, and my friends agreed.

The first step was to write to that extraordinary organization, Amnesty International. I had several friends at Taipei who had been helping me smuggle letters out of Formosa for quite some time. With their help I wrote briefly to Stockholm asking the Amnesty International representative there if my case could be put to the Swedish government. If I suddenly appeared at a Swedish port or airport without passport or visa, could I be granted political asylum?

In early February 1969, I received an affirmative answer. Some of my friends wanted me to leave immediately, for they were deeply concerned for my safety. This was impossible; there were too many details to be arranged, and all through a most indirect correspondence. We could not trust the ordinary international mails. Some letters were mailed in Tokyo, some in Hong Kong, and some were hand-carried to the United States or to Europe. I had to locate cooperative and trustworthy people at intermediate points. Financial problems had to be solved. I needed to arrange to have a substantial sum available in Sweden, for it might be a long time before I could earn my own way, once I had reached there. Planning an itinerary became an absorbing game; it was as if I were planning a trip to the moon, with as many variables and uncertainties and dangers along the way. It would not be easy for a one-armed man to travel undetected, halfway around the world.

By late spring the details began to fall into place. I was urged to go, but the matter of a disguise was my most serious problem, and it would be easier in winter, when everyone would be wearing heavy overcoats and capes. I tried all kinds of disguises. At one time I tried growing a beard and at another shaved my head like a Japanese soldier. My mother thought I was becoming too eccentric.

In midsummer I began to condition my guards by going out less and less often. Whenever I did venture out and wherever I

went the agents were with me. If I shopped they pushed forward
to watch the purchase closely, and then asked the shopkeepers
detailed and often absurd questions. Sometimes I remained indoors for two or three weeks at a time, then went out to shops,
restaurants, or hotels, by taxi or by bus. Sometimes I merely
walked around the local university housing area, so that the
agents could see that I was still there. By the end of the year,
they were thoroughly accustomed to these long periods of apparent inactivity. More and more often I went out at midnight or
just after, for few of the agents bothered to stay at their post
after midnight.

In the autumn months I began to feel exhilarated. I had *something* to do, *something* to look forward to, however full of danger
this project was certain to be. I invented a code in English. For
example, if my friends along the way received a cable using certain phrases, it meant that I would leave on the following day.
Another phrase meant that my departure was postponed, and so
forth. Five relay stations were set up along the way at which I
would be met, provided with necessary funds, and helped in any
way required.

For one brief period it looked as if all plans would fall apart. A
letter from New York said that someone there had been over-
heard to say, "You know, Peng may escape from Formosa." Was
this a leak? After a month of double-checking, we found that it
had been no more than an idle speculation. We decided to go
ahead.

The most delicate operation of all was arranging for certain
friends to visit Formosa at an appropriate time, once we had settled upon a date. Some were strangers to me whose cooperation
was arranged and vouched for by mutual friends acting as inter-
mediaries. They would know me in disguise by prearranged sig-
nals, and some of them would keep me in sight at all times until
I was safely away. If I were seized or shot on the spot, they
would bear witness.

Knowing that my house would be searched thoroughly, I sorted my papers and burned most of them. My wife, my son, and my daughter thought my behavior was strange in these weeks, and I think my son became quite suspicious but said nothing. I spent many hours at my desk, writing notes in English and in Chinese to my wife, my mother, and to other members of my family. I prepared a statement explaining the reasons for my decision to leave Formosa. The treatment accorded me 'after my release from prison, portrayed as a gracious amnesty on the part of Chiang Kai-shek, made it impossible to go on. All my friends and associates were in danger as long as I had any relations with them. I declared that if I were arrested I repudiated in advance any confessions wrung from me by any means or any document purporting to come from my hand. Two copies of this were to be kept secretly in Formosa and three were sent out, in advance, to be published in Hong Kong, Japan, and the United States if I failed to make my escape. I burned the diary I had kept since childhood.

After carefully measuring the time required to grow a good beard, I shaved it off and showed my face in public again. It was time to pay a last visit to my mother at Kaohsiung. My guards were accustomed to my making this trip, for I often went down the island on family anniversaries, and my routine of local visits was usually the same. My mother was not very well and kept much to her own rooms on the second floor of her house, which adjoined my brother's home. Her telephone, however, was downstairs, and I decided on this trip that she should have an extension installed. It was the last thing I could do for her. I arranged for this, and then, buying some flowers, I went alone to visit my father's grave.

I learned later that my mother thought that I was contemplating suicide. She betrayed no hint of this, but an hour or two before I was to take the train for Taipei, she rather sternly said to me, "You must believe in God. You must believe in an afterlife."

And with what seemed then to me to be almost a note of anger in her voice, "You must have faith. You must believe, otherwise your life will be useless."

I was depressed. It was the last time I would see her, and it hurt that we were not parting a little more warmly than this. I realize now she was fighting hard to conceal her deepest emotions.

I returned to Taipei, secluded myself once more, and immediately began to grow a beard. A few weeks later all necessary telegrams were out, my disguise was ready, and by prearrangement a friend from abroad was in town. The last day had come. I proposed to leave my house after midnight. It was extremely difficult to maintain the appearance of normal routine, and my son mentioned my odd behavior to his mother who turned aside the questions. As my daughter and son made ready for bed I called them to me and measured them for height. They were a bit puzzled but said nothing unusual as I bid them a goodnight which in my own heart had to mean good-bye.

All my necessary gear had been taken elsewhere, piece by piece. I was therefore able to slip away from the house after midnight, as usual, and to reach my friends' home across town. There I stayed throughout the next day. A go-between met with my escort-to-be from abroad to make a final check upon the marks of identification each would look for. We were not actually to meet or to exchange greetings. In human weakness that evening I called my home to say that I had to go down to Taichung on business, and that after that I would make a tour of the island. I would not return for a week or so. I then entrusted my friends with two large, thick envelopes, one to be opened if I failed in my escape, and the other to be opened when they had heard that I was successful and beyond the reach of Chiang's agents. The second day in my friends' house was spent in perfecting my disguise and getting comfortably used to it. Some photographs were taken. I found that I was not nervous but rather felt a sense of curious calm, of suspension, knowing now that the last and final step had to be taken.

I had congratulated myself upon my capacity to keep my emotions under control, even when saying my silent good-bye to my son and daughter. But now on this last evening, my friends undid me; at our last evening dinner they began to sing familiar songs, and I was compelled to go into my own room and cry. I had not shed tears since those first homesick days in Japan and later in Canada.

My hosts were rather embarrassed. As there were still nearly two hours before I could leave the house, someone proposed that we play "Oh Hell," a card game, to kill time. One of them remarked that he had played it just before his wedding to relieve his nervousness. It certainly took our minds off the unbearable tension for a few minutes.

We were all relieved when at last the moment came to leave the house. Our plan was minutely detailed. It had been arranged to have witnesses nearby for every move I now had to make. I went to the point of departure and there I immediately recognized the person who would stay near me for the next several hours. Other persons were posted at vantage points to watch my movements. I am told that my watching friends "died" every time it seemed a hitch might develop and I would be caught.

As I went through the last barrier I signaled good-bye. I watched as the island slowly disappeared. For the first time in six years, I felt light in heart and spirit.

At the first stopover I was met by someone whom I had known in earlier years. He had engaged a hotel room in which he stayed the night with me, merely calling his wife to report that all had gone well thus far and that I was fine. We talked until nearly 3 o'clock in the morning but even then I could not sleep. I was beginning to feel the physical and emotional strain under which I had been living through the preceding days. We were called at 4:30 A.M. and in the darkness before dawn took a taxi to the point of departure. Later this friend sent the following eyewitness account to our mutual friends.

I was not certain who I would see, much less what they(he) would look like. I noticed . . . then saw this goofy looking beatnik following them. Glory be! I had made arrangements at a local hotel for a twin bed room. Since the hour was not early (that's Chinese sentence pattern translated into English) and we anticipated an early departure, I felt the hotel bit was best. It also kept down possible recognition on a. . . . Too, our area is uncertain in terms of where one's loyalties stand. We just didn't want some lovely . . . recognizing our (Peng) . . . went on to . . . and we two stayed together. (Peng) was so filled with excitement and disbelief that he couldn't even think of sleep. We sat up until 3:30 talking and then I begged for an hour's sleep. The nutty guy at the hotel desk called us at 4:30 (I had asked him to call at 5:30) (Peng) was up and brushing his mop and fixing his boxing glove. What a sight it was. One of the loveliest sights was to see him peel off all that garb he was wearing. When he finally got near humanity, I could see the results of his previous months of worrying and concern. He had really lost a lot of weight. But the spirit and twinkle of eye were still with him.

We took a cab to the . . . about 6:00 and arrived in quick time. I had spent days working through all the possibilities . . . and found each possibility had its inherent danger. (Peng) felt no fear about laying over in . . . so he agreed with my plan. We felt the chance of laying over in . . . for from 1-8 hours was better than waiting so long here. Hopefully our decision was correct. (Peng) was so excited that he started down the stairs without even saying good-bye. He caught himself and turned to say good-bye and thanks. I was touched from tail to toe. (A second recollection. While sitting on our beds chatting, I said to (Peng), "It's a wonderful feeling to know that when there is someone in the world who is concerned for human dignity, freedom and self-expression for a given people, that there are persons around willing and eager to help." Peng thought for a minute and then said, "That's what is so humbling about the whole thing.")

I went back to my spot on . . . and . . . watched . . . marking the beginning of new hope for those we love. The beginning of a new day.

I felt safer and more relaxed at the second stop. After wandering around for several hours, I resumed my trip. At the last stop before I reached Sweden I called Mrs. Gawell at Lidingo. We had been writing to each other since I was released from prison in 1965. I knew Mrs. Gawell and other Swedish friends were most anxious about my fate. When the phone call got through and she knew I had successfully escaped from Formosa, she exclaimed: "It can't bé true!"

I arrived at Stockholm at about 12:30 A.M. in the darkness of a January night and on what proved to be the coldest day of the year. Officials had been alerted who knew that I would arrive without travel documents of any sort. The temperature was twenty-five degrees below zero. Three couples had come to welcome me, bringing sweaters, boots, gloves, a muffler, and a fur hat, all of which they insisted I put on, on the spot. I must have looked grotesque. We paused in a building for about ten minutes while the police made a simple record of my name only and requested very politely that I return the following day to complete the required information after I had had a chance to rest. I was indeed in a new world.

These new Swedish friends were very kind. They were active and efficient members of Amnesty International. They had been notified of the approximate time I would leave Formosa, and they had been exceedingly concerned until they received my telephone call. These hours, they knew, were the most critical in the life of every political escapee. I also learned later that one of the friends who greeted me had been called next morning by another member of the Amnesty group. When asked, "How is he? What is he like?" she had answered, "He looks horrible!" Undoubtedly my disguise and beard had created a most unattractive sight.

I was driven to the suburban home of a couple who had

agreed to take me in. They welcomed me most cordially, although it was by then 2:30 in the morning. There were flowers in my room and cards welcoming me to Sweden. I showered and fell into bed, exhausted, but even so my last thoughts before sleep were of the contrast between this civilized world and the world of fear and of cynical politics from which I had now escaped.

The next morning my hosts, Mr. Lunden and his British wife, accompanied by Mrs. Karin Gawell of Amnesty International, took me to complete the entry formalities left unfinished in the early morning hours. The first thing that I had to do for the Swedish authorities was to prove that I was really Peng Mingmin. Fortunately, some years earlier I had had an occasion to present an autographed copy of my French book to a noted professor in Göteborg who now volunteered to confirm my identity and professional reputation. Opinions had been solicited from others who were familiar with Formosan affairs or with my academic career in Canada and France.

The immigration officers were most courteous at every point, but they questioned me with meticulous care. Our interview required more than three hours.

Political asylum in Sweden requires formal approval at the cabinet level, hence about one month was required to complete the certification. After spending four days at the Lundens' home, I was invited to move into the home of a most distinguished Swedish scientist, Professor Carl Gustav Bernhard, a member of the Nobel Committee and later president of the Swedish Royal Academy of Science. It was a big house, superbly located, commanding a sweeping view of the harbor below. Here I had the good fortune to stay while I remained in Sweden.

ONCE THE IMMIGRATION RECORDS were set in order and I was safely in Sweden my first problem was how to break the news in Formosa. It could not be delayed too long, but it had been agreed that I should wait until certain people had left the island, those who had come in to help me and had made the project a success. They were to cable me in code when all was clear.

No message came. Ten days had passed since my departure. My escape might be discovered at any time. Had they been trapped? I was beginning to be deeply troubled when at last the signal came. They had been so relaxed after I left that they had decided to enjoy their stay, making a leisurely ten day tour around the island.

On reaching Stockholm I had written to friends in New York to say all was well and to be ready to release the brief announcement I had prepared. But there was a premature leak in New York, my friends in Japan were alerted, and called me in Sweden. We agreed that the announcement should be made immediately. First, however, I sent an open cable to my wife saying, "Sorry I left without warning you. I am safe and in good spirits."

My wife received this message. The government was notified by the cable office but refused to believe its authenticity. The first thought was that a sympathizer had sent it, just to cause trouble, or that it was premature. At once a great alert went out, fishing ports, airports, Keelung and Kaohsiung were blocked, and all people leaving the island were carefully examined. Scores of my friends and known political activists were picked up for questioning and had their houses searched. Li Ao, Hsieh, and Wei were detained for prolonged interrogation.

Immediately after my escape became known at Taipei, my wife and son and other members of my family there were seized, and my brother, arrested at Kaohsiung, was flown to the capital. All were subjected to twenty-four hours of continuous interrogation before being released, but were strictly forbidden to tell anyone of the ordeal. My son bore up very well under this grueling examination.

As I rested among friends during these first few days of freedom I thought of my family. From the beginning to the end of the ordeal they all behaved with extreme courage, calmness, and understanding. No one complained. My mother, my sister, my brothers, my wife, and my children all gave me tremendous support and the spiritual strength to resist demands of the party apparatus, the military, and the Investigation Bureau agents. Although they did not know it, they gave me courage to plan my escape. My son was only thirteen years old at the time of my arrest, a junior high school student. He had sensed the importance of this upheaval in our family life but did not complain. He had been doing extremely well in school before the crisis, and in the next term his grades dropped a bit, but then went back up. My daughter was not quite eight years old in September 1964, too young to comprehend all the details of the case but well aware of a crisis. The house was raided and then closely watched, but she never showed fear nor did she mention it to her mother, thus sparing my wife the difficulty of attempting explanations. At the time of my escape both children were again doing very well in school.

My successful escape had stirred up a hornet's nest. Senior government officers were certain that I could not be in Sweden because their records, the reports of their subordinates, showed that I had been traveling here and there in Formosa until the very day the news of my escape became known, almost three weeks after I left my house in Taipei. According to these reports, I had been staying in the best hotels, eating at expensive restaurants, and enjoying the cinema. The proof in their hands were the police bills charged against the special account for my surveillance.

Then the truth became evident. During the months in which I had so often secluded myself for long periods, and probably since I was released from prison in 1965, and during the weeks *after* I had left the island, my guards, the Investigation Bureau agents, and the police had been submitting falsified accounts, false expense vouchers and claims, and pocketing the money.

Many senior officers in the Investigation Bureau lost their jobs. Wang Kan was dismissed. Director Shen, in true Chinese fashion, asked "to be punished." Although he was spared, the deputy director was dismissed. The agents who were supposed to have been watching me around the clock were jailed, and so were others in the I.B. hierarchy who should have been checking them out and may have been taking a percentage of the unearned expense payments. The department chief who had so viciously threatened me as we sat around the Christmas tree at the Investigation Bureau clubhouse was the highest ranking man to be sent to prison. He was the scapegoat at the higher levels, charged now with having pressed me too hard.

The rumor spread, prompted by the Nationalist government, that I left Formosa with the assistance of the CIA. Many people seem to suspect the CIA because they cannot imagine how anyone could escape from Formosa without the aid of the CIA. Unfortunately since so many people were involved, I am still unable to explain how I escaped without endangering those brave and loyal friends. I can say, however, that I have received no help from any government except, of course, the Swedish government which gave me political asylum.

I knew that many people who had stood up for me, had advocated lenience or had shown friendship and sympathy, might now be harassed. To counter this as best I could, I sent a number of letters, registering them so that they would attract attention, and in the expectation that they would be intercepted and read. To Mr. Liang, my lawyer, I explained briefly that I had found life unbearable under the Nationalist police regime and thanked him for his help in times past. To some I apologized for having been the cause of so much trouble, and asked them to understand my decision.

On the evening that the news broke in Formosa, my host Dr. Bernhard happened to be giving a party. Among the guests was the editor of a big Stockholm newspaper. Thinking to do him a favor, Dr. Bernhard introduced me with a brief comment upon my peculiar arrival in Sweden as a political refugee. He was polite but seemed not too much interested. On the following morning, when he had made his rather leisurely appearance at the downtown editorial offices, he found that wires were coming in from many quarters asking for information on my escape. He called me at once, asking me not to talk to other newspapers for twenty-four hours so he could have an exclusive interview. For a few days there was a stir of interest and within the week a local television interview was broadcast.

Immediately a crank letter came in, written by a member of a "Swedish-Chinese Friendship Association," the type of group the Nationalists have sponsored to lobby for them throughout the world. This abusive note had been addressed to me in care of the Soviet embassy and had passed from there to the Immigration Office and so reached my hands. It accused me of being a traitor and a Communist.

This sort of thing could be expected and was unimportant, but I was altogether unprepared for the Japanese reaction in Sweden.

Immediately after my escape became known, the angry Nationalists asked governments around the world to bar me. They were particularly insistent in Washington and Tokyo, for the Independence Movement was gaining strength in the United States and Japan, and each had a Formosan resident population numbering in the thousands. An arrest warrant was issued in Taipei. To back this up, every Nationalist agency abroad was instructed to blacken my name and brand me as a criminal.

I did not know then what Washington's reaction might be, but I knew that Japan had no doctrine of political asylum and was generally very callous on the subject. I learned that the Japanese government had taken up my case at the cabinet level. The decision was to cooperate with Taipei. Taipei and Tokyo were in conflict just then. The Sato government was under great domestic pressure to expand commerce with Communist China, but at the same time Japan had large investments in and a most profitable trade with Formosa. Taipei had often protested Japan's trade with continental China. My case seemed to offer Tokyo an opportunity to appease the Nationalists to some degree at no cost to

Japan. No one in the government showed much interest in the humanitarian aspects of such a case, and there were precedents in which Formosan expatriates living in Japan had been delivered over to the Nationalists, sacrificed in heartless political and economic deals.

The Japanese ambassador at Stockholm was instructed to find out where my next destination might be, and made himself slightly ridiculous. Apparently it was thought I might try to smuggle myself into Japan. The ambassador himself called on the director of the Swedish Immigration Office. He was told that my future destination was not known nor was it of interest to Sweden. The ambassador then sent his secretary to the Immigration Office to state clearly that Japan would not admit me. Since I had no intention of going to Japan, this was absurd, and the absurdity was compounded when the ambassador again sent a request that the Swedish government prevent my going to Japan. The astonished Swedish officials observed that it was up to Tokyo to prevent my entry into Japan, not Stockholm; moreover, it was not Sweden's responsibility or privilege to tell me what I should do.

Meanwhile I had taken temporary employment while waiting the formal Swedish cabinet decision concerning political asylum. In the first weeks after my arrival I was extremely tired. Relaxation of tension made itself felt. I was quite prepared to learn the Swedish language, but this would take some time. Fortunately the husband of one of the Amnesty International's active members was curator of the Asian Section of the Stockholm Museum of Ethnography and was custodian of materials relating to the Sven Hedin expeditions, books, documents, maps, which had not yet been fully catalogued. There was a budget for the work, and I received a temporary appointment as specialist cataloguer. My host, Professor Bernhard, with great kindness, took me to the museum every day on his way into the Karolinska Institute, where he was a Professor of Medicine.

Within the month formal action was taken by the Swedish

government. I was granted political asylum, an alien passport was issued, and I was now free to travel. I felt that I had an identity again, and this official act on my behalf brought great relief.

I asked the Swedish government to admit my family if it could be arranged for them to leave Formosa. Permission was granted. I learned then that my wife had already written directly to Yen Chia-kan, the premier and vice-president, requesting permission to leave the island with the two children. She pointed out that although my son was now of military age, he would be exempted from conscription because of a hyperthyroid condition, and under the supervision of the *Taita* Medical School specialists, he constantly had to take certain drugs. The hospital records were available to support the case. She registered the letter in order to secure a record of receipt. The receipt-acknowledgment form was returned, but there was no reply. I could only conclude that my family were considered hostages.

The American press carried stories of my successful transit to Sweden. Soon letters began to reach me from old friends. Through *Newsweek's* London office a letter was forwarded to me from the Stanford girls, living in New York and in California, who offered to assist me in any way they could. One of them launched a letter-writing campaign among her friends, designed to urge the State Department to admit me to the United States.

To my surprise, the Japanese embassy at Stockholm continued to pursue a curious course. I could only assume that Tokyo was eager to do Taipei a special favor just then, or that Taipei had attached a price to something Tokyo desired. Soon after I took up my temporary work at the Ethnographical Museum, the embassy's first secretary invited the museum's Asian section chief to have lunch with him and then in rather tactless fashion attempted to find out how I had been introduced to the museum, under what circumstances I was living, and what I proposed to do. He showed great concern lest I might try to slip into Japan, and made it clear that if I did, I would be arrested and sent to

Formosa. He then asked his luncheon guest to please notify the embassy if I were ever absent from my job, or showed any interest in leaving Sweden. The museum representative bluntly told him that he was not interested in spying on behalf of the Japanese embassy. The matter should have ended there, but the ambassador's underlings kept calling the museum on his behalf from time to time to ask if I were still working there.

I remained at the museum for about one month, clearing up a backlog of uncatalogued materials. My hosts had a lovely house at the seaside about two and one-half hours' drive from the city, and we went there with the children to spend quiet weekends. Soon I began to receive letters and inquiries from branches of Amnesty International in Europe. Chatham House in London, the Institute for International Affairs, the London School of Oriental Studies, and the British offices for Amnesty International each invited me to London to speak on Formosan problems and to discuss the general problem of political prisoners. A schedule was arranged.

To my surprise, when I applied for a British visa, complications arose. There was delay after delay. When my London hosts pressed for information at the British Foreign Office, they were told that the matter was under consideration. Up through the bureaucratic ranks it went, until one Sunday I received a call telling me that the question was now being discussed with the foreign minister himself. Finally, less than twenty-four hours before I was to leave for London, word came that my visa had been granted. Although it was Saturday, when the British consulate in Stockholm was usually closed, the appropriate officer most kindly arranged for me to come in for the necessary stamp on my papers. On reaching London, however, I was amazed to learn that the foreign ministry had instructed its people to stay away from any social or formal meetings at which I would be present. None showed up at Chatham House, for example, when I spoke there. I was given to understand that this avoidance was not personal, but had rather to do with Peking and the extremely delicate problem of British subjects then being held by the Peking government. I was being described as a "Formosan Independence Movement leader," and the Communists, like the Nationalists, were determined that the island of Formosa and its people must remain Chinese whether they wished to or not. The release of British subjects had to take precedence in London, and anything prejudicial to that object had to be avoided.

This was my second visit to London. I had not been much impressed by it in 1953 when I was a young tourist. This time I fell in love with the great city. In the week that I was there I managed to visit the Amnesty International offices almost daily. I had been warned that they were very plain, occupying a narrow, old, four-storied house with overcrowded rooms cluttered with desks, chairs, people, and papers. A full-time staff of a dozen persons with some part-time employees and some volunteers carried on with a spirit of devotion and great energy. The cluttered appearance belied an operation of great efficiency. I was discovering that Amnesty International attracts first-rate people. This organization was tremendously impressive to one who had so recently been helped to gain new life.

Soon after I returned to Stockholm and my job at the museum, I was invited again to London to attend the annual meeting of the British section of Amnesty International and from there flew to Geneva, Switzerland, to give some talks at meetings of the World Council of Churches.

The invitation to speak at Geneva on the situation in Formosa had come to me largely through Mrs. Richard Frank, a graduate of the Harvard Law School whose husband, also a Harvard Law School graduate, had been in the State Department and was now in private business in Switzerland. In Geneva Mrs. Frank worked as an administrative assistant to the Commission on International Affairs within the World Council of Churches. I had met her at a conference in Stockholm, young, idealistic, and dedicated to working toward a more humanistic and liberal relationship among governments and peoples. She had become interested in the Formosa problem and in the troubles of the Formosan Presbyterian church, and thus had asked me to visit Geneva for conversations with council members.

The Franks met me at the airport, took me to their home in the suburbs, and on the first evening entertained me at a country restaurant. It was my first glimpse of the French countryside in ten years. As we relaxed in the Franks' living room, and cows grazed quietly just outside the windows, we discussed the Far Eastern situation and Formosa's unhappy position on the edge of the Chinese world. I then spent some days in a round of talks with staff members of the World Council discussing the political and religious situation in Formosa, and talked with representatives of the International Red Cross. Members of the official International Red Cross Committee were obviously reluctant to meet me, stiff and unbending, meticulously careful to preserve and insist upon the apolitical, neutral character of the organization. They dealt with governments rather than with individuals. In the Geneva offices of the League of Red Cross Societies, on the other hand, the reception was much more open, and the only concern seemed to be humanitarian interest. I brought up the subject of my family, telling them of my wife's appeal to Premier Yen Chia-kan for an exit permit. These Red Cross officials noted that since the "villain" was gone and Sweden was willing to receive my family, there was no point for the Nationalists in keeping them. Obviously Taipei was holding them as hostages. The Geneva office had made informal inquiries at Taipei and there had been no response.

I flew back to Sweden, but was soon off to London again, where I received a letter from Canadian friends inviting me to visit them. This seemed to be a good idea. On application to the Canadian consulate I received a tourist visa with no difficulty and flew to Montreal and then to Toronto. There I renewed acquaintance with old friends, met with Formosan students, and after an exceedingly busy ten days, flew back to London for one week.

That was a very interesting week during which I enjoyed meeting my friends at Amnesty International and Formosans living in London and I had conversations with the editor of the *China Quarterly*. I also met the high commissioner for the Indian government in London. He had been stationed in Peking at the time of my escape. He said the Communists had made an outcry, indistinguishable in some respects from the outcry at Taipei. I was a "traitor to China," an "American stooge brought out of Taiwan to become active in the two Chinas plot," and much more in the same vein. Radio broadcasts and magazines, including the English-language *Peking Review,* had made a shrill attack, causing the foreign diplomatic corps to ask, "What's this all about?" There had been much discussion of the significance of these angry Chinese reactions in Peking as well as Taipei.

Then I received an urgent telephone call from Mrs. Bernhard in Stockholm saying that she had received a telephone call from a stranger who identified himself as a Chinese just arrived from Formosa. He had said that he was eager to see me, but as the conversation went on, she became suspicious and troubled. The caller's English was poor, interspersed with some Russian and a few words of Swedish, and he was somewhat rude in his manner. Mrs. Bernhard told him that I was not available, and she did not know when I would return. Then he became heated and sarcastic, saying, "Peng lives with you, and you say you don't know? So it's a secret? I'll ask you one question: What kind of passport did he use?" Mrs. Bernhard firmly repeated that she did not know, and hung up, but she was troubled; some years before a political refugee had been shot and the assassin had successfully left Sweden by plane. She therefore reported the incident to the police, and when I flew back to Stockholm after a month's absence, the chief of the airport police detail met me at planeside. Dr. Bernhard was also there, with his huge German shepherd dog, and we returned to the house without incident. Despite this excitement, I felt relaxed to be back home in Sweden, and on the next day we all went to the country for a sailing holiday.

This was all very pleasant, but my work at the museum was temporary. I had to look about for something of a more lasting nature and I resumed correspondence with the academic world in America. Professor Whitmore Gray at the University of Michigan Law School wrote assuring me of continuing interest at Michigan in the projects we had begun to discuss in 1966. He was to be in Moscow briefly and telegraphed that he would meet me in Stockholm at a certain place and hour, asking me to confirm this by wire at his hotel in Prague. I did this, but on the appointed day in Stockholm he failed to appear. I heard nothing further for ten days until he telephoned to me from Michigan, saying that he had not received my wire at Prague, and therefore had not stopped in Sweden. Was I still interested in a Michigan appointment?

Of course I was, and in the long correspondence that followed, I expressed my appreciation for the continuing interest and renewed offer. Professor Rhoads Murphey joined in the exchange in his capacity as director for the Center for Chinese Studies, and a joint appointment was proposed. The law school would provide office space and the center would become my academic base for research. I proposed to make an analysis of the prevailing legal system in Formosa under the Nationalist occupation.

The University asked if I could take the appointment in April 1970. It was then February and many technical problems had to be overcome, including visa problems.

When my Swedish friends learned that I contemplated going to Michigan, they protested. From a Swedish point of view it seemed a dangerous thing for me to do. European newspapers were filled with stories of violence in the American cities and of a crisis in law and order. My friends argued that it was suicidal. The Nationalists could easily arrange to have me killed. I raised this question in my correspondence and with American journalists who had come to interview me in Stockholm. The consensus seemed to be that although it was true that violence in the streets was a serious problem in many American cities, the Nationalists would be stupid to do me any physical harm. Public indignation would heavily damage the regime's reputation in the United States and might be fatal.

Although aware that political behavior, especially of the Nationalist Chinese, would not necessarily follow the reasoning or the logic advanced by my friends, I decided to apply for a visa permitting me to proceed to Michigan.

XIII

The View
from America

I was in touch with friends in America who made private inquiries at the State Department. We wanted to be fairly certain that I would be admitted to the country before I made formal application for a visa. The State Department made no commitment, but there was optimism. I was warned that there might be some delay, but that things would be worked out in due course.

Bearing a letter of introduction from Dr. Bernhard, one day I went to the American consulate in Stockholm, completed an application for a tourist visa, and presented it to a vice-consul. He was discouraging: I was a political refugee and unemployed, therefore I could not be considered a genuine tourist. Nevertheless, he agreed to forward the application to Washington. Then on April 24, 1970, two young Formosans attempted to assassinate General Chiang Ching-kuo in the lobby of a New York hotel. My friends became quite pessimistic, believing that now the State Department would be most reluctant to admit me to this country. The department was said to feel that the wounds created by my escape were still too fresh in Taipei and Peking; it was too soon to admit me to the United States.

But the academic year was approaching. We decided to act.

On July 31, I presented my formal application for an exchange visa, backed up by the university's formal invitation. The consulate had been expecting me to come in again, and I was invited to talk with a consul and a lady vice-consul. I began by saying that I understood this was a complicated matter, but that the university and I had to know soon what our course of action should be.

The consul was polite but blunt in letting me know that the embassy would have preferred that I did not request entry. "What is your purpose in applying for a visa?" he asked. I pointed out that the formal university invitation, in his hands, made my purpose clear.

"Are you going to engage in political activity?"

"How do you define political activity?" I asked. I observed that my field had been the study of political science and public law. My life has been devoted to research and teaching. I considered that my professional duties included making known my views on current affairs. I believed this was within the legitimate boundary of my academic work if I went to the United States. Professional comment on political matters would not constitute political activity in my view.

"But if, for example," the consul said, "a retired ambassador should recommend recognition of Communist China, I would consider that political activity." He then asked if I would seek out the media people to present my views.

"I don't know that I will seek them out, but I must say that if they seek me out, I shall not refuse my comment on current affairs."

Our prolonged conversation took a rather surprising turn when the consul asked if I would allow my name to be used on any letterhead. I replied that was unlikely; I had never done that sort of thing. He then asked me what I would do if my visa were refused. I could only say that I did not know. I said to myself that I would certainly not commit suicide.

My interrogator now pointed to the fine print on the application form. "Perhaps you have noticed that in this article there is a question about criminal record. Have you noticed this?" I replied that of course I had, but that I did not consider my case a criminal one.

He then asked, "Will you please write down the details of your case?" and I replied that it would not be necessary. The American embassy in Taipei had a full file on my case and I was sure they would supply details if they were asked to do so.

The consul seemed somewhat taken aback, saying only, "You must realize that every embassy does its own independent work," and on this rather embarrassing note he ended our conversation with the obsrevation that the ultimate decision on my application would be made in Washington.

During the next four weeks of that beautiful summer with the Bernhards I began to realize how deeply attached I had become to Sweden and my Swedish friends. I suspect that the Bernhard family secretly hoped in their hearts that it would prove impossible for me to enter the United States. Professor Bernhard had occasion to visit New York and Boston on professional business, and there he sought to solve my financial problem by approaching certain publishers. On returning to Stockholm he urged me to forget about going to the United States. "Stay here and write a book," he said.

I was not ready to contemplate a serious project, and I was entirely charmed with the atmosphere of Stockholm and overwhelmed by the kindness of my hosts and my Swedish friends. I was being treated like a member of the Bernhard family. We enjoyed good conversation and made many delightful excursions into the beautiful countryside. But from a professional point of view I was ill prepared to make a living. I could not continue to work in a museum, although I found it interesting. Almost everyone in Sweden seemed to speak English, but I could not speak Swedish, which was an enormous handicap professionally.

Six weeks passed and I was still waiting to hear from the

American consulate when one September morning the telephone rang before eight o'clock. The voice of the young vice-consul said, "Congratulations! A cablegram from Washington says that you are to get your visa. There is still some paper work, but I suggest you go ahead with your medical check."

On September 17, I took my documents to the embassy to receive my visa. This time I was greeted by a different consul in a more pleasant mood, who also congratulated me and made some flattering remarks. He was obviously well informed of my earlier career. As he handed me my completed papers he smiled broadly and said, "Of course you understand you are going to the university to do research and we hope you will not deviate from your original purpose. . . ."

When it became known that, at last, Washington had granted me permission to enter the country and take up my research program at the University of Michigan, the Nationalist government made a strong protest to the American ambassador in Taipei, and Taipei's ambassador to Washington went in person to the State Department to emphasize his government's objection.

The "sin of kinship" had its penalties; the board of directors of the Tamsui Institute of Business Administration had steadfastly resisted pressure to force my sister's resignation as president of the school, but now they were informed that the Ministry of Education would intervene directly and force the change by decree if she did not withdraw voluntarily. She was called by someone in the Nationalist party office who very politely advised her to resign, smoothly alluding to the Thomas Liao case when Liao's sister was imprisoned and his nephew condemned to death, until he gave up his political activities in Tokyo and returned to an informal captivity on Formosa.

The hint was unmistakable. The church synod under which the college operates arranged to meet earlier than usual, and in December 1970, accepted my sister's resignation, but refused to yield to a demand that it should be said that she had been removed for incompetence. Concurrently, the wife of a distant cousin, a woman who enjoyed traveling abroad, was abruptly notified that her passport had been canceled, and that she could no longer leave the island.

At the time my visa was granted, I had accepted two invitations, one to speak at a Swedish university and another to address a meeting of Amnesty International being held in Oslo. The first of these I canceled since I prepared to fly to the United States by way of Norway and England. Parting with my Swedish hosts and Amnesty International friends and leaving Sweden was difficult. This was the country that had given me asylum when my life was in danger and these friends had received me with a warmth and kindness it would be impossible to forget.

The Oslo meeting was held in a superbly beautiful ski resort not far from the city. Here I met many London friends, staff members of Amnesty International, and spoke to the conference on behalf of political prisoners throughout the world:

> Between those who are punished because they express their conscience honestly in words or in deeds, there seems to be a certain invisible, spiritual tie which binds them closely together despite the time and space which separates them and despite the fact that most of them have never known or seen each other. Such a tie which makes them feel like close comrades-in-arms results not only from the common predicaments in which they find themselves but also and especially from the firm conviction they share regarding certain basic rights, fundamental freedom and human dignity (although their personal positions may differ greatly concerning any particular political or social issue). On the strength of this spiritual and invisible solidarity which exists between these people, may I be permitted to say a few words on their behalf.
>
> First, on behalf of those, like myself, who have already been punished and spent time in prison, but were fortunate enough to survive those unfortunate experiences and have regained our freedom—on their behalf I wish to say that words cannot express our

gratitude to *Amnesty International*. We owe, to no small degree, our new freedom to this group and it has helped us to rediscover the real value of freedom and liberty.

Second, on behalf of those prisoners who have already been adopted by *Amnesty International* but are still languishing behind prison bars in many corners of the world—on their behalf I wish to express to you their deep appreciation for what you have done and are doing for them. They know that the efforts of *Amnesty International* may not necessarily result in their immediate release but these efforts constantly remind them that they are not forgotten. They feel that someone beyond the prison walls still cares about them. This knowledge brings them indescribable consolation and joy, if one can speak of any joy in prison. You give them the only hope to live for, you give them moral strength, you inspire their spirits, and you keep them from completely losing their faith in mankind in spite of the fact that they are living in painful and humiliating conditions of physical and mental torture.

Third, on behalf of those who are imprisoned because of the honest expression of their own conscience but whose imprisonment is not yet known to the outside world and to *Amnesty International*—on their behalf I wish to convey a desperate cry for discovery and an urgent appeal for whatever assistance could be extended to those who are still living in darkness and despair.

Last, on behalf of those who are in trouble because of the honest expression of their conscience, who are not yet imprisoned but who are in the precarious situation of being subject to arrest at any time—on their behalf I wish to express the hope that the existence of *Amnesty International* will be some sort of deterrent factor, and its worldwide activities will lessen the danger they are in and will offer them certain protection.

One is unfortunately accustomed to verbally dividing the world in various ways, such as East and West, Christian and non-Christian, capitalist and socialist, free world and enslaved world, developed and underdeveloped, civilized and uncivilized—whatever these words mean. However, I believe many of us have lived long enough and have seen enough to realize how superficial and meaningless this kind of dichotomy is.

If one really has to divide the world into two parts, I think the only significant way to do it is to speak of the part in which the honest and free expression of one's own conscience is considered as one of the supreme virtues to be exalted and the other part in which the free and honest expression of one's conscience is considered as an unpardonable crime to be severely punished.

It is my earnest wish that *Amnesty International* will not only be the guardian of "prisoners of conscience" but also will become the guardian of the very conscience of all humanity itself. On behalf of all those I have mentioned I would like to say thank you again from the bottom of my heart.

I flew from Oslo to Detroit via London and Montreal at the moment of the 1970 hijacking crisis, and at London airport passengers were searched and all baggage taken off for a thorough check. On the afternoon of September 29, I came through customs at Detroit, reentering the United States for the first time in nearly ten years. My last entry had been on a diplomatic passport issued by Nationalist China; this time I traveled on papers issued in Sweden on behalf of a political refugee.

My new life in America began with a very pleasant call on Professor Rhoads Murphey, director of the Center for Chinese Studies in the University of Michigan. He tactfully sought to discover if I planned to become politically active while in the States and if I had any special understanding with the State Department on this point. In other words, had the department exacted any pledge limiting my freedom of speech or action? I replied by telling him what I had told the consular officers in Stockholm. I still considered myself an academic, I expected to do my work in law and political science, and in the course of my work I would undoubtedly comment on current world affairs.

Professor Murphey observed in turn that he saw no reason I should not be as free as any American professor in the same field. I had been invited to Michigan to write on any subjects I might choose, and I had proposed to prepare a study of "Law and the Politics of 'National Emergency' in Formosa." The invitation to Ann Arbor had been issued first in 1968 and had been repeated in the following years when I was under surveillance in Taipei. To some scholars in the Chinese field, Formosa was "only a part of China" and the only part to which they had access for field research. A question was raised: "Will Peng's presence at the Center for Chinese Studies now jeopardize its delicate relationship with the Nationalist government of Taiwan?" Some center associates suggested that I should be warned not to engage in political activity that might affect the center's interests, strain its relations with Taipei, or hamper the university's programs in Formosa. But, after discussion, it was left to individual faculty members to make their views known to me, and in subsequent weeks they did. I found the intellectual atmosphere stimulating, and my research project was soon expanded to cover the international legal history and status of Formosa during the last hundred years.

Soon I began to receive invitations to speak to academic groups, church organizations, public forums on international affairs, and Formosan student meetings. Newspapers and magazines asked for articles concerning the Formosa problem. Using weekends, holidays and inter-session vacations, I traveled across the United States, attending seminars, meeting students, and addressing groups interested in international affairs.

My first trip away from the University of Michigan was to Kansas State University in Manhattan, Kansas, where nearly 300 Formosans held a Formosan Thanksgiving dinner. I was deeply impressed by the enthusiasm and warm spirit of those present. On that occasion I made several new friends with whom I still maintain a close association.

On one occasion I spent ten days at Harvard, then went to the West Coast to visit the California Institute of Technology, Stanford University, and the University of California at Berkeley. My position was stated in the public speeches I made in those institutions.

I pointed out that as far as the political situation within and without Formosa is concerned, it is as though time has been suspended for more than twenty years. The political calendar of Formosa still reads 1949, the year when the Chinese Nationalist government went into exile on Formosa. Since then, there has been complete stagnation. The position taken by the Nationalist government remains the same, that is, that it is the only legitimate government of all of China, the Communist victory on the mainland is but a temporary state of Communist rebellion, and that the government in Formosa will soon reconquer the whole of China. It has become a cliché to say that the government in Formosa in the past twenty years has been government by fiction and government by myth—the fiction that this government is the government of the whole of China, and the myth that this government is going to return to China in the very near future.

Domestically, the state of siege and martial law proclaimed in 1949 by the government in Formosa has been maintained down to the present and, according to the government, this state must continue until the day of the Nationalists' reconquest of all of China—that is, indefinitely. For more than twenty years, the government in Formosa has been practicing what might be called "the politics of national emergency." Constitutional guarantees have been suspended and demonstrations, petitions, and strikes are forbidden under penalty of death. Ostensibly to combat the national crisis, emergency policies have been adopted, emergency laws passed, and emergency practices established. The peculiarity of the situation is that those emergency measures have often been invoked not to remove the cause of the national crisis, but rather to perpetuate the state of emergency itself, because this is the most expedient means, and perhaps even the only one for preserving the life and power of the regime. The application of the politics of national emergency in defense of Nationalist political myths has had devastating effects on community life in Formosa.

I also noted that the international picture was not much more encouraging. The Nationalist Chinese government, which in fact represented no one, had incredibly been assumed to represent

China at all international forums for the past twenty years, to the great detriment of international order. One can say that this government does not represent anyone because, since the people of China clearly rejected it more than twenty years ago, it cannot represent the people of China. Nor does it represent the people of Formosa, because in the past twenty years there has been no general election there on the national level, and eighty-five percent of the population have only three percent of the seats in the national legislative bodies.

I noted also at the same time, a new and rather unsettling tendency developing among some of the enlightened and liberal leaders in various countries. Appalled by the absurdities of the myths of the Nationalist Chinese government, which are certainly an affront to their reason, intelligence, and common sense, and eager to reject them, they sometimes tend to go to the opposite extreme and begin to embrace a new set of myths. These seem to be no more realistic and no more constructive than the old. These new myths are as follows: first, that Formosa has been, and therefore will always be, an integral and inalienable part of China; and second, that in order to bring to an end China's semicolonial status, in order that China may achieve recognition as a sovereign equal and regain her national self-respect, it is necessary to le her purely and simply annex Formosa.

This is but another set of myths, but the myths are supported and nourished by strong emotional and sentimental feelings. These are several and quite understandable. First, there is the deep and lingering sense of guilt troubling the Western conscience due to the extended period of injustice and humiliation inflicted upon China by the Western powers. Second, there is the resultant urge to atone for this guilt. Third, the West is fascinated and transfixed as it witnesses the dizzying sight of the birth, growth, leap, and convulsions of the new China. Fourth, there is an increasing fear haunting the Western mind, confronted with the prospect of China's emergence as a major nuclear power. These feelings—guilt, fascination, consternation, and fear—are all justified to some extent. I believe that to react to such feelings by meekly accepting whatever China says and does as good and reasonable is irresponsible. I respect the sincerity and honorable motives of those who tend to embrace these new myths, but I couldn't help questioning the degree of their understanding of the situation in Formosa. I thought that in reference to these new myths some facts about Formosa should be brought into the open.

The first myth is that Formosa has been, and will have to remain, an integral and inalienable part of China. It seemed to me to be useful to examine this from the perspective of Formosan history and international law. As a noted historian in this field has pointed out, Formosan history is largely the record of a search for self-determination and autonomy. Throughout Formosan history, the descendants of Chinese immigrants who settled on this frontier island have struggled constantly to reduce continental Chinese influence in the island's affairs, and even to remove themselves from continental control altogether. This is illustrated in a saying known to all historians in this field: "Formosa experiences every three years an uprising, every five years a rebellion." On the other hand, historically, China's attitude toward Formosa has not exactly been one of fervent affection. China has always regarded Formosa as a barbarous island inhabited by rebels, bandits, pirates, misfits, and opium addicts— which it probably was. In the seventeenth century because of the difficulties the island was causing the Chinese government, Peking once even seriously considered evacuating those few Chinese settlers who had by then settled on the island. As late as the latter part of the nineteenth century, when the crews of foreign vessels wrecked offshore from Formosa were massacred by the inhabitants, the Chinese government once took the position that it could not be held responsible for acts committed "outside its jurisdiction." In 1869, the Chinese government went so far as to allow the head of eighteen aboriginal tribes in Formosa to conclude a treaty with the United States. After her defeat in the

Japanese-Chinese War in 1895, China ceded Formosa to Japan. This caused resentment among Formosans, who were angry that China was willing to sacrifice them, and led to an abortive attempt to remove themselves altogether from both Chinese and Japanese control and establish an independent Republic of Formosa. This republic lasted only 148 days, but the incident is symbolic in the history of relations between Formosa and China. Japanese administration in Formosa lasted a half century, during which Formosa was completely cut off politically and culturally from China. Then, at the end of the Second World War, the Nationalist Chinese government took over Formosa, but only four years later, in 1949, Formosa was again politically separated from China, and Formosa and China have been ruled ever since then by different regimes. In other words, the connection between Formosa and China before 1895 was so loose as to be almost nominal, and relations were tumultuous; Formosa was constantly trying to remove itself from continental control. Furthermore, during the seventy-five years from 1895 to the present, there have been only four years of political union between Formosa and China, from 1945 to 1949, and those four years were by no means the happiest in Formosan history. It was during this period, on February 28, 1947, that there was a general uprising of Formosans against Chinese rule, which resulted in the massacre by Chinese troops of over 20,000 Formosan leaders.

Who are the inhabitants of Formosa? Among the fourteen million people on the island, eighty-five percent are native Formosans. To be sure, they are of Chinese extraction, but their ancestors began to immigrate to the island in the thirteenth century. Immigration continued until 1895, when Japanese prohibitions on Chinese immigration to Formosa cut off all contact with the mainland. As a result, they have undergone centuries of experience which is different from that of the Chinese. They have acquired and developed their own personality and identity which is different from that of the Chinese. After the Second World War, over two million continental Chinese have joined in the experience of these native Formosans, and further shaped Formosan distinctiveness. By now the inhabitants of Formosa are about as Chinese as Americans or Australians are British.

Moreover, from the point of view of international law, in the seventy-five years since 1895, when Formosa was formally ceded by China to Japan, there has been no international treaty or act with legal binding force reattaching Formosa to China. The Cairo Declaration of 1943 and the Potsdam Declaration of 1945, which stated that Formosa should be given to China, have no legal binding force. They are merely statements of the common purpose of the war. The Instrument of Surrender signed by Japan on September 2, 1945, which accepted these two declarations, is at most a commitment on the part of Japan to renounce its sovereignty over Formosa at a later time. The Peace Treaty signed between Japan and the Allied Powers in 1951, and the Peace Treaty signed between the Nationalist government and Japan in 1952 merely stated that Japan renounced its rights, claims, and title over Formosa, but nowhere did these treaties specify the beneficiary of the Japanese renunciation. On the other hand, the Atlantic Charter of 1941 stated that there should be "no territorial changes that do not accord with the freely expressed wishes of the people concerned." Article 1 of the United Nations Charter provides that "the principle of equal rights and self-determination of peoples" should be one of the basic guiding principles of international relations, and the Charter further stipulates in Article 103 that in the event of conflict between the obligations of the members of the United Nations under the Charter and their obligations under any other international agreements, the obligations under the Charter shall prevail. In view of the foregoing, so far as Formosa is concerned, the Cairo Declaration and the Potsdam Proclamation not only lack legal effect, they violate the letter and spirit of the United Nations Charter and must be regarded as superseded by the latter. Therefore, from the point of view of international law, it can only be said that Formosa was detached from Japan, but has not been attached to any other country. That is, Formosa's international legal status has been undetermined since the end of the Second World War. It is not suggested that international affairs should or could be solved entirely on legalistic grounds, but, given the present international and domestic circumstances of Formosa, the fact that its legal status has not been settled since the end of the war must have some bearing on its future.

Those are the facts which I brought up in reference to the myth that Formosa has been and so will have to remain an integral and inalienable part of China. From these facts one can clearly see the fallacy in this first myth.

As for the second myth, that is, that in order to end China's semicolonial status, in order that she may achieve international recognition as a sovereign equal, and regain her national self-respect, it is necessary to let China purely and simply annex Formosa. The fact is that now, two decades after the revolution, the new China *has* ended the old China's semicolonial status. It *has* achieved international recognition as a sovereign equal. It *has* regained its national self-respect. Perhaps the Western conscience needs to be troubled by what the West has done to the old China, but it need not, because of its guilty conscience, accept whatever the new China says or demands. In any event, China's emotional claims to Formosa have nothing to do with her semicolonial status, her sovereign equality, or her self-respect. They have to do with civil war, with the Nationalist government, and with the maintenance of that government on Formosa by the United States. The truth is that during the early period of this century, when China was desperately struggling to end its semicolonial status, to abolish the unequal treaties and achieve recognition as a sovereign equal, and to regain its national self-respect, Formosa was never the most important issue. China has accepted the fact that Formosa was legally separated from it. Chairman Mao Tse-tung himself has recognized the permanent separation of Formosa from China. It was only after 1949, when the Nationalist government was exiled to Formosa and, supported by the United States, continued to wage war against China, to proclaim its intention to reconquer China, and to disseminate inflammatory propaganda against China—it was only after this that China began to make such emotional claims to Formosa.

Those are the historical facts and realities which I thought should be mentioned in my lectures in reference to the second myth that Formosa be given to China as a price to be paid for the reconciliation of China and the West.

I said, if we discard all fiction and myth and try to see a genuine solution to the Formosan problem, it seems that there are certain basic points which must be taken into consideration. First, it would be unrealistic on the part of the United States to think it can maintain its military presence in Formosa permanently. Second, it would be unrealistic on the part of China to think it can simply annex Formosa as an integral part of its territory. Third, it would be foolish on the part of the Nationalist Chinese on Formosa to think they can maintain their totalitarian rule in Formosa forever. Fourth, in view of Formosa's geographic proximity to China and their geopolitical relations, it would be foolish on the part of the inhabitants in Formosa to imagine that they can live in a state of hostility with China. Fifth, it would be unfair, to say the least, to the people in Formosa to disregard their particular history, distinctiveness, and identity, which result from their unique history, and to deny their aspiration to govern themselves, to decide for themselves their own destiny. This aspiration is only natural, human, and legitimate. In discussing the possible solutions to the Formosan problem it would seem to be fair and sound to accept the basic proposition that no one can speak for Formosans but Formosans themselves, no one can dictate to them where and to whom they should belong, and no one has the right to ask them to accept liberation by some outside power, as true liberation can only come from the people directly concerned.

I emphasized that the real solution to the Formosan problem

was in the hands of the Formosans themselves; that is to say, Formosans should be allowed to decide their own destiny. Let them decide their own political future for themselves.

I appreciated that it is difficult for the Chinese to understand that modern nation-states are not formed on the basis of biological origin, culture, religion, or language, but rather on a sense of common destiny and a belief in shared interests. There are subjective feelings which rise out of a common history, and are not necessarily related to these objective criteria of biological origin, culture, religion, and language. In modern history, examples abound in which people of similar biological origins and religious, cultural, and linguistic backgrounds constitute separate nation-states because they lack these feelings, and examples also abound in which people of different origins and backgrounds constitute a single nation-state as a result of these feelings of commonalty. No state has the right to claim sovereignty over a territory based only on some biological, cultural, religious, or linguistic affinities with the inhabitants of the territory in disregard of the will of the people themselves.

I urged the Chinese to accept the principle that any group of people, given certain geographical and historical conditions, are entitled to decide for themselves their own political future, and should even be entitled to constitute an independent political entity if they so desire, regardless of their biological, cultural, religious, or linguistic affinities to other political entities.

I also said the Chinese should discard their archaic, almost feudalistic, obsession to claim as a member of the Chinese family anyone of Chinese ancestry, however removed from China geographically or historically.

I asked the Chinese to distinguish ethnic origin, culture, and language on the one hand, and politics and law on the other, and to abandon the idea that those who are ethnically, culturally, and linguistically Chinese must be politically and legally Chinese as well. I asked them to stop vilifying as traitors those who desire self-determination for themselves. I pointed out that if for his own convenience, an individual Chinese becomes a naturalized citizen of another country such as the United States, and this is not regarded as an act of treason toward China—and I believe it should not be so regarded—if this is the case, then neither should the legitimate aspirations, based on historical and political realities, of a group of people of Chinese ancestry to constitute a political entity and create their own nation be so regarded.

I wanted the Chinese to understand that one can be proud of his Chinese ethnic and cultural heritage and still wish to be politically and legally separate from China, in the same way as General Dwight D. Eisenhower, who was proud of his German ancestry, was not considered a traitor because he led the Allied armies against Germany.

I thought that if international organizations, and especially the United Nations, still have any reason for being, any significant role to play in international politics, the case of Formosa is precisely one into which they should move to help work out a fair solution.

I observed that those who advocate solving the Formosan problem in accordance with the principle of self-determination have often been identified with the Free Formosa Movement. It is quite clear that Formosans resent the totalitarian repressive regime on Formosa today, that they are not prepared to accept the Communist government in China, and that they want to extricate themselves once and for all from the interminable conflict between China's Nationalist and Communist parties. So, it is also quite clear that, given a free choice, Formosans would probably choose to constitute a political entity separate from both Nationalist and Communist China.

I knew that in view of Chinese claims to Formosa, some doubt had been cast upon its viability as a separate political entity. But, I said, I believe China constantly vows to liberate Formosa because the Nationalist Chinese regime remains in Formosa, supported by the United States, and continues to proclaim its intention to invade China, intentionally maintaining an inflammatory situation in the Straits of Formosa. This prolongs the Chinese civil war and keeps Formosan-Chinese relations in a state of permanent hostility. But I believe the Formosan people bear no grudge against the Chinese people—on the contrary, they want to live in close and friendly association with the Chinese people. Once the Formosan people free themselves from the Nationalist Chinese regime and form a genuine representative government of their own, I believe they will declare to the world their *de facto* and *de jure* severance from past Chinese internal conflict. I believe the new Formosan government will spare no effort to establish close economic, commercial, and cultural relations with China. It may even be willing to explore the possibility of working out with China a formula through which the basic national and foreign policy of the two countries could be coordinated, provided China does not meddle in the domestic affairs of the island and does not interfere with its free social, political, and cultural development. Then Formosa will be able to contribute freely and to no small degree to the economic, social, and industrial construction of China. At the same time, I believe the Formosan people will do their best to maintain close and friendly relations with all countries regardless of their political views.

I hoped that China would realize it could gain more by recognizing and respecting a free Formosa than by forcibly annexing Formosa, that there was no reason why it should insist on conquering Formosa, which it could do only to the great detriment of its own image, prestige, and basic interests. If, as has often been pointed out, the Chinese Communist leaders, despite their often belligerent utterances, are in fact cautious and pragmatic in their actions, I saw no reason why they should not be persuaded to accept the above arrangement, which they would discover in time to be practical, fair, and in the best interests of all concerned. If, after all, China is pragmatic enough to tolerate the existence of Hong Kong, which it could take in three hours, or Macao, which it could take in thirty minutes, and if it is pragmatic enough to leave an independent state like Singapore alone, although it is composed predominantly of ethnic Chinese, I saw no reason why it could not be persuaded to be equally tolerant, reasonable and practical toward a peaceful, friendly Formosa, which could offer it considerable advantage. I was not saying that the status of Formosa is similar in every respect to that of Hong Kong, Macao, or Singapore, but was merely saying that I believe in the basic pragmatism of the Peking leaders, present and future, despite their militant words and revolutionary zeal, and I saw the possibility for negotiation and compromise, once the provocation that the Nationalist Government on Formosa constitutes is removed. I admitted the obstacles and difficulties which lie in the way of a solution to the Formosan problem should certainly not be underestimated. However, there is no easy way out of the Formosan impasse.

My classroom lectures concerned international law, criminal law, and case studies illustrating Chinese criminal procedures. In the semipublic lectures and in meeting with church groups and Formosan students I tried to present a Formosan view of the domestic and international situation as objectively as possible. In question-and-answer periods the subject of Formosa's future was invariably raised.

All this give-and-take with the American public was exhilarating. Perhaps few in my audience could appreciate what such freedom of speech and assembly means to one who has been arrested, court-martialed, and imprisoned for criticizing an administration. As I traveled, the local reactions of Nationalist Chinese agents revealed certain common patterns in Massachusetts, Michigan, California, Wisconsin, Ohio, and Canada. Apparently the Nationalist agencies in the United States believed they could destroy me by distributing a series of slanderous pamphlets describing me variously as a "Communist," "adventurer," "rapist," "CIA agent," and "stooge of the United States and Japan."

When it is announced that I am to appear in public somewhere, these agents release such pamphlets and distribute them to the people concerned a few days in advance. Next there is an attempt to mobilize Chinese students in the area. The Chinese consul for the region then arranges a dinner to which only Chinese students are invited. At the dinner-meeting I am described as a traitor, and the students are urged to protest my appearance, to demonstrate, picket, and disrupt proceedings and discussions in any way possible. Since the same questions are asked by students on each occasion, it becomes clear that the procedure has been worked out without much creative imagination. Some of the questions are fantastic, and one is inevitable: "You say there is no freedom in Taiwan, but if there is no freedom, how did you escape?" My audience laughs when I say that if someone manages to escape from prison, it does not mean democracy or freedom exists there; perhaps it means only that I was smarter than my jailors.

Another invariable comment runs: "You say Taiwan is so bad. Why then could you teach there, be a professor of political science and chairman of the university's department, and an advisor to the U.N. delegation?" My answer at almost every public meeting has had to be that "I became professor and chairman because of my academic record. I am a student of political science, and the more I examined the situation in Formosa, the more intolerable it became."

Running through all the questions is the moralistic criticism that I was awarded my positions in Formosa as personal favors from Chiang Kai-shek, and that I have now betrayed him. I have to assure my audiences that there is nothing personal in this; had I wanted to enjoy great personal advantage and to become more important at Taipei, I could have done so. On the contrary, I have chosen the uncomfortable life of a political exile.

A third standard question has been, "Are you a Chinese? If you are a Chinese, how can you do this sort of thing? Taiwan has always been part of China!" On this I have to remind my audiences that if historical connection becomes the basis of territorial claims, then England would have a claim upon the people of Massachusetts and Virginia, and Spain could revive claims upon the southwestern regions of the United States. I must remind my audience that seventeenth-century Europeans first opened Formosa to civilization, not China, and that as recently as 1875 the imperial laws of China forbade free migration from China to the island lying a hundred miles distant at sea. Formosa was not declared to be a province of China until 1887, and then only eight years later Peking ceded it to Japan. Formosa was settled by Chinese emigrants who were trying to leave China and make a new life for themselves overseas.

It has been no great surprise to learn that in some instances individual Chinese students have been paid as much as forty dollars for raising these questions.

On one occasion I accepted an invitation to speak at the University of Wisconsin on the topic, chosen by my hosts, of "Political Life in Formosa in the Past Twenty Years." This was a general subject not connected to the Formosan Independence Movement. The meeting went well from every point of view but when we came to the question-and-answer period, a Chinese stood up to demand that we talk about "my" independence movement. I noted that it was not "my" movement, and that it was not the subject for the evening. If I were invited to do so I would be glad to discuss problems of Formosa's future as I had already done on many occasions, but I was not prepared to talk about it in an off-hand or fragmentary manner and at this time. Then followed a typical reaction. When this Wisconsin meeting was written up by a Nationalist agent and published in a Hong Kong journal, it was said that I was a stupid fellow; if an American politician refused to discuss America's future and asked time to think about it, it would be political suicide.

On my tour of the West Coast in February, 1971, I was followed by a Chinese refugee employed in one of the largest West Coast academic research centers. He had taken time out from his proper duties to perform a special job, which was to heckle me. In the question-and-answer period following my presentation at

Cal Tech at Los Angeles, he attempted to respond to a question I had put to the audience, but his manner was so utterly absurd and nonsensical, and his English so awkward, that members of the audience laughed, and the pro-Nationalist Chinese among them were visibly embarrassed. He reappeared in my audience, busily taking notes, when I moved on to the University of California at Berkeley, 350 miles away. Then within a few weeks a series of Chinese-language articles began to appear in Hong Kong and in the United States. These carried "inside stories" with such titles as "How I Talked with Peng Ming-min" and "My Meetings with Peng Ming-min." The content was pure fantasy.

At every announced meeting, some representative of the Nationalist government is present. They are uninvited and have no proper business in the classrooms. At public lectures, Nationalist agents and officials, standing at the doors, attempt to recognize and identify every Formosan who attends. On some occasions, for example, at Stanford, Nationalist photographers have taken pictures of every Formosan who stands to ask questions. This is an obvious attempt to intimidate as well as to identify the suspect Formosan. The academic sponsors at Stanford protested but were met with the challenging retort, "This is a public meeting and a free country, isn't it?"

Nationalist versions of these meetings have been published in Chinese-language newspapers and magazines in the United States, Tokyo, and Hong Kong, distorting and often reversing the sense of my remarks. Very often they report things that I have never said and it is standard to say that my English was exceptionally poor, my presentations awkward, and my comments on the Taipei government libelous. On one occasion it was said that I was so pressed by my interrogators and so incapable of answering them, that I withdrew from the platform pleading an upset stomach!

Once when I was speaking at the University of Wisconsin on the subject of Formosa's complicated international legal status, I noticed several local Nationalist agents in the audience, together with a Chinese who had once been my student in Formosa and was known to be a Nationalist employee in the Chicago area. Some weeks later a similar scholastic gathering to discuss the same topic was arranged at the University of Michigan. Notices were not posted about campus until the morning of the event; nevertheless, when the evening session began, I saw this man again in the audience. He was not alone, however, for he had brought with him two militant blacks whose tough appearance and behavior can only have been intended to intimidate me.

As McGill University was celebrating its one hundred and fiftieth anniversary, the former Institute of International Air Law, renamed the Institute of Air and Space Law, celebrated its twentieth year. I was invited to be a guest speaker at the anniversary banquet but when I learned that there was some consternation elsewhere in Montreal because my hosts had asked me to speak on "The Chinese Representation Problem in the United Nations," I offered to give my place to some other less controversial speaker. The sponsors insisted that I accept, and some of the audience seemed surprised when I confined myself entirely to technical legal aspects of the case. This seems to have been the only public occasion at which the Nationalists did not have an agent present.

Curiously enough, the worst experience I have encountered in public speaking occurred in Canada soon after Ottawa recognized Peking. Although Nationalist Chinese officials had withdrawn, a considerable number of Nationalist student-agents remained in Canada. In addressing a scholastic group at the University of Windsor I attempted to explain the uneasy relationship between the great majority of Formosans and the two million continental Chinese now in Formosa. I was suddenly interrupted and challenged as a scholar to cite the book, chapter, page, and exact line on which I could find proof that the number of continental Chinese was two million, not more, not less. There was a physical attempt to disrupt our meeting, and for a moment it seemed as if these agents would actually attack me. The professor who chaired the meeting had to threaten to evict the trouble-makers before some degree of order was restored.

One day I was invited to take part in a luncheon-meeting panel discussion in New York, sponsored by a church organization. Too late and to the embarrassment of my hosts, it was realized that Taipei's ambassador to the United Nations had also accepted an invitation. We met agreeably enough and shook hands, but then the unhappy ambassador had a miserable time. He would not give direct answers to direct questions, preferring to ramble on about "Communist evil" and "the free world and the slave world." The chairman rather bluntly attempted to pull him back to specifics and a discussion of the Formosan problem, but without success; he refused to keep to the subject. Some little time later several prominent members of the International League for the Rights of Man sought a formal appointment with officials of the Nationalist United Nations Delegation. The reception was cold, for Taipei's U.N. office staff was troubled and puzzled by the allusion to the "rights of man," not quite knowing the purpose of the visit. Delay followed delay, but at last the three visitors were received. When they asked that the ambassador relay to Taipei a request, made on humanitarian grounds, that my family be granted exit permits and allowed to join me in exile, the official who had received them replied rudely and with a show of anger, "Peng is a criminal: He has deserted his family and this is against Chinese morality!" Nettled by this, one of the visitors retorted, "Is it not against Chinese ethics to keep families separated?"

It was a fruitless request. Nothing came of it, and my wife and children remained hostages.

The Chinese embassy in Washington continued to protest to the State Department about my presence in the United States. I am told that every public and semipublic appearance I had made in this country had been listed, and my discussions of Formosa's legal status and future were condemned as subversive activity. It was intimated that the Formosans in the United States were planning violence within the country; further assassination attempts, for example. I assume that this claim was designed to build up prejudice in the State Department and to jeopardize renewal of my visa. The University of Michigan authorities were told informally that a strong Nationalist protest had been made, and some faculty members passed the word along to me.

I often detect an unwitting romanticism among Chinese residing in America and in Chinese-American publications. They are very critical of Chiang Kai-shek. Until Ping-Pong diplomacy set in, followed by President Nixon's announced plans to travel to Peking, most articulate Chinese-Americans speaking in public were also carefully critical of Peking. Nevertheless they always talk of a beloved motherland, China. It is an abstraction, and it is to that abstraction that they seem to believe the Formosan people should belong. The fact is all those "Chinese patriots" have themselves chosen a long time ago to live under *neither* Chinese Communist *nor* Chinese Nationalist regimes. It seems to me presumptuous for them, now comfortably settled here, to try to dictate to the fourteen million Formosans that they must accept the rule of a government from which these "patriots" have themselves successfully escaped and to which they never intend to return.

My comments sometimes bring the retort that everyone knows both Nationalists and Communists are bad, but that someday all China must be one again, even if we have to wait fifty or a hundred years. I have to point out that it is easy for them, sitting here in America in safety and comfort, to declare that "Formosa must go back to China." I say let the future be the choice of our children, fifty or a hundred years hence. Formosans are suffering enough now; let them liberate themselves from the present regime and let them enjoy freedom and liberty *right now*.

There are about ten thousand Formosans living in the United States. They are graduate students and professional men and women for the most part, but even living here they are under great restraint. Harassment can take many forms. Some therefore say nothing, some do nothing more than give anonymous financial support to Formosan organizations. Every Formosan knows that there are Nationalist agents on every major university campus in the United States, watching them and reporting upon their activities. Members of their families at home may lose jobs, and bank credit may be denied their relatives. At worst, their passports may be canceled, forcing them to return to the island or to seek political asylum elsewhere.

This harassment is directed toward Formosans and not simply toward all critics of the Nationalist government. Many Chinese holding Chinese Nationalist passports have dared to be extremely critical of Taipei or to be openly in sympathy with Peking. This is a fact well known to the Nationalist authorities here and in Formosa, but there has yet to be a single case in which passports of such critics have been revoked, for they have not made the mistake of advocating a freedom of choice for the island people.

Taipei has been making great effort to destroy our Formosan identity. In recent years every student leaving Formosa has been individually warned by the garrison command that he must not belong to any Formosan organization of any kind. He is told, "If you want to belong to something, belong to a *Chinese* organization." Nevertheless, there are a number of Formosan social organizations at the larger student centers. Those who have become officers of these social groups, presidents or vice-presidents, have had their passports revoked. Meanwhile there are many Chinese social organizations based upon continental regional identities; only *Formosan* clubs are prohibited.

I sometimes encounter a line of criticism that runs as follows:

You are correct in calling for a drastic change in the Taipei administration, but the Formosan activists are only interested in a transfer of power from the Nationalist elite to your own elite. The majority of your young leaders are the sons of former landlords, well-to-do merchants, and professional people. You haven't considered the fundamental social and economic conditions of Formosa. You never talk with equal concern of the interests of the masses. Even if you do wrest power from the Nationalists within Formosa, it will mean little change for the common people.

Such criticism is as unfair as it is uninformed. The movement for Formosan self-determination has not been conceived as a political party movement, but has grown out of universal protest against the exploitation experienced by one and all since 1945. As an organization it has become a symbol of the aspirations of the great majority of Formosans since the tragic experience of February and March, 1947. That experience destroyed popular trust in the continental Chinese and revived the old antagonisms of the 18th and 19th centuries. We insist that the Taipei administration must undergo drastic change, open the government to Formosan participation, and create a framework in which *all* elements of the island population can compete freely for place within Formosa. The farmers must be relieved of the enormous tax burden that now supports Chiang's armed forces and so-called "central government of China," in addition to a necessary government for the island itself. The total population should be free to choose the form of government under which it is willing to live. The island people should not be compelled to accept any one or another regime imposed upon it from outside or by the armed agencies of the present regime.

It is true that the present leadership of the Movement is an elite, but an intellectual elite drawn from all economic levels of Formosan life. In many countries there are masses of helpless people who may not even be aware that they are subject to economic and political exploitation. It is the responsibility of the observant, reflective, and articulate elite to make them conscious of the improvement in living conditions to which they may aspire. They must be made aware of their own rights. I have on occasion pointed out that some of the most powerful leaders of revolution have come of the bourgeoisie, Chou En-lai and Chu Teh, for example, or Ho Chi Minh, or the leaders of the American and French revolutions. I have also reminded them of the sacrifices on behalf of all Formosans made by my friends Wei, a farmer's son, and Hsieh, a businessman's son.

In March I received the news that Hsieh Tsung-ming and Wei Ting-chao were arrested again, together with Li Ao and other Formosan and Chinese intellectuals. Later I learned that they were charged with attempting to overthrow the government. The prosecutors are asking the death penalty for Hsieh and Wei and a prison term of more than ten years for Li.

Some critics have created a new scenario for their own argumentative purpose. They now attack the Formosan movement for self-determination because Peking chooses to attack it, and charge that the independence movement organization is nothing but a cover-up for CIA operations. The line of reasoning seems to be: The United States sees no more hope for Chiang to hold on, and therefore promotes Formosan independence in order to prepare a fall-back position. American support for independence will enable Washington to maintain the American military presence in Formosa.

Some American radicals and liberals appear to be as bemused by "Great China" as the missionaries of the nineteenth century and the "Friends of China" in recent years who have given such uncritical and emotional support to the Chiangs. In support of the thesis that Formosa must be an integral part of China they are as ardent as the most dedicated Nationalists and Communists. They criticize the Formosan self-determination movement leaders as an elite and ignore the fact that the people of Formosa are mute and have no way of expressing themselves short of violent uprisings.

These Americans are highly intelligent, extremely individualistic, very critical and nonconformist, and almost rebellious towards any established authority. Yet when it comes to the People's Republic of China, many of them go limp, losing their independent mind and critical spirit, and simply admire and worship whatever China says or does. These are the people who looked, with contempt, on those who were invited by the Nationalist government to visit Formosa, received lavish hospitality and returned to the United States singing the praises of the Nationalist regime. It is ironic that this is exactly what is happening to them in their relationship to Peking. It is hard to comprehend how, while feeling such aversion to any infringement of personal freedom and to any attempt of regimentation in the United States, they could be so full of admiration for the regime in Peking. They are such indomitable fighters for human rights and fundamental freedoms and yet they are so insensitive to the rights of and aspirations of the more than fourteen million native Formosans. One suspects that some of these critics are not totally unselfish; they are eager to be invited to China and to be hailed as champions of the government of one-fourth of the world's population. To ask for consideration of Formosan interests would jeopardize their chances for the pilgrimage to Peking.

I think we have no need to apologize if Formosan interests happen to run parallel with the interests of any other nation. We only ask that the Formosa question be examined from all sides and as objectively as possible. Truly disinterested and nonpolitical scholarship, it seems to me, would require some investigation of the history, character, and claims of the island people. To us, silence maintained in deference to either Taipei or Peking is a form of negative political activity and a betrayal of objective scholarship.

This may be too much to expect at this late hour. At the sudden apparent thaw in Sino-American relations a number of influential academic specialists began to exhibit certain strong personal and political interests. Those who feared to offend the Nationalists by public discussion of the Formosa question now live in greater fear that such a discussion might jeopardize their hopes and interests in Peking. Very few have had the courage, exhibited by Professor Fairbank of Harvard, to raise the issue of Formosan rights and interests in debates concerning recognition of Peking and the fate of Formosa.

To our misfortune, the term "self-determination" seems to have become an unsavory phrase in the American vocabulary. So much has been sacrificed for so little in Vietnam in the proclaimed interest of "self-determination" in Saigon. The disillusioning one-man race for the presidency there in 1971 provoked outraged editorial comment in the American press from coast to coast, but we search in vain for reference to American sponsorship of Generalissimo Chiang's lifetime presidency, the pretense of a "central government of China" at Taipei, and the farce of an "elective legislature" formed through a rigged election on the continent in 1947.

President Nixon's visit to Peking and the debates on the Chinese representation problem in the United Nations underscored once again the tangle of the Formosan issue. On September 18, 1971, the eve of the United Nations Twenty-Sixth General Assembly, which finally voted to seat the People's Republic of China in the U.N. and expel the Nationalists, the leaders and representatives of the Formosan people gathered in New York to express their extreme concern over the future of Formosa. They wanted to speak out on behalf of the great majority of the inhabitants of the island, who are silenced by the present regime there. At the press conference held on the same day, I made the following observations:

1. Over 1200 Formosans from the United States and Canada participated in this meeting. In view of the fact that they are scattered all over the United States and Canada, the rate of attendance is extraordinary. The number of Formosans who participated constitute over ten percent of all Formosan citizens in the United States and Canada. If, for example, the black population in the United States turned out in the same proportion, the number attending would be over two million. We also received a considerable number of telegrams and letters from Formosans in Japan and Europe expressing solidarity with us.

2. This is the largest spontaneous political rally to be held either within or outside of Formosa since World War II. The participants come from all walks of life and all parts of Formosa. They include young students, housewives, businessmen, academic personnel, doctors, lawyers and religious leaders. All of them have families and friends in Formosa so they are highly representative, and can speak for the great majority in For-

mosa. The fact that this kind of rally could not be held or even imagined in Formosa attests to the nature of the regime and the political situation there.

3. All Formosans are firmly united in demanding the recognition of their right to self-determination of their political future. The real issue is not whether or not Formosa should be an independent state, but rather whether or not those more than fourteen million Formosans are entitled to say something about their own future. The fact is that for the past 400 years these people have been kicked around. We have heard enough about what Peking says about Formosa. We have heard enough of what the Nationalist government, which represents no one, says about Formosa. We have heard enough about what the United States government says about Formosa. All of those who gathered for this meeting came to ask in substance just one question, "What about the Formosans?"

The following statement was made at the conference.

1. The Formosa issue cannot be dealt with as if this were merely litigation concerning a piece of real estate. The fact that the fate of more than fourteen million people is involved must be borne in mind throughout debate, negotiation and resolution.

2. These millions—including those who came to Formosa after 1945—will insist on their right to determine by themselves their political future. Their basic interests and legitimate aspirations must not be ignored again, as they were ignored in 1895 and in 1945. The tragedies of the past must not be repeated in another unrestricted transfer.

3. The issue of the sovereignty over Formosa should be settled by international negotiation in which the people of Formosa are fully and effectively represented. No one from the outside has the right to dictate to whom they should belong. Neither the government of the People's Republic of China nor the government of the United States can speak for them.

4. The present Nationalist regime in Taipei has never spoken legitimately for the great majority of the people on Formosa. It cannot do so hereafter unless a drastic change takes place there and the Formosan majority is represented effectively at every level in the government.

5. The Formosans demand, at a minimum, a reasonable time to bring about this reorganization and to prepare for an ultimate choice of sovereignty. The island has a viable economy and a literate people who wish to live in peace, threatening no one. They want to see the immediate and total withdrawal from Quemoy and Matsu of the army conscripted in Formosa by the National regime and the speedy restoration to China of all

Chinese national treasures and other public properties brought to Formosa by the same regime.

6. Toward the end of a specified period and under conditions agreed upon by the parties concerned, the people of Formosa should be allowed to reach a decision concerning their future course and status. Given freedom of choice, without intimidation, they may prefer to form a distinct political entity, or they may opt for a special association with China. Whatever the outcome, the choice should be theirs, a Formosan decision.

All the participants in the conference were convinced that whatever decision was made by the United Nations regarding the Chinese representation problem, the Formosan issue would remain unsettled for some time to come.

A month later, on October 18, in New York City and simultaneously all over the world, groups of Formosans chained themselves together in a dramatic attempt to call the world's attention to their demand for an independent Formosa free from Chinese control—whether Nationalist or Communist. They called for recognition of the People's Republic of China by the United Nations as full, legal, and rightful holder of the China seat. At the same time they urged the member-states to keep the doors of the United Nations open for the more than fourteen million people of Formosa and to give their support for a freely chosen Republic of Formosa—a future member of the United Nations.

The United Nations vote in October 1971 settled the problem of Chinese representation in the U.N.; it has not solved the Taiwan issue. A long, arducus struggle lies ahead for the Formosan people in the fight for their right to self-determination and their road to freedom.

Index